MEXICAN AMERICANS
AND THE
MASS MEDIA

COMMUNICATION AND INFORMATION SCIENCE
A Series of Monographs, Treatises, and Texts
Edited by
MELVIN J. VOIGT
University of California, San Diego

William C. Adams • Television Coverage of International Affairs

William C. Adams • Television Coverage of the Middle East

William C. Adams • Television Coverage of the 1980 Presidential Campaign

Mary Cassata and Thomas Skill • Life on Daytime Television: Tuning-In American Serial Drama

Hewitt D. Crane • The New Social Marketplace: Notes on Effecting Social Change in America's Third Century

Rhonda J. Crane • The Politics of International Standards: France and the Color TV War

Herbert S. Dordick, Helen G. Bradley, and Burt Nanus • The Emerging Network Marketplace

Glen Fisher • American Communication in a Global Society

Oscar H. Gandy, Jr. • Beyond Agenda Setting: Information Subsidies and Public Policy

Oscar H. Gandy, Jr., Paul Espinosa and Janusz Ordover • Proceedings of the Tenth Annual Telecommunications Policy Research Conference

Edmund Glenn • Man and Mankind: Conflict and Communication Between Cultures

Bradley S. Greenberg • Life on Television: Content Analyses of U.S. TV Drama

Cees J. Hamelink • Finance and Information: A Study of Converging Interests

Robert M. Landau, James H. Bair, and Jean Siegman • Emerging Office Systems

John S. Lawrence and Bernard M. Timberg • Fair Use and Free Inquiry: Copyright Law and the New Media

Robert G. Meadow • Politics as Communication

William H. Melody, Liora R. Salter, and Paul Heyer • Culture, Communication, and Dependency: The Tradition of H.A. Innis

Vincent Mosco • Broadcasting in the United States: Innovative Challenge and Organizational Control

Vincent Mosco • Pushbutton Fantasies: Critical Perspectives on Videotex and Information Technology

Kaarle Nordenstreng and Herbert I. Schiller • National Sovereignty and International Communication: A Reader

Ithiel de Sola Pool • Forecasting The Telephone: A Retrospective Technology Assessment

Dan Schiller • Telematics and Government

Herbert I. Schiller • Who Knows: Information in the Age of the Fortune 500

Indu B. Singh • Telecommunications in the Year 2000: National and International Perspectives

Dallas W. Smythe • Dependency Road: Communications, Capitalism, Consciousness and Canada

Janet Wasko • Movies and Money: Financing the American Film Industry

In Preparation:

Gerald Goldhaber, Harry S. Dennis, III, Gary M. Richetto, and Osmo A. Wiio • Information Strategies: New Pathways to Corporate Productivity

Bradley S. Greenberg • Mexican Americans and the Mass Media

Heather Hudson • Telecommunications and Development

Armand Mattelart and Hector Schmucler • Communication and Information Technologies: Freedom of Choice for Latin America

Kaarle Nordenstreng • The Mass Media Declaration of UNESCO

Jorge A. Schnitman • Dependency and Development in the Latin American Film Industries

Jennifer D. Slack • Communication Technologies and Society: Conceptions of Causality and the Politics of Technological Intervention

Sari Thomas • Studies in Mass Media and Technology Volumes 1-2

Tran van Dinh • Independence, Liberation, Revolution

Georgette Wang and Wimal Dissanayake • Continuity and Change in Communication Systems

Osmo Wiio • Information and Communication Systems

MEXICAN AMERICANS AND THE MASS MEDIA

BRADLEY S. GREENBERG
MICHAEL BURGOON
JUDEE K. BURGOON
FELIPE KORZENNY

ABLEX Publishing Corporation
Norwood, New Jersey 07648

Printed in the United States of America

Library of Congress Cataloging in Publication Data

Main entry under title:

Mexican Americans and the mass media.

  (Communication and information sciences)
  Bibliography: p.
  Includes index.
  1. Mexican Americans and mass media. I. Greenberg,
Bradley S. II. Series.
P94.5.M47M4   1982   302.2'34'0896872073   82-11658
ISBN 0-89391-126-7

ABLEX Publishing Corporation
355 Chestnut Street
Norwood, New Jersey 07648

CONTENTS

I
WHAT IS KNOWN?

1
Mass Communication and Mexican Americans 7

Bradley S. Greenberg
Carrie Heeter
David Graef
Kurt Doctor
Judee K. Burgoon
Michael Burgoon
Felipe Korzenny

v

FOREWORD

ALLEN H. NEUHARTH
Chairman and President, Gannett, Co., Inc.

Gannett began this study of the communications attitudes of Hispanic Americans because our newspapers and broadcast stations have the potential of reaching Hispanics in more than half of the top 30 Hispanic markets across the United States.

From Phoenix to Denver, from Santa Fe to Stockton, and from San Diego to Salinas, Gannett's voices reach millions of Hispanic Americans every day.

Gannett's recent acquisition of the largest Spanish-language daily newspaper in the mainland U.S., *El Diario-La Prensa*, is another measure of our commitment to serve Spanish-speaking audiences. We believe we can use our resources to help *El Diario* reach a larger percentage of Hispanics in its New York City base, and reach out to provide improved news and information services to the rapidly growing Hispanic population in many other areas of the country.

After we started the study, we ran a corporate advertisement in several leading newspapers and magazines about our attempts to learn more about Hispanic Americans. That advertisement, called ''Sounding Hispanic Freedom,'' generated hundreds of responses.

The mail is usually a pretty good barometer of the way Americans feel about something. The overwhelming majority of that mail—about 95 percent—was very positive about Gannett and the research project. Many of the letters were from Hispanic Americans who often seemed surprised and especially grateful that someone had taken such an interest in them. They aren't used to interest and attention that focuses on Hispanic Americans in a positive way.

One letter from that 5 percent who were not very complimentary of our efforts shows the need for better coverage of Hispanic-American issues. It said, in part: "Does your concern . . . extend to all the illegal aliens who are breaking our laws and are costing our taxpayers a bundle by resisting assimilation? Either they want to be Americans or Hispanics, it's that simple. Your effort can lead to nothing but destruction. If your motto is 'A World of Different Voices,' why concentrate on one?"

The letter reached John Quinn, the President of Gannett News Service and the chief news executive of the Gannett Co. Quinn wrote back: "Gannett makes no apologies for any efforts to help share the many benefits of the American way of life with those who are less fortunate. And that includes working hard to deliver the First Amendment rights of a free press to the Hispanic-American community."

We are also making—and have been making for years—similar efforts to reach and understand all the audiences served by all our voices.

We received a second noteworthy letter, this one from Sister Teresa McGahan, who lives in Louisville, Ky. Sister Teresa wrote: "As a person whose life has been enriched by Hispanic people, I applaud you. May your efforts be blessed with continuing success. May we as Americans be helped to recognize the richness which is ours in our diversity."

All of us at Gannett appreciate the opportunity we have had to learn more, firsthand, about that richness and that diversity. We intend to try very hard to make use of what we have learned, so that all our voices can better serve our Hispanic-American readers, listeners, and viewers in the future.

PREFACE

In the summer of 1979, a group of communication researchers at Michigan State University began discussing the absence of empirical data on the mass media orientations of Hispanic Americans, the fastest-growing minority group in the United States. Two of these researchers, Michael and Judee Burgoon, had been consulting with Gannett Co., Inc., a media company with substantial newspaper holdings in areas of the United States with large Hispanic-American populations. After informal conversations, a letter proposal was drafted by four co-investigators—the Burgoons, Bradley Greenberg and Felipe Korzenny—in August 1979. A favorable response to that proposal led to a full-scale proposal submission in September, and within a month, the Gannett organization agreed to fund the study, which began in January 1980. The research proposed the following:

> To "provide original and seminal research on the mass communication behaviors of Hispanic Americans"
>
> To conduct "a programmatic, synthesized series of studies"
>
> To "generate significant baseline data for all newspapers (and other media) interested in better addressing the needs of their Hispanic-American communities"

The work was commissioned for a 12-month period; it required 16 months for all reports to be prepared. During that period, the following studies were executed:

1. Survey interviews with 820 Hispanic Americans and 765 Anglo adult residents in seven cities in the West and Southwest.
2. Questionnaires administered to 464 Hispanic Americans and 271 Anglo fifth graders and tenth graders in five of the seven cities.
3. Focused interviews with 88 Hispanic American community leaders in six of the cities, including educators, religious leaders, business and other professionals, and grass-roots leaders.
4. Focused interviews with newspaper executives and reports from all seven sites.
5. A content analysis of the newspaper coverage of Hispanic Americans in six sites.
6. A stylistic analysis of newspaper stories reporting on Hispanic-American individuals and events in six markets.
7. A comprehensive review of the research on the mass-communication and interpersonal-communication orientations of Hispanic Americans.
8. A national conference, in Washington, D.C., to report to Hispanic-American organizations the results of the projects.

This volume reports the findings and implications of this research program. It is testimony as much to the foresight of the Gannett organization, its interest in the problem posed, and the obvious speed of its response as to the amount of work conducted. It is to be hoped that the quality of the work merits the investment from all parties.

Project CASA—Communication Among Spanish-speaking Americans—was created to document what Hispanic Americans were doing with the mass media during 1980. As study parameters were established, the largest subgroup of Hispanic Americans in the United States—Mexican Americans—became the focus group. The West and Southwest have the largest concentrations of Mexican Americans, and thus study sites were chosen from those areas. Two considerations for specific selection of cities were preeminent: (1) based on figures from the 1970 Census, at least 20 percent of a city's population had to be classified as Hispanic American; (2) cities with Gannett newspaper properties were preferred, but not mandated, because of the need for rapid, local cooperation from media personnel, community leaders, and school officials. A variety of city population sizes and a range of mean incomes among Hispanic Americans were also sought. As a result of this screening process, studies were done in San Bernardino, Salinas, Stockton, and Visalia, California; Tucson, Arizona; Santa Fe, New Mexico; and El Paso, Texas. In the first five of these cities, the population proportion of Mexican Americans was at least 20 percent; in the sixth and seventh, it was well over 50 percent.

The first step in the study process was to examine the existing literature: What had been reported about the communication behaviors and attitudes of
Hispanic Americans? Precious little, the answer came back. Much would have to
take the form of exploratory, ground-breaking investigation. Two significant
steps followed. First, newspaper executives and some reporters in the chosen sites
convened in San Francisco. They were quizzed about their problems in reporting
on the Mexican-American communities in their cities and on their strengths and
weaknesses in doing so, and they were asked to gauge the perceptions held by the
Mexican-American community toward their paper and other media in the city.
Second, Felipe Korzenny and Betty Ann Griffis visited six of the study cities and
met in both individual and small group sessions with leaders of the Hispanic-
American communities. The leaders were quizzed along the same lines, except
now they were reporting on their own attitudes toward the local media and
projecting the attitudes of their constituencies.

The results of these intense interviews were fed back to the research
team principals. From those interviews, from the literature review, and from
their own extensive research experience, the research principals developed draft
questionnaires to focus on these issues:

1. Use of the English-language mass media, including newspapers, radio, TV,
   magazines and other print material, and movies

2. Use of Spanish-language mass media

3. Content preferences within those media

4. Perceptions of and attitudes toward the media, including perceived biases
   and strengths; image characteristics; the credibility of the different media;
   and satisfaction with the performance of the media

5. Functions of the mass media for community residents

To provide a comparative base for results, it was determined to
collect parallel responses from equivalent samples of Anglos in the study sites.

At the outset of the project, before field work had begun, the principal investigators identified the need for an advisory group, one that would consist
exclusively of Hispanic Americans, to react to and critique the multiple study
phases and approaches of the project. The National Advisory Panel to Project
CASA was then established. Its members included:

Antonio Guernica, Executive Vice President of the National Association of
Spanish Broadcasters

Félix Gutiérrez, School of Jounalism, University of Southern California

Olga Lozano, Deputy Director of the Michigan Commission on Spanish-
Speaking Affairs

Rosa Morales, a public information specialist then with the Governor's
Community Development Cabinet for the State of Michigan

Jorge Schement, Annenberg School of Communications, University of Southern California

This group was first convened to review draft instruments and preliminary reports. Their insight and experience were helpful throughout the project, and individual members of the panel repeatedly provided critical assistance.

After the panel had examined our materials, and suggested revisions, the telephone questionnaire was translated into Spanish and analyzed. Pretesting and redrafting occurred, final questionnaires were created, and field studies of both adults and young people were conducted. Concurrently, the content and stylistic analyses were begun. The project then took off, with one team of researchers working relatively independently on each of the major project phases.

Throughout this effort, several key executives at Gannett provided the researchers with a great deal more than just fiscal support. Allen Neuharth, Chief Executive Officer of Gannett, provided us and the industry with a model of commitment to the First Amendment rights of the people. John Quinn, Chief News Executive of Gannett, believed in us and the project from the initial conversation and provided us with assistance from beginning to end. Walt Wurfel, Vice President for Corporate Communications, provided valuable assistance in disseminating the results of this research. Tom Curley, Gannett's Director of Research, was one of the project's principal promoters as well as its monitor. He advocated the project, cajoled support for it, criticized it, forgave our errors, and helped to make the results dissemination phase into a first-class project. Robert Whittington, president of the Gannett West Newspaper Group, had a deep personal and professional commitment to this project; it would not have developed as it did without his help. Gannett carried their policy of local autonomy forward to a group of researchers. We had their support but were never constrained nor inhibited in our search for knowledge, regardless of the form it might take. They never asked for, nor were they given, any prior approval of public releases. In fact, it was their notion that the public had the right to know about the data at the same time results were reported to Gannett. Our Washington conference served to inform both the project sponsor and the public.

More than 100 people have been involved in this set of studies, not all of whom can be acknowledged here. All have our gratitude. Those people identified here performed services without which the project would not have emerged. A major portion are or were Michigan State University graduate and undergraduate students. The key research assistants on the project were Steven Burch, Carrie Heeter, Kim Neuendorf, Rodney Reynolds, Lori Roscoe, and Bethann Witcher. Significant assistance also came from G. Blake Armstrong, Roger Carvalho, Bernardo Donoso, Eric Eisenberg, Scott Garrison, Susan Goldstein, David Graef, Ronnie Kurchner-Hawkins, and Terry Slater. Many of these researchers are also recognized as coauthors of various chapters of this book. Coders for the content analysis and youth study were Chris Chirio, Susan Flynn, Sandra Hernandez, Barbara Jacobi, Elana Kreinen, and Elizabeth Vega.

Don Ellis, a colleague at Michigan State, assisted on the stylistic analyses reported in Chapter 7.

Bilingual interviewers included Zusel Pordominsky, Rose Trevino, Luis Uribe-Gamboa, Janet Haskell, Rebeca Aguilar, Rose Anguiano, Manuel Barrientos, Nancy Corral, Lupe Aguilar Cortez, Ana Gatrell, Mike George, Susan Howell, Gilberto Izquierdo, Bonnie Joustra, Jaime Martinez, Duane Millar, Liliana Mina, Barbara Place, Patricia Rojas, Rosalia Solozano, Russell Stubbert, Murat Ucer, and Manuel Villoreal.

Local Hispanic-American consultants were Hector Gonzalez, Juan Marinez, and Gumecindo Salas. Armando Valdez and Gordon Dahnke were part of the youth study data collection team. Community leaders who made special arrangements for the project were Roberto Melendez of Salinas, Raul Grijalva of Tucson, Richard Padilla of Santa Fe, Ralph Hernandez of San Bernardino, Ramona Lopez of Stockton, and Fred Ortiz of Visalia. MSU secretaries, whose patience, as well as skill we appreciate include Annette Oliver, Kami Merritt, Michelle Torres, and Linda Yared.

At the National Conference, WXIA-TV of Atlanta (a Gannett station) videotaped the conference.

Cooperating school districts and individual schools in each community included the Salinas School District, the Salinas Union High School, Roosevelt Elementary School, Lincoln Elementary School, and Alisal High School, all in Salinas; the San Bernardino City Unified School District and San Gorgonia High School in San Bernardino; the Santa Fe Public Schools, Tinon Elementary School, and Santa Fe High School in Santa Fe; the Tucson Unified School District, Van Buskirk Elementary School, Kellond Elementary School, and Tucson High School in Tucson; and the Visalia Unified School District, Mineral King Elementary School and Golden West High School in Visalia.

Newspaper people who participated in our San Francisco meeting and other aspects of the project include Frank Feuille, publisher of the *El Paso Times*; Walt Ryals, publisher, and Bob Storey of the Santa Fe *New Mexican*; Bob Huttenhoff, publisher, Harry Nordwick, Roberto Robledo, and Toni Wiggins of the *Salinas Californian*; Bob Uecker, publisher, Armando Durazo, and Jim Hushaw of the *Stockton Record*; Bill Honeysett, publisher, and Jaime Guerra and Kathy Rebello-Rees of the San Bernardino *Sun*; James Geehan, publisher, and Maria Vigil of the *Tucson Citizen*; and Margaret Jean Boyer, publisher, and Bob Conley of the *Visalia Times-Delta*.

INTRODUCTION

The 1980's promise to be the decade of Hispanic Americans. Just as the 1960's brought increased awareness of Blacks and the 1970's, of women, so the 1980's have already displayed a heightened awareness of the needs, preferences, and behaviors of Hispanic Americans. As the fastest-growing minority group, expected to become the largest by the year 2000, it is not surprising that Hispanic Americans should become the target of unprecedented attention from the media, advertisers, marketers, political and social action groups, and the public as a whole. In this context, in-depth study of Hispanic Americans and their relationship to the media seemed to be an idea whose time had come.

We had several motives in undertaking this multifaceted study. One was intellectual. As academics, we were interested in extending our knowledge of media evaluations and practices to a relatively little-known segment of the American populace. We were interested in knowing as much as possible about the workings of print and broadcast media and the generalizability of their effects on people, and the extent to which Hispanic Americans converge with or diverge from the majority culture in evaluating and using media. We were equally curious about the degree to which Hispanic Americans are a homogeneous or heterogeneous subpopulation in their media practices. The dearth of systematic research on the communication habits of Hispanic Americans had given rise to a number of assumptions and stereotypes that we felt should be empirically tested. We hoped that this research, by addressing the questions from multiple vantage points, would enlighten us not only about this important segment of the American public but also about the interrelationships among a number of attitudes and behaviors of media consumers in general.

Our desire to broaden our knowledge about the current state of broadcast and print media was equaled, if not surpassed, by that of practicing journalists, who expressed great frustration at knowing so little about a key segment of their market. Discussions with journalists prior to this project revealed that many of them were keenly interested in better serving minorities but ignorant about assessing and meeting their needs. The concerns of such journalists partly prompted the proposal for this project.

Beyond these desires of academics and practicing journalists to learn more about Hispanic-American media habits, there was a philosophical motivation for undertaking this project, one that revolves around First Amendment obligations. With the privileges of free speech and a free press come obligations to serve the information needs of the entire community. That responsibility looms larger when a newspaper is the only news organization in a community. In this day of declining numbers of daily newspapers, many smaller towns and cities face the prospect or the reality of only one daily newspaper, a circumstance sometimes coupled with the absence of any local television stations. Media organizations that are sensitive to their public trust recognize the need to learn as much as possible, and as soon as possible, about the public they are charged with serving. By doing so, and by using the assembled information responsibly, media organizations are most likely to contribute to protecting a free press. Aiding the media to reach out to all segments of their community was yet another motivation for this study, and a particularly important one.

Finally, this project was prompted by the economic implications for media industries in assessing the needs and wants of such a substantial segment of the consuming public. For the newspaper industry especially, there was the prospect of boosting sagging circulations by producing a product better tailored to the needs of Hispanic Americans. For all commercial media there was the dual prospect of attracting more advertising by demonstrating the ability to reach this as yet untapped market. Thus, such "bottom-line" considerations also played a role in the decision to sponsor this project. That media and advertising people should see a profit motive in studying Hispanic Americans has been applauded by many who believe it means that Hispanic Americans will now be wooed rather than ignored.

While these various motivations influenced the decision to undertake this project, the issues addressed and the methods used were shaped by another set of criteria. First, we wanted to be able to integrate new data with knowledge we had already acquired. The principal investigators each approached the project with strong personal research backgrounds in subsets of the study foci, and their experience and expertise formed a substantial foundation for the research process. Prior to the inception of this project, two of the principal investigators had amassed newspaper-readership data (and secondarily, broadcast-use data) from nearly 24,000 adults. We wished to ask some of the same questions so that we would have a well-grounded knowledge base from which to interpret some of the replies. Issues addressed in prior research that we chose to carry over to this project included frequency and amount of time spent with newspapers, radio, and television; content preferences; satisfaction with and perception of the various media; functions for which newspapers and television are used (in addition to demographic characteristics); and the role of writing style in stories about Hispanic Americans. Research that two other principal investigators had been engaged in prompted us to look at portrayals and coverage of Hispanic Americans. by the media; young people's use of media and their attitudes, motives, and preferences in media decisions; the role of parent-child interaction in the use of the media; the perceived reality of television; and the relative credibility of each medium.

Because so little systematic empirical research on Hispanic-American media patterns had been done, we considered it essential to pursue multiple avenues in familiarizing ourselves with those media-related issues most pertinent to Hispanic Americans. To achieve a broader perspective, we decided to create a national advisory panel and to interview people on both the production and consumer sides of the media—publishers, reporters, and community leaders from each of the sites chosen for study. We felt that this multifaceted, extensive consultation would not only sharpen the focus of the study, helping us to center on the most useful and as yet unanswered questions, but would also provide an invaluable frame of reference for interpretation of the actual results.

Our decision to undertake in-depth interviews with newspaper personnel and community leaders was also part of another objective of this project—to study Hispanic Americans and the media from as many different methodological vantage points as possible. It was our conviction that greater validity and generalizability could be achieved by arriving at conclusions from several different directions and kinds of data. Accordingly, the interviews with publishers and their staff and with community leaders from diverse backgrounds were designed to provide a wealth of anecdotal data that could produce a kind of gestalt impression of how the media are currently being produced, used, and evaluated. We felt such preliminary qualitative data would have considerable pay-off in painting the "big picture."

We were equally convinced of the need to gather more objective forms of data. Toward that end, we used three additional methodological approaches. The bulk of our effort went into the development of written questionnaires, one to be used with adults and another with children. These survey instruments—the former administered by telephone, the latter in mass administrations at the children's schools—supplied the majority of quantitative data for this project. Second, we performed detailed content analyses of the newspapers published in the chosen communities during the study. These examined how and to what extent Hispanic Americans were being covered by the various newspapers. Third, we completed stylistic analyses on the same newspapers to determine if language and readability differed for Hispanic-related and other types of stories.

A final objective of this project was to maximize its generalizability. This was accomplished partly by conducting the study in multiple sites, permitting us to identify general trends across locations, trends that could not be attributed to unique demographic characteristics of a given locale or properties of a given newspaper. While the conclusions drawn are best limited to the Southwest and predominantly to Mexican Americans, the geographic breadth of this project is substantially greater than that of most other empirical studies of Hispanic Americans. Generalizability also was enhanced by collecting parallel data on Anglos as much as possible. This allowed us to explore some important issues in media use, evaluation, and preference that transcend the issue of ethnicity and also allowed us to determine the degree of similarity and dissimilarity between Hispanic Americans and Anglos.

In its totality, then, this project offers a mosaic of how Hispanic Americans and their Anglo counterparts use and evaluate the media and how the media in turn treat members of each group. We believe the wealth of information available from this project is unsurpassed in the academic and industrial literature.

The chapters that follow are divided into four sections. Section I consists of two chapters that summarize existing research literature on Mexican Americans' mass communication and interpersonal communication practices and evaluations. Section II lays out the expectations we developed from interviews with community leaders, newspaper executives, and reporters. Section III presents the results we obtained, broken down into four chapters covering results from adults, results from youths, the content analysis, and the stylistic analysis. Section IV offers some commentary on the project and suggestions for the future: Chapter 8 summarizes the results; Chapter 9 presents a retrospective analysis of the project by two members of the national advisory panel; and Chapter 10 discusses implications of the study for media professionals, Hispanic Americans, and communication researchers.

I
WHAT IS KNOWN?

1

MASS COMMUNICATION
AND MEXICAN AMERICANS

BRADLEY S. GREENBERG

CARRIE HEETER

DAVID GRAEF

KURT DOCTOR

JUDEE K. BURGOON

MICHAEL BURGOON

FELIPE KORZENNY

This chapter represents the first effort to review comprehensively the research literature on the mass communication behaviors of Hispanic Americans. It analyzes the existing information on a broad range of mass media *consumption patterns* and *attitudes, bilingual* and *bicultural* programming, the *image* of Hispanic Americans in the commercial media, and the extensive research on *public television for Hispanic-American children*. This review was a prelude to the research program reported throughout this volume.

Hispanic American was the comprehensive term chosen for this review, intended to suggest an individual living in the U.S. whose ancestry, language, and/or cultural orientation is or has been in some way related to a Spanish-speaking country.

Hispanic Americans are a heterogeneous group. Their length of family residence in the U.S. ranges from centuries to hours. A national population of approximately 12 million self-identified Hispanics was reported in the U.S. Census Survey of March 1978. This figure may be low due to difficulties in counting "illegals" and migrants. Fifty-nine percent identified themselves as of Mexican origin, 15 percent Puerto Rican, 6 percent Cuban, 7 percent Central or South American, and 13 percent of other Spanish-speaking origins (U.S. Bureau of the Census, 1979).

Research about Hispanics may be generalizable only to the Spanish-origin group most abundant in the locations sampled. Mexican-origin Hispanics predominate in the Southwest, Puerto Ricans in New York City and along the east coast, and Cubans in Florida and the southeast coast. Seventy-nine percent of Puerto Ricans live in central (large) cities, compared to 46 percent of Mexicans and 37 percent of Cubans. There is selective dispersion of each of the groups.

Despite their diversity, Hispanic Americans are grouped in this synthesis because they tend to share four pertinent traits:

1. Hispanics as a group are economically and educationally disadvantaged when compared to non-Hispanics. The median income for all Hispanics is lower than for non-Hispanics, with Puerto Ricans having the lowest and Cubans the highest incomes. Hispanics over age 25 have completed fewer years of school than have non-Hispanics, with Mexicans and Puerto Ricans completing the least and Cubans the most. Hispanics share a so-called minority status.

2. Four of five Hispanics report that they speak Spanish (although proficiency in both Spanish and English varies greatly, and different dialects of Spanish are spoken). Inability to speak English is a handicap for some Hispanics, but the ability to speak Spanish is viewed as an asset, and there is a strong desire to preserve bilingualism among most Hispanics.

3. In addition to language, Hispanic Americans tend to share some degree of identification with a Hispanic culture as well as with the dominant U.S. culture. There is a desire to thrive in both cultures.

4. The Hispanic-American population in the U.S. is growing quickly. In some cities, Hispanics outnumber Anglos. Based on continued high immigration and the relative youth of the Hispanic population, Hispanics are expected to become the "majority minority" in the U.S. no later than the year 2000. Increasing awareness by Hispanics and non-Hispanics of this growth is accompanied by increasing interest in the social, economic, and political impact of Hispanics.

For these reasons, among others, there are stronger signals of interest in Hispanics within the media and among media researchers. The media face questions regarding employment, imagery, and news coverage of Hispanics. Researchers cannot easily ignore such a large population whose potential as readers and viewers permit cross-cultural and intracultural issues to be examined without leaving the country. Both media professionals and researchers can recall that their interest in another population subgroup, Black Americans, dates back less than two decades. In one sense, history may be repeating—a flush of excitement about Hispanics to parallel earlier zeal about "doing something with (or for) Blacks.'' This review identifies what is known at this time.[1] It is organized into four basic sections:

1. The first section examines Hispanic American access, use, content preferences and preferred sources of information, primarily among English-language media.
2. The second section examines current and past practices of Spanish-language and bicultural media, with a specific examination of Spanish-language media use.
3. The third section examines the available programming and research that have originated with public television's efforts in creating series for Hispanic-American children.
4. The final section characterizes the portrayal of Hispanics in English-language mass media.

MASS MEDIA HABITS OF HISPANIC AMERICANS

Access to the Mass Media

There appear to be very few differences between this group's access to the mass media and that of other identified subgroups or majority groups in the U.S. Data have been collected in Los Angeles and three communities in Texas—San Antonio, Austin, and Lubbock. We will begin with Los Angeles, and then identify the extent to which there are any significant deviations from the pattern there. In Los Angeles, Lopez and Enos (1973) indicate that 99 percent of Hispanic citizens had one or more television sets, with 50 percent having two or more working sets. This compares with census data that 95 percent of the general population had one or more television sets, with 32 percent having two or

---

[1]The actual mechanics of conducting such a literature search and review require certain judgments. We have synthesized pertinent empirical articles, books, and reports written between January 1970 and February 1980. Some descriptive pieces of special interest or insight have been included. The search and the summary were intended to be comprehensive but are probably not exhaustive. The primary sources included the following: several abstracting services (*Psychological, Sociological, Communication, Journalism,* and *Anthropological Abstracts,* and *Topicator*); computer-based bibliographies (ERIC, Social Science Citation Index); communication conference listings of delivered papers; relevant journals (*Advertising Age, American Sociological Review, Broadcasting, Journal of Broadcasting, Journal of Communication, Journalism Quarterly, Public Opinion Quarterly, Television/Radio Age*); available Hispanic bibliographies; and personal searches with Hispanic research centers, researchers, and publications. Perhaps 1,000 titles emerged after an initial screening. About 200 were examined in more detail, and abstracts were created for a few more than 100 of them. That set of information is integrated in this reivew.

more. A study of 400 Latinos in the barrios of Chicago (Duran and Monroe, 1977) also yielded the 95 percent figure. In Los Angeles, 45 percent of this sample had black and white sets only; 55 percent indicated ownership of a color set. For radio ownership, 70 percent had two or more AM radios, 26 percent had one, and 4 percent had none. For FM radios, 43 percent had two or more, 41 percent had one, and the remainder had none. Eighty percent of this sample indicated that they had some form of record player or tape/cassette player. About half the sample had a newspaper delivered regularly.

In Lubbock (Hsia, 1973) the data were not dissimilar. Ninety-five percent of Chicanos owned at least one television set, and for 46 percent there was a color set. All respondents owned a radio; the average number owned by Chicano respondents was 2.11. Slightly more than half subscribed to a newspaper. Thus the small city of Lubbock, Texas, and the large city of Los Angeles reflected virtually identical media access patterns. Turning to the other two Texas cities, as reported by Valenzuela (1973), we find remarkable parallelism. In the combined data for San Antonio and Austin, 95 percent owned a television set; for 41 percent, this included a color set. More than 90 percent had some kind of radio; for 90 percent this included an AM radio and for 71 percent an FM radio. Newspaper subscription data apparently were not collected in this study. Individual access to the broadcast media is virtually universal. Newspaper penetration, by comparison, is at only half the available level. There appears to have been a deliberate avoidance of English-language newspapers.

Use of the Mass Media

First let us look at newspapers. Pasqua (1975) found adults in his Chicano sample averaging a little more than 20 minutes a day reading the newspaper. In Hsia's Texas study (1973), slightly more than half the respondents subscribed to newspapers; Marshall et al. (1974) found half to be regular readers. However, a large proportion of nonsubscribers also did some newspaper reading; only 18 percent of Hsia's respondents read no newspapers at all. This may be a slight underestimate, inasmuch as 8 percent of respondents did not answer the newspaper readership question. As many as 25 percent of his respondents were unlikely to be newspaper readers. Of those who did read a newspaper, his time estimates were about 10 minutes higher than those reported by Pasqua for weekday reading. His figures showed about half an hour a day on weekdays and about 45 minutes for the Sunday newspaper. For teenagers, Justin (1973) reported that 45 percent of Anglo respondents and 38 percent of Chicanos read a paper every day. In Chicago, two-thirds of the 400 Mexican, Cuban, and Puerto Rican respondents reported regular reading of one or more newspapers in the last year. Newspaper reading was associated with education and being male. Thirty-four percent read one newspaper regularly, 19 percent read two of them, and 7 percent read three or more. Seven of the top 10 newspapers cited were Spanish-language, but the top two were English.

Hsia (1973) and Valenzuela (1973) provided information about radio listening. Hsia indicated that the national average is slightly under 2 hours per day; he found that low a level only among his most affluent Anglo respondents. Essentially, he found Anglos and Chicanos at an average 2.5 hours of radio listening per day; his Black sample averaged more listening and did so on both weekdays and weekends. Valenzuela, in contrast, found an average listening habit of 3.7 hours per day estimated in San Antonio and Austin. Actually, his Austin average was 2.0, a figure not very different from the Lubbock figure reported by Hsia; both cities house major Texas universities. In the more urban surrounds of San Antonio, Valenzuela found 4.1 hours per day. Valenzuela pointedly noted that there were three all-Spanish-language radio stations in San Antonio broadcasting about 300 hours per week. He contrasted that with about 40 hours of Spanish-language programming in Austin per week; those Austin hours all occurred between 6 and 10 A.M.

Rosenthal (1978) examined Arbitron data for television usage. He concluded that Hispanic viewing and general-public viewing were nearly identical, with Latino children and teens slightly higher viewers, and women and men slightly lower viewers. He indicated further that adult viewing from 4:30 to 6:00 P.M. was higher among Hispanics than among the general population. Barba (1978), reporting a study of more than 2,000 Spanish homes in New York City, indicated that one-fourth of the respondents watched only Spanish-language television stations, 72 percent viewed both Spanish and English, and only 4 percent viewed solely English-language TV stations. This reflects an orientation even in those homes where English is a primary language to view available Spanish-language television programs. Hsia reported a viewing figure for Chicano males and females of 3.75 hours per weekday, with no gender difference. He further reported 6 hours on Saturday and Sunday for Chicano males and slightly more than 5 hours for Chicano females. The weekend figures for Chicano males were substantially larger by at least an hour and a half than for any of the other ethnic groups in his study. The weekend rates for females were no different by ethnic groups. Valenzuela's study has somewhat larger TV-viewing averages. He reported the mean number of hours of television viewing as 4.4 per day; 59 percent of his respondents watched television from 2 to 6 hours a day. In San Antonio, where Spanish-language TV programming was more available, respondents watched a little longer, 4.7 hours per day, than in Austin. In those two cities, about one-fifth of the respondents watched television 6 or more hours per day.

Additional media usage data are provided by Hsia (1973) for two other media. His Chicano sample read 2.2 magazines per month, a figure greater than that obtained from his Black sample but less than from his Anglo sample. The time spent with magazines was not different across these ethnic groups, averaging a little more than 30 minutes when magazines were read. Hsia also asked about monthly movie attendance. He found that Blacks averaged 2.5 movies per month, Chicanos 2, and Anglos 1 movie per month.

The viewing of public television (PTV) by Mexican-American adults was examined by Valenzuela (1974) in a study of more than 4,000 persons in California, Texas, and Arizona. He found (1) an average of 30–40 percent of the respondents had watched public television in the last month, a percentage that corresponds to non-Hispanic viewership of public television; (2) preferred programs tended to be those specifically produced to attract a Mexican-American audience, with one exception: "Sesame Street"; next most popular were bilingual children's shows and locally produced adult shows targeted for the Hispanic audience; (3) PTV viewers among Mexican Americans showed the same differentiating characteristics—higher education and higher socioeconomic status—as PTV viewers in general.

From a more theoretical basis, Neuendorf, et al. (1980) examined television orientations of a sample of 149 Spanish-surnamed Michigan residents as they related to the "cultural identity" of the respondents. The main measure of cultural identity was the self-classification by respondents as American, Hispanic-American (including Mexican-American, Hispanic American, Cuban-American, Spanish-American), and Hispanic (including Chicano, Mexican, Latino, Cuban, Mejicano). They tested a series of hypotheses relating cultural identity to television orientations and found the following: (1) no support for the expectation that greater watching of English-language television would be associated with a more "American" cultural identity; (2) no support for the expectation that available Spanish-language programming would be less watched by those with a more "American" cultural identity; (3) no support for the hypothesis that the more "American" the identity the more exposure to news content; (4) no support for the hypothesis that the more "Hispanic" the identity, the greater the watching of soap operas.

This same study also adds to our store of descriptive information regarding television usage and attitudes. The average television viewing in this sample was just under 4 hours per day. The most viewed content areas were the evening news, game shows, situation comedies, sports, and evening movies. Most interesting is the sample's reactions to a series of statements regarding their perception of the portrayal of Hispanic Americans on television. There was more agreement than disagreement that characters are usually shown on television as "lawbreakers," "in humorous roles," and as "lazy." There was most disagreement with the proposition that they are shown "in important roles" or as "well educated."

Content Preferences

In Tucson, a large audience study of Mexican-Americans by Marshall et al. (1974) identified movies on television as the favorite program type of just under one-fourth of the sample. One-fifth had no favorite, and 10 percent identified musicals, soap operas, and Mexican theater as favorite and/or preferred programming. If the interview was conducted in Spanish, it was more likely that Spanish-language programs were specifically cited and requested by the respondents. An earlier report by Eiselein and Marshall (1971) asked what content preferences its Mexican-American respondents had in terms of news and public-affairs programming, as contrasted with entertainment-programming preferences. The primary responses, the top 10, of this large Mexican-American sample were: (1) Mexican-American news and sports; (2) homemaking; (3) consumer economics; (4) agency information (HUD, FICA, etc.); (5) job information; (6) legal information; (7) youth problems information; (8) educational opportunities; (9) history and cultural affairs; and (10) the Chicano movement.

Valenzuela (1973) spanned several media in terms of content preferences. Radio music preferences of Hispanic respondents in Austin and San Antonio were Mexican, 41 percent; all types, 22 percent; Rancheras or Western music, 14 percent; rock, 12 percent; and some others. For television programming, the major content preferences were soap operas, 39 percent; Mexican- or Spanish-language programs, 30 percent; movies, 28 percent; variety shows, 25 percent; dramas, 23 percent; comedy variety, detective programs, and westerns, all 22 percent; and situation comedies, 18 percent. Across studies then, the two primary content choices of Spanish and Mexican programs and movies emerged as the most strongly desired types of programming. The preferred list also emphasized soap operas.

Valenzuela also asked his respondents what type of news and information they would like to have more of. The primary responses were more local news and more news in general. This study also asked about individual preferences for Spanish-language programming. With regard to radio, one-third preferred Spanish language, one-third preferred English language, and one-fourth mentioned both types as preferred. As for television, where Spanish-language programs were available, the Mexican-American respondents said they preferred to watch them; where they were not as available, the respondents said they wanted more of them. In this survey, one-third said they desired bilingual television programming, one-third said they desired Spanish-language programming, and one-fourth preferred English-language programming. Recall the Barba (1978) study showing that one-quarter of his New York respondents watched only the Spanish-language stations. This same variation occurred in terms of news and information programming preferences. The split in language preferences is large, and the need for media agencies to accommodate both sets of preferences may be equally large. Language preference is a content-free request inasmuch as the distributions of preferred language remain very similar whether one is talking about news or entertainment, about different types of entertainment, or about very different media.

Hsia (1973) asked his respondents what their news interests were. In descending order, but not going below 70 percent as an expressed level of interest, his Chicano-sample study identified local news, women's-page-type news, news about murders, the comics, movie reviews, and ads as their most preferred informational categories.

Sources of Information

The reviewed studies identify television as the most relied on source of news information. Perhaps most noteworthy among the data collected from Hispanics is the prominence of radio as a second major source of news information. These conclusions emerge from several field studies; here we will provide some of the specific supporting evidence. Marshall et al. (1974) determined that 85 percent of their Mexican-American sample watched television news with some regularity and that 80 percent listened regularly to radio news programs. Less than two-thirds of their respondents regularly read the newspaper. Asked differently, but with similar results, Valenzuela (1973) determined from his large sample that 39 percent identified television as their primary news and information source, 30 percent radio, 26 percent newspapers, and the remainder a more miscellaneous collection of sources. Hsia (1973) found that 49 percent of his sample cited television as their most important source and 15 percent cited radio. No other news sources achieved either of those levels.

Even among community leaders, the greater reliance on broadcast media as more useful sources of information is repeated (Korman and Valenzuela, 1973). Their study of Anglo and Chicano community leaders resulted in a preference by Chicano leaders for television and radio as more trustworthy than newspapers and magazines. In that sample group, "other people" were also considered more trustworthy than were the print media. Nearly parallel results were obtained from a set of questions that asked which media were preferred for the dissemination of messages. Television and radio were primary choices. Both in terms of trustworthiness and preference, the broadcast media emerged in a singular position, and the print media lagged considerably. The leader respondents were asked what they thought the average citizen preferred as sources of information; both Chicano and Anglo community leaders first identified electronic media. The Anglo leaders believed the print media would be a second choice; the Chicano community leaders identified people as a second choice. Throughout these study data there is a strong orientation to the electronic media by both sets of community leaders. The authors concluded that there was a strong lack of positive feelings about the print media among the Chicano community leaders.

Lopez and Enos (1973) surveyed a sample of Hispanic Americans in Los Angeles county. They found that media trust was largely a function of age and that age in turn reflected recency of immigration to the U.S. The older, less-educated, poorer respondents typically watched more Spanish-language television and trusted it more. The younger, better-educated, U.S.-born respondents typically watched and trusted English-language media more. The reference to media in this part of their study dealt with the truthfulness and accuracy of television news.

One study (Tan, 1978) explored another dimension of media evaluations. He asked some 200 adult Mexican Americans in Texas about different characteristics of the several media. Tan found that a majority of the Mexican Americans believed that most television shows appealed to their ethnic groups, but there was intense discontent about the frequency of representation of their ethnic group on television. The major predictor of that television assessment was the age of the respondent. The older respondents were more favorable and the younger respondents less favorable toward what television was doing with Mexican Americans. The study also reported a negative relationship between self-esteem and evaluations of commercial television; the lower the self-esteem, the more positive the evaluation of television. With regard to newspapers, a majority of the Mexican-American respondents believed that newspapers were not reporting enough positive news about Mexican Americans. There was less consensus as to whether the newspapers were treating Mexican Americans fairly in their news columns. Again, age was significantly and positively related to these newspaper evaluations; younger respondents were less favorable toward what the newspapers were doing. Self-esteem was not correlated with the newspaper evaluation.

Research by Valenzuela (1974) in seven sites—San Antonio, Austin, Nogales, San Diego, Phoenix, Tucson, and Casa Grande-Collidge-Eloy (Arizona)—explored many of the media variables reviewed in this section. Access, use, content preferences, language orientation, and news source preferences in that study support the basic findings and conclusions identified throughout this summary.

SPANISH/BICULTURAL PROGRAMMING

This section synthesizes the available research and literature on media and programming directed toward Hispanic Americans. Gutierrez (1980b) identified three types of media that relate to Hispanic Americans: *Anglo media,*

Spanish-language media, and *bilingual/bicultural media.* The first of these is dealt with extensively elsewhere; this summary will address the last two.

Spanish-Language Media

Spanish-language media are media directed at a Hispanic-American audience. Gutierrez (1980b) added another characteristic for this media type: it tends to be imported from Mexico and Latin America. Hispanics in the U.S. are largely a secondary audience for much of the Spanish-language media directed toward them.

Twenty television stations broadcasting in Spanish to U.S. audiences (five from the Mexican side of the border) are listed in the 1978 *Broadcasting Yearbook.* Full-time Spanish-language TV stations are located in most major Southwestern metropolitan areas, as well as in Chicago, New York, and Miami.

Spanish-language television is dominated by the Spanish International Network (SIN), which is 75-percent owned by Mexico's Televisa television network. SIN is affiliated with or owns 16 stations in major cities and is carried by several hundred cable-TV stations (Galavision: Pay TV with a difference, 1979), SIN receives 80 percent of the $20 million spent on advertising on Spanish-language television annually and claims billings with 23 of the top 25 U.S. advertisers (Gutierrez, 1978a).

SIN broadcasts 70 hours of imported programs from Mexico and Latin America, including dramas, comedies, variety, news, music, sports, and special-events shows. Fourteen hours per week are produced in the U.S., including a one-hour international news program and weekly international boxing, with a focus still on Mexico and Latin America (Galavision: Pay TV with a difference, 1979).

The president of SIN is also the president of Galavision, a new pay-TV cable service offering 8 to 10 first-run Spanish-language movies per month, as well as novelas (serials), sports events, and variety specials, all currently imported from Latin America (Galavision, 1980).

A report by Velasquez and Warner (1980) on the cable-TV service to be introduced to the unincorporated county area of Los Angeles illustrated the extent of dominance of Latin American programming, despite the potential for diversity inherent in cable-TV technology. The cable system (Buena Vista Cable TV) will feature four Spanish-language channels: SIN, Galavision, a television station cabled directly from Mexico City, and a teletype news printout in Spanish.

Spanish-language radio is the most widespread and the fastest growing Spanish-language medium. The 1978 *Broadcasting Yearbook* listed over 600 radio stations airing Spanish programs, about 100 on a full-time basis. Gutierrez (1980b) asserted that most stations are managed and owned by Anglos and staffed by Hispanics from Latin America, not by local Hispanics. Station formats depend heavily on music (most of it imported), with a sprinkling of news, public affairs, and other information.

In a study based on the 1974 *Broadcasting Yearbook* and the October 1, 1973 **Spot Radio**, Gutierrez and Schement (1979) identified 485 stations broadcasting all or part of their programs in Spanish. In addition, 35 Mexican-licensed radio stations broadcast to audiences in the U.S. Seventy percent of the U.S. stations that broadcast in Spanish did so for nine hours or less; 11 percent broadcast 10 to 19 hours; 6 percent broadcast 20 to 39 hours; and 11 percent, 40 hours to full time. Much of this analysis compared *Primary Spanish-Language Radio* stations (PSLRs, which broadcast 50 percent or more of the time in Spanish) and *Secondary Spanish-Language Radio* stations (SSLRs, which broadcast less than 50 percent in Spanish). Of the 485 stations identified, 11 percent were codable as PSLRs and 88 percent were SSLRs.

Even PSLR stations are predominantly owned by Anglos. Only 24 percent of all PSLRs listed Spanish-surnamed owners. Twenty to thirty percent listed Spanish-surnamed employees in top management and in sales; 70 percent or more listed Spanish-surnamed employees in programming, news, and promotion slots. No Spanish-surnamed engineers were listed.

The distribution of Spanish-language radio parallels the Hispanic population distribution. Seventeen percent of all Spanish stations were located in California, 19 percent in Texas, and 1 to 5 percent in each of 36 other states. PSLRs were concentrated in areas with large Hispanic populations, while SSLRs occurred more frequently in areas with medium to small Hispanic populations.

Gutierrez and Schement (1979) found significant differences between the broadcast licenses of PSLRs and SSLRs. Seventy-five percent of all Spanish-language radio broadcast on AM. Thirty-six percent of AM PSLRs, compared to 56 percent of AM SSLRs, were licensed to broadcast full time. One-hundred percent of all PSLRs were licensed commercial, compared to 84 percent of all SSLRs (58 percent of FM SSLRs were limited to educational uses).

In terms of network characteristics, SSLRs were significantly more likely to be affiliated with a national and/or regional network, which provides programming and/or advertising. PSLRs affiliations were more sales oriented. They were significantly more likely to be associated with national or regional sales representative agencies and with organizations that specialize in selling commercials for Spanish-language radio.

Gutierrez and Schement also conducted a content analysis comparing news broadcasts and public service announcements (PSAs) of a primary English-language station (KONO) and a primary Spanish-language station (KCOR) in San Antonio in 1975. Both stations had reputations for superior news coverage. The English-language station was found to report more total news stories, devote more time to news broadcasts, and offer more news stories in every content area except local crime than the Spanish-language station. Local crime reporting accounted for 29 percent of KCOR local news, and 9 percent for KONO.

The PSA findings indicated two very different information channels. English-language PSAs appeared to serve as a local community voice, with 70 percent of them originating locally, 19 percent of which were government sponsored. Spanish-language PSAs seemed to be a channel for nonlocal organizations (61 percent), particularly government (51 percent), and non-Hispanic messages. The English-language station drew more PSAs from Hispanic areas than the Spanish-language station did.

One problem faced by Spanish-language broadcast media is the alleged undercounting of the Hispanic audience by the national rating services, which results in loss of advertising revenues (Wolin, 1980). An estimated 25 percent of Hispanics in Los Angeles do not have telephones, and Hispanics have a much higher interview refusal rate than the general public. Wolin writes that Arbitron and Nielsen admit to undercounting Hispanics; both have tried various methods to compensate for the discrepancies, but they have yet to find an economically feasible solution.

Nonbroadcast Spanish-language media follow a similar pattern to radio and television. A 1970 compilation identified nearly 200 Spanish-language newspapers published in five southwest states between 1848 and 1942. In 1979, there were nine U.S. Spanish dailies (Gutierrez, 1980b). Spanish-language newspapers, records and tapes, and movies for Hispanic Americans are also highly dependent on imports from Latin countries. Gutierrez described Spanish-language media in the U.S. as dependent on attracting "a large Latino audience with low-cost programming to deliver that audience to advertisers." Thus, "Latinos share with other Third World people a basic contradiction in dealing with the media that considers them their main audience: The media are operated for the benefit of the dominating group and not the audience."

Spanish Language Media Use

Evidence from several studies identifies the fact that age is a key predictor of use of and preference for Spanish-language media. In the adult and older-adult segment of the Hispanic population, there is a distinctly stronger preference for Spanish-language media than among younger Hispanics. For example, an analysis of audience data in *Television/Radio Age* (Spanish-language market study, 1977) indicated that Spanish-format radio carried a 45 share of Spanish-speaking persons, for which group it ranked number one over eight other radio formats; across the total population, both Hispanic and non-Hispanic, Spanish-format radio carried a 6 share. However, among Spanish-speaking teenagers aged 12 to 17, the share was only 14. The combination of age and lower social status made the Spanish-language orientation even stronger

(Williams et al., 1973a). Among adults, Spanish-format radio gained a larger share of the female audience than the male audience. Rosenthal (1978) reconfirmed these findings from Arbitron audience surveys. He reported that 41 percent of all radio listening by Hispanics was to Spanish-format radio stations, 28 percent to contemporary Anglo stations, 7 percent to Black radio formats, and the remainder miscellaneous. He also identified a small but consistent gender difference: Spanish women listened to Spanish stations 50 percent of the time, compared with 30 percent for Spanish men. Latino teenagers, on the other hand, listened 65 percent of the time to contemporary stations and only 11 percent to Spanish stations.

Lopez and Enos (1973), with a major survey in Los Angeles County, determined that a Spanish-language UHF TV station was the favorite in a Spanish-speaking sample, chosen by 35 percent of the respondents. The choice of that station was positively related with speaking Spanish at home and negatively correlated among those respondents primarily speaking English at home. A network affiliate acquired 27 percent of the favored station responses, and no other station exceeded 10 percent. This study also asked the extent of watching Spanish-language television. Fifteen percent of the respondents said it was what they watched exclusively, 31 percent said frequently, 36 percent said seldom, and 18 percent said never. That is a symmetrical distribution of responses and most likely reflects the age and language orientation of the respondents. When asked what television programs the respondent and their children watched, the responses were easily categorizable in terms of the language orientation of the household. The favorite television programs for English-speaking, U.S.-born Hispanics were identical to the top 10 in the nation at the time. The favorite television programs for Spanish-speaking citizens were more likely to include Spanish-language programs.

A study by Marshall et al. (1974) is appropriately mentioned here. Their research focused on assessing the impact of a specific Spanish-language, Mexican-American series, "Fiesta." They found that the series was viewed equally by those living in heavily Anglo areas and by those in the barrios. However, "Fiesta," broadcast in Spanish, was much more likely to reach people who preferred to speak Spanish than it was to reach those who preferred English. Age was closely associated with this factor in the sense that teenagers who typically preferred English were less likely to have watched this Spanish-language series.

A study that relates both to Spanish- and English-language media was conducted by Dunn (1975). He factor-analyzed media habits and preferences with specific social and demographic characteristics. This factor analysis yielded results that pertain in part to the present depiction of Spanish-language media usage and preferences. One cluster of respondents received the label *Traditional*. Here were older persons, most typically housewives, for whom the interviews were conducted in Spanish and who called themselves Mexicans or Mexican

Americans. This cluster of respondents preferred Spanish-language radio and television. A second cluster was labelled *Nontraditional*. Here were the younger, better-educated respondents whose interviews were either bilingual or in English. These respondents preferred English-language radio and television, and they used print media as a primary source of news and information. The factor analysis affirms many of the more isolated data pieces we have tried to group. There is a strong cleavage in the Hispanic community in utilization of Spanish-language and English-language media; that cleavage appears to be focused principally on cross-generational differences.

Subervi-Velez (1979) examined the relationship between Spanish-language and English-language media exposure and a series of perceived discrimination scales among a sample of 115 Puerto Ricans, 162 Mexican Americans, and 111 Cubans. This was a secondary analysis of data collected by Duran and Monroe (1977). The scales assessed perceptions of discrimination in *regulatory* organizations (e.g., police, landlords, labor unions), *consumer* organizations (e.g., department stores and the telephone company), *social* organizations (e.g., public schools and radio and television stations), and *employment opportunity* organizations (e.g., public and private employers). The basic finding indicated that exposure to Spanish-language media was negatively related to perceptions of discrimination across all these organizational comments but that English-language press exposure was positively and statistically associated with each of them.

Schement (1977) reviewed six audience studies done of Mexican Americans. His critical analysis led to these conclusions: (1) Chicanos are broadcast-oriented to the relative exclusion of the print media; (2) programming in Spanish will almost certainly draw a Chicano audience; (3) personal communication channels, particularly oral ones, are preferred to less personal ones, including media; and (4) a substantial segment of the Mexican American community prefers Spanish-language activity.

Bilingual/Bicultural Media

Bilingual/bicultural programming is specifically directed toward Hispanic Americans. It can be in English or Spanish or a combination, and it is frequently produced by Hispanic Americans. Gutierrez (1980b) suggests that "Latino alternative media are most often operated as part of a community organization or media collective, staffed by community members who are often not media professionals, and provide information not usually presented by the established media." Bilingual/bicultural media include periodicals, alternative radio programs, guerrilla teatros (theater groups), independent films and video tapes, books, and community cable television (Guernica, 1977a; Gutierrez, 1980b). Bicultural broadcast programming frequently must find air time on Anglo media.

Parra (1976) and Abrams (1977) identified lack of funds, poor management, and lack of media experience as major problems encountered in attempts at bicultural programming. Abrams examined a Black and Hispanic community news service that folded in 1976 and found no running coverage of breaking stories, hand-delivered stories, high staff turnover, extreme variance in quantity and quality of stories, and lack of any effort to become self-sufficient as reasons for the failure.

Parra (1976) also discussed a general lack of direction in programming quality and minimal commitment by station managers to the importance of Hispanic programming. Del Solar (1976) asserted that station managers were looking for minority programming that is relevant, timely, and cheap.

Although public television devotes only a small fraction of its broadcast time to Hispanics, some of its programming efforts qualify as bicultural programming. Public television's attempt to program for Hispanics and measure Hispanic media attitudes and preferences accounts for much of the existing research on Hispanic audiences.

Public reaction to "Junta De Amigos," a bilingual program designed to make local public television in central Michigan a vital force in the Hispanic community, was generally well received. Subjects ranged from boycotts to dating behavior to attitudes of the older generation. Rapp (1971) found audience complaints ranging from judgments that subject matter was too controversial to its not being controversial enough. Complaints about the bilingualism were also found, leading Rapp to conclude that it is impossible to please everyone.

The "Fiesta" project, a public television Spanish-language program designed to attract, retain, and realistically help a Hispanic-American audience in southern Arizona, reached 60 percent of its target audience (Eiselein and Marshall, 1971, 1976; Marshall et al., 1974). One quarter of the program's nonviewers (10 percent) were not aware of its existence. Some households indicated difficulty in receiving the appropriate broadcast channel. Twelve percent of "Fiesta" nonviewers did not watch the series because of the times it was aired. Eighty-five percent of "Fiesta" viewers indicated that they liked the series in general. Ascertainment research suggested that Hispanic community relations with the station improved.

Research on the Hispanic-American audience has included content preferences in bicultural programming. Eiselein and Marshall (1971, 1976) found that Mexican music was what viewers liked best about the "Fiesta" series. Rapp (1971) found that viewers preferred segments about Hispanic-American heritage. In addition to Mexican music and Hispanic-American heritage, there was a desire for bicultural programming to include information and news segments. Eiselein and Marshall (1971, 1976) found that viewers wanted more local and regional Mexican-American news, news about education and the schools, and sports.

Other types of bicultural programming requested in civic studies include musical-varieties, movies, soap operas, educational programs, and informational programs. Informational topics desired include homemaking, consumer economics, agency information (i.e., social security, model cities, etc.), job information, legal matters, youth programs, and historical and cultural affairs.

There was a strong desire for more bicultural programs (Marshall et al., 1974). The "Fiesta" series was changed from the originally planned five 2-hour specials to 20 30-minute shows. Valenzuela (1973) surveyed Hispanic Americans in Austin and San Antonio for the public television "Teletemas" series. Where Spanish-language programs were available (in San Antonio), respondents preferred to watch them; where they were not available (Austin), respondents said they desired more Spanish-language programs.

Valenzuela also asked about language preferences in bicultural programming. Thirty-five percent desired bilingual programs, 30 percent desired Spanish, and 25 percent wanted only English programming. Seventy-seven percent of the respondents watched Mexican programs. Mexican music (mentioned by 46 percent) and Spanish-language (40 percent) were the most-liked features; commercials were least liked.

Efforts to increase bicultural programming persist. *Enfoque Nacional*, a weekly Spanish-language news program is produced in San Diego and broadcast over National Public Radio (National Association of Spanish Broadcasters, 1979–80). Various Hispanic groups are attempting to purchase cable-TV systems and commercial stations (Guernica, 1977a,b,c; 1978).

The Latino Consortium is a group of public televisions stations that share the best in locally produced programs by and about Hispanic Americans. One of the major goals of the Consortium is to promote stronger ties among public television stations, independent Hispanic producers, and the Hispanic-American communities (Tejada-Flores, 1979). Currently, the Consortium has more than 100 member stations (increased from 39 between June 1979 and March 1980). The Consortium distributes a national series, "Presente," a collection of quality local productions by member stations. "Presente" is divided into three categories of programs: *documentos*, documentaries; *expresiones*, "expressions," or cultural and artistic; and *puentes*, "bridges," or acquisitions from independent producers and foreign sources.

The Consortium newsletter reported that of the 73 program proposals submitted for funding to the national PBS schedule for 1981, 12 were Hispanic. However, not one of the Hispanic program proposals survived the voting for funding by the PBS stations.

Gutierrez (1980a) offers some predictions about Hispanic Americans and broadcasting in the 1980s: (1) greater organizational efforts of Hispanic media professionals; (2) more emphasis by nonmedia Hispanic organizations on media issues; (3) increased visibility of Hispanics in Anglo news and entertainment media; (4) continued advertising expenditures to attract Hispanic consumers, thus encouraging the growth of Spanish-language and bicultural programming; (5) particular growth in bicultural media and domestic program production; (6) greater interest on the part of Anglo media in attracting Hispanic audiences; and (7) increased employment of Hispanics in the media.

PUBLIC TELEVISION AND HISPANIC AMERICAN CHILDREN

Public television (PTV) is currently the primary source of children's programming for minorities. Principal funding for these shows has come from the Emergency School Aid Act, with additional monies from private foundations and corporations. Therefore, most children's programs targeted at minorities are funded by, produced by, and broadcast on majority culture systems.

Both Cheng (1976) and Barrera (1976) raise the issue of majority culture control of minority programming. Barrera, producer and originator of the PTV series "Carrascolendas," changed the series format from a half hour complete musical storyline to a "more Anglo" modular format with multiple short sketches in order to continue to receive national level funding and exposure.

Majority dominated or not, children's programs on PTV are more racially balanced than adult PTV shows (Task Force on Minorities in Public Broadcasting, 1978). PTV children's shows tend to have clearly defined instructional objectives, are sensitive to the existence and presentation of minority cultures, and are usually characterized by extensive research into program effectiveness.

This section will describe the children's programming designed for Hispanics that has been currently or recently available on PTV and will summarize research results.

Available Programming

Programming for Hispanic children can be classified by its target audience. Some programs emphasize cultural diversity, presenting multiethnic content; others are geared primarily for Hispanics, and still others are intended for specific Hispanic subgroups. Programs for Hispanics are likely to be bilingual.

Hispanic children's programs can also be grouped in terms of educational objectives. Some programs have very specific *academic instructional* goals, primarily modular-format shows designed for early elementary students, that seek to improve basic scholastic skills. Other programs have a more *sociological orientation* designed primarily to present and encourage children to examine minority-related aspects of Hispanic lifestyle, culture, and problems. The sociological Hispanic programs are more often intended for older children (ages 12 and up), tend to be directed to specific Hispanic subgroups, and are presented more often in dramatization formats. Both groupings share a common goal of enhancing self-image and cultural pride in Hispanic children.

"Sesame Street," "Infinity Factory," and "Electric Company" are examples of multiethnic, academic-oriented series.

"Sesame Street" is intended primarily for preschoolers, with a general set of 34 cognitive instructional objectives, including the recognition and naming of letters, numbers, and forms and prereading skills (Filep et al., 1971). In addition to the general objectives, "Sesame Street" has numerous specific objectives for audience subgroups. Cooney (1977) lists the objectives for Hispanics: (1) to use Spanish language, customs, art forms, and Spanish-speaking performers to reinforce cultural identity and pride; (2) to make the "Sesame Street" curriculum more comprehensible to the Spanish-speaking by presenting "Sesame Street" goals in Spanish and by labeling in Spanish sight words that are encountered in the child's environment; and (3) to familiarize non-Spanish-speaking children with the Spanish language and culture.

"Sesame Street" scripts are subjected to extensive formative evaluation and continue to be analyzed after they are produced. The Chicano Study Center (Children's Television Workshop, 1974) was asked by the "Sesame Street" research staff in 1973–74 to critique the Spanish segments broadcast that year. Overall, reaction was favorable. Many of the criticisms centered on improper or inappropriate Spanish-language usage. A related comment was that many of the Spanish segments were translated English segments, with no relationship to Hispanic culture.

Harvey et al. (1976a,b) describe the cognitive and affective objectives of "Infinity Factory." The series is aimed mostly at Black and Latino children ages 8 to 11 and attempts to present mathematics in a useful way to the children. "Infinity Factory" also is intended to reinforce children's feelings about their ethnic group, to represent the inner city positively, and to stress equality, self-respect, and cooperation.

"Electric Company" teaches basic reading skills to elementary school youngsters, using adventure, humor, dramatic skits and live action.

Multicultural children's series that emphasize sociological objectives include "Rebop," "Vegetable Soup," "Gettin' Over," and "As*We*See*It." They tend not to be as thoroughly pretested as programs with academic goals. They are presumed to be effective, but direct research evidence has not been located.

"Rebop" is designed for ages 7 to 14; it uses a half-hour magazine format to present three film portraits of ethnic children in real-life situations (Bureau of Elementary and Secondary Education, 1976). "Vegetable Soup" uses cartoons, animated puppets, and film serials to encourage racial understanding. "Gettin' Over" is a half-hour series where teenagers "rap" and investigate issues pertaining to minorities. "As*We*See*It" is intended for ages 12 and up.

In a format that includes role playing and dramatization, it explores the tensions of desegregation.

Academically oriented series designed for Hispanics include "Carrascolendas" and "Villa Alegre."

"Carrascolendas" is a half-hour modular-format series designed for Hispanics—primarily Mexican Americans aged 3 to 9—but the program also appeals to Anglos. Williams and Natalicio (1972) cite five content objectives: (1) to help children understand their multicultural environment; (2) to improve Spanish- and English-language skills; (3) to teach numbers; (4) to improve recognition and naming of objects in the physical environment; and (5) to assist in concept development, e.g., temperature, weight, size. Content for these objectives is presented in both Spanish and English.

"Villa Alegre" has 234 half-hour programs currently available for broadcast. The series is designed especially, but not exclusively, for Spanish-speaking 4- to 8-year olds. The format switched to modular in 1976. "Villa Alegre" is intended to help children see their cultural duality as a special good fortune and to sense their own value and importance, while teaching them about human relations, the natural environment, food and nutrition, energy, and man-made objects.

Hispanic children's series with predominantly sociological objectives include: "Mundo Real," "¿Qué Pasa, U.S.A.?," "La Esquina," and "Sonrisas," according to ESAA director Elwood Bland. "Mundo Real," a bilingual series for ages 7 to 12, presents Puerto Rican family life and relationships. "¿Qué Pasa, U.S.A.?," a Spanish-English situation comedy series for ages 12 and older, is about the generation gap in a typical Cuban-American family. "La Esquina," for ages 12 and older, dramatizes problems of Mexican-American and Anglo adolescents. "Sonrisas" is designed for Latinos and Anglos ages 8 to 12, focusing on adventures and fantasy in an urban community center.

Program Research Results

Most of the literature on Hispanic children's programming effectiveness deals with "Sesame Street," "Infinity Factory," and "Carrascolendas." Research results fit into six categories: (1) cognitive (academic) learning effects; (2) attitudinal (self-image) changes; (3) comparative cognitive effects between different viewing situations; (4) viewing behaviors; (5) program appeal; and (6) parent and teacher attitudes.

Cognitive Effects. Bogatz and Ball (1971), Filep et al. (1971), Williams and Natalicio (1972), Williams et al. (1973a,b), Van Wart (1974) and Harvey et al. (1976a,b,c) *all demonstrated direct significant cognitive learning effects for the programs they studied, although program results were not always consistent.*

"Sesame Street" researchers Bogatz and Ball and Filep et al. found consistent improvements in viewers across most of the desired content areas. Williams and Natalicio, Williams et al., and Van Wart found definite improvements in some areas for "Carrascolendas" but no improvement and occasionally regressions in a substantial number of other areas. The improvement areas varied with the year of study and the grade levels studied within each year. Harvey et al. demonstrated significant gains in math content for "Infinity Factory," the extent of which varied with viewer ethnicity and age.

More specifically, "Carrascolendas" was tested along the five program objectives in Spanish and in English, in 1972–74. Williams and Natalicio (1972) found significant improvements in three of the 10 areas, all in English: understanding multicultural environment, recognizing and naming objects in the physical environment, and concept development. There was no significant improvement in any of the five Spanish areas or in the other two English areas.

Series effectiveness was tested the next year by Williams et al. (1973a,b), and significant improvements were found in only two of the 10 areas—Spanish history and culture. First graders, considered alone, improved in five of the 10 areas. Second graders and kindergartners benefited less. When Van Wart (1974) evaluated "Carrascolendas," improvements were found in six of the 10 areas: Spanish history, culture, and reading, and English history, culture and science. In both Spanish and English, math training had the least impact.

Williams et al. (1973a,b) also considered Spanish and English fluency and responding in the correct (same) language to test interview questions and found no significant difference.

"Sesame Street" research in 1970 showed that frequent viewers in a small group of Spanish-speaking children sharply outgained all other sample groups. Bogatz and Ball (1971) attempted to verify this result but could not, due to problems with the control group. They did find that children who watched the most scored the highest. There appeared to be no significant difference between advantaged and disadvantaged children.

The second year, "Sesame Street" set more ambitious goals, which were not met as fully as the first year's goals. However, viewers who watched both years continued to learn, primarily in the new goal areas. Specific age groups appeared to gain more in specific areas.

Teacher rankings showed that "Sesame Street" viewers are generally better prepared for the school experience than nonviewers. The Peabody Picture Test indicated that "Sesame Street" had a positive effect on the verbal vocabulary of preschoolers. Limited evidence points to the fact that the show may have a positive effect on viewer IQ and mental age.

Self Image. As stated earlier, all minority-oriented children's programs share the common goal of enhancing self-image. Research testing whether or not this occurs is somewhat contradictory. Filep et al. (1971), testing

"Sesame Street," define *self-image* in terms of observable, "socially desirable" behavior, and the data indicate significant improvements in viewers. "Carras-colendas" studies vary in their results. Williams et al. (1973a,b) found no significant difference between viewer and nonviewer self-concepts. Van Wart (1974) found few significant gains between viewers and nonviewers, although scores varied regionally. Van Wart suggested dropping self-concept enhancement as a program objective because of the poor results.

Although testing of viewers did not yield significant results, surveys of parent and teacher attitudes for "Carrascolendas" and "Sesame Street" (Williams et al., 1973a,b; Van Wart, 1974; and Filep et al., 1971) indicated that increases in cultural pride, self-confidence, increased usage of Spanish, increased class participation, and improved interpersonal cooperation were perceived to have occurred.

Weisgerber and Coles (1971) produced a film designed to enhance minority self-image, and a teacher training film to demonstrate how teachers should hold follow-up discussions to reinforce learning from the film. Perceived control over one's future was one criterion of self-image the film was designed to improve. After viewing the film, all three ethnic groups felt they had less control over their futures than the control group did. Viewers were more self-critical than nonviewers, again a reverse effect. The only ethnic difference was that Hispanics with high self-image tended to have a lower average self-image than Blacks and Anglos with high self-image. Self-images were modified, but not in any consistent way and not in the intended direction. Weisgerber and Coles suggest that the film raised more questions than it answered, and it may have led the viewers to consider self-image questions for the first time.

Viewing Situations. Each of the television series research reports stressed the importance of follow-up discussions—particularly in school settings. Only one study measured the effects of such discussions. Filep et al. (1971) examined the effectiveness of the "Sesame Street" Mother Project, an attempt to increase learning from "Sesame Street" by having preschoolers view it in groups with a volunteer mother who held follow-up discussions after the show. The results reported here are from the East Los Angeles test group, comprised entirely of Hispanics.

The children were divided into categories of high involvement (involved in the project for 7 months to 1 year) and low involvement (less than 7 months) and were divided into large (45) and small (8 to 10) viewing groups. Filep et al. found that Spanish-speaking high-involvement viewers improved significantly more than frequent "Sesame Street" viewers not involved in the Mother Project. High-involvement viewers improved more than low-involvement viewers, although both groups improved. Small groups improved more, but not significantly more, than large groups. The results suggest that *follow-up discussions may increase learning from television.*

Viewing Behavior. Laosa (1974, 1976) studied children's behavior while viewing "Carrascolendas." Hispanic subgroup comparisons were made for Puerto Rican Americans, Cuban Americans, Mexican Americans, and Anglo Americans on the variables of eye contact, smiles and laughter, verbal and physical modeling, and program-related verbalizations. The results were comparable in both study years.

Laosa found that for eye contact, Puerto Ricans exhibited the most, followed by Mexican Americans, Cuban Americans, and Anglos. Girls generally exhibited more eye contact than boys. Higher eye contact was associated with fewer verbalizations and less modeling. Anglos showed fewer smiles and laughter than the other groups. There was very little physical modeling, but Cuban Americans exhibited by far the most.

Anglo Americans and Mexican Americans performed better on the posttest, possibly because they had had previous exposure to the series.

Program Appeal. Children's overall reactions to the series tested were very positive. "Sesame Street's" target audience is preschoolers, and program penetration research can be considered a measure of its appeal. Reports of studies done for CTW, the Children's Television Workshop (1970, 1974) indicate avid watching of "Sesame Street" by Hispanic youngsters. In two different studies that included the predominantly Spanish-speaking community of East Harlem, intensive data were collected from the parents of Hispanic children regarding their "Sesame Street" viewing habits. In 1970, 78 percent reported that their children watched "Sesame Street"; in 1971, 86 percent answered yes. The vast majority of those parents answering yes in both years indicated that "Sesame Street" was most recently viewed either that day or the day before. Virtually all the children qualified as regular viewers by watching at least two or three times a week. A majority of the children watched daily, and a similar majority tuned in the programs themselves without asking the parent to do so. Half the Hispanic households in this study had children aged 6 to 12, older than the target audience of children aged 2 to 5. In those households with older children, 90 percent also watched "Sesame Street," two-thirds on a regular basis. The mothers interviewed were impressed by what they considered the educational value of the program. They indicated that "Sesame Street" appeared to be playing a vital role in helping their children adapt to both the culture and language of the U.S. CTW contends that it may help older Hispanic children and mothers learn English. Viewing of "Sesame Street" was higher in the Hispanic test groups than in the Black test groups.

Harvey et al. (1976a,b) found very high student appeal ratings for "Infinity Factory." "Carrascolendas" was listed among Mexican Americans' and Anglo Americans' favorite television programs (Laosa, 1974), although Puerto Rican Americans did not list the series. Hispanic subgroup preferences may differ from each as much as they differ from Anglos'.

Parent and Teacher Attitude. Overall parent and teacher reactions were very high for all series. Harvey et al. (1976a,b) found the least positive teacher attitudes for "Infinity Factory." Even there, complaints dealt primarily with the lack of an adequate teacher's guide and accompanying material. "Infinity Factory" was felt to be more appropriate for younger children.

"Carrascolendas" benefited both Anglos and Hispanics according to teachers surveyed by Williams et al. (1973a,b). Over half of all parents surveyed were aware that their children watched "Carrascolendas" in school, and they approved partially because they want their children to speak both Spanish and English.

"Sesame Street" parents and the "Sesame Street" mothers who participated in the Filep et al. study were extremely positive about the program. CTW (1971) found that Puerto Rican mothers in East Harlem stressed the educational values of the program more than Blacks in Bedford-Stuyvesant did. Generally, Hispanics felt "Sesame Street" helped their children adapt to the culture and language of the U.S.

THE HISPANIC-AMERICAN IMAGE IN ANGLO MASS MEDIA

Newspapers

A number of studies investigated the image of Mexican Americans in newspapers. Gutierrez (1978b) was concerned with the effects of the news treatment of Mexican Americans and the responses of other sectors of American society to such coverage. An initial finding was that coverage of Chicanos was not balanced, adequate, or objective. Gutierrez, Chavira (1977), and Fishman and Casiano (1969) found that Chicano coverage was greatest in times of social unrest or threat to the established order. In such coverage, stereotypical symbols have been used by mass media sources to designate Chicano groups. Terms like *wetback* and *illegal alien* have negative connotations and were used as descriptions in much coverage of Chicano-related news events. Gutierrez observed that some papers have shifted from the use of the term *Mexican* to more negatively connoted terms just when problems with the minority group began to surface. He concluded that the use of unfavorable, stereotypical symbols may trigger stereotypical images of all Chicanos in Anglo minds and breed unfavorable feelings where they previously did not exist, similar to comments by Martinez (1969) about the effects of advertising that involves Chicanos. More recently, Gutierrez (1980b) reported that there remained a tendency for news stories to focus on Latinos as "problem people," causing or beset by problems. A 14-month analysis of California newspaper reporting of immigration in 1977 and 1978 revealed that reporters relied heavily on law-enforcement and other public officials in seeking information. Less than 1 percent of the stories even quoted or cited the undocumented workers themselves as sources.

Sanchez (1973) examined the treatment of Mexican Americans in 10 daily newspapers, including the *New York Times, Denver Post, Los Angeles Times, Arizona Republic,* and *Albuquerque Journal.* Nineteen dates between January and June 1970 were analyzed. He found (1) no support for the proposition that newspaper coverage of Mexican Americans would decrease in total stories or total space as the distance from the centers of Mexican-American activity increases; (2) most of the newspaper articles about Mexican Americans analyzed were negative, dealing with conflict as opposed to cooperation or resolution of conflict; (3) the negative news stories were no longer in average length than the positive stories; and (4) a minority of the news stories involving Mexican Americans used sources who were Mexican American, and those which did were no more likely to be positive.

Broadcasting

In considering the Hispanic-American image portrayed on television, several studies revealed similar findings. Seggar (1977), Lewels (1978), Greenberg and Baptista-Fernandez (1980), and Larez (1973) all found that Hispanic-Americans are underrepresented on television. Greenberg and Baptista-Fernandez found that 1.5 percent of the TV characters considered were Hispanic, while the Bureau of the Census estimates a total U.S. Hispanic population of around 9 percent. They said, "If you watched 300 television characters say something, you'd find less than a handful of Hispanics." This study also noted that when Hispanics are cast, it is in stereotypical roles, usually as crooks, cops, or comics. Gutierrez (1980b) related that television in the 1950s brought Desi Arnaz with his heavily accented English and a tendency to lapse into fast-paced Spanish when Lucy made him angry. Other early stereotyped characters included Frank, the Chicano gardener on "Father Knows Best"; Pepino, the farmhand on "The Real McCoys"; Sergeant Garcia, the bumbling soldier on "Zorro"; and most of the secondary characters on "The Flying Nun."

Greenberg and Baptista-Fernandez (1980) also found that (1) not more than two or three Hispanic characters were on successful shows, i.e., returning for another season; (2) half of all the Hispanic TV characters identified appeared on just four shows; (3) five of every six were male; and (4) only two Hispanic characters appeared on Saturday mornings during the three seasons analyzed. They concluded, "Television has yet to do much with or for the Hispanic American, either as a television character or as a viewer. It might be improper to characterize them as invisible, but the portrayal is blurred and hard to follow."

Larez (1973) explains that TV has created an unfavorable and unflattering stereotype of Mexican Americans based on and generating racism. Seggar (1977) found that the mass media treatment of Blacks improved significantly between 1971 and 1975. All other minority groups fell further from equal or proportional representation in television drama.

Lewels (1978) and Good (1977) concur that a major reason for media underrepresentation is the lack of minority employment in the broadcast industry. Since salaries are generally low, few educated minorities can be attracted to the industry. Until entry-level salaries can be boosted, this problem will remain.

Further problems exist because the vast majority of broadcast management and decision makers are Anglos. Good (1977) states that minority stories often are considered not important enough to run because the people making the decisions are not sensitive to minority issues. Lewels (1978) adds that "Minority problems are given a low priority on the news and reported through the eyes of people not sensitive to the problems of the minority involved."

Film

Considering the film medium and its treatment of Latinos, Whitney (1978) proposes that there have been four phases of film stereotyping. The first, earliest stage (the era of silent pictures) portrayed the Latino as "the greasy Mexican bandit, generally repulsive and/or irredeemably evil."

A second phase began in the 1930s and lasted for about 10 to 15 years. Then, the Latino was portrayed in the new role of the "Latin lover." The Latino would rarely be seen unless singing or dancing and demonstrating a sensuality unmatched by Anglo performers. Ironically, the Latino would consistently find himself losing to the Anglo figure in competition for love.

Phase three returned to the "bandito" image, the Latino playing the role of robber, sidekick, or stupid peasant. This period began in the 1940s and has lasted until the present. Whitney sees the future as the fourth phase of development, in which the Latino should be portrayed as he or she really lives, doing away with the traditional stereotypes that have followed the Hispanic Americans through the various stages of treatment in films.

Literature

A number of studies have dealt with stereotypical imagery in children's literature. This area has attracted researchers because most contend that children learn from and can be influenced by the reading materials they encounter. Uribe and Martinez (1975) summarized research that found that a culturally diverse curriculum of reading materials for children could improve the self-concepts of both white and nonwhite students, and that when children's actual backgrounds and experiences are depicted in books, children identify more readily with the story characters. Stories that consistently involve only Anglo children do not allow identification and self-concept development in minority children.

Gast (1967) found that the stereotypes of the Mexican as dark, uneducated, and unmotivated are also present in children's books. Hornburger (1975) stated that young readers should be taught to be critical of the materials presented to them and when possible, to discuss the stereotypes found.

Morgan (1973) found that a basic story line emerges in the children's literature dealing with minority groups. Typically, a Latino family moves to New York, lives in a bad neighborhood, and finds trouble with school officials and/or police, who are nearly always Anglo. Eventually, the family lives happily ever after, once the "American way" is made clear to them by helpful and loving public officials, usually police officers, social workers, and teachers.

Blatt (1968) observed that while Mexican and Mexican-American cultures are very different, books often present them as being identical. Morgan further pointed out that so-called Puerto Rican traits, customs, dress, and food were often actually of Italian or Mexican origin. The resulting cultural conglomeration served primarily to confuse readers.

Gast (1967) concluded that recent children's literature has become more representative of the differing cultural backgrounds likely to be held by those for whom the works are intended. He argued that modern trends in children's literature were positive in nature, aimed at the elimination of racial stereotyping and portraying minority characters in a favorable light. This positive trend seemed to be strongest in children's fiction and less evident in modern textbooks and nonfiction designed for use by children.

An underlying theme in most, if not all, studies considered is the fact that minority issues are discussed and presented in the mass media primarily in the context of the problems or difficulties that they pose for Anglo society, whereas their cultural activity and creativity is, by and large, overlooked.

The media image seems to convey these major shortcomings:

1. Mexican Americans are often portrayed as crooks, drunks, sneaks, overweight, and in need of a bath.

2. The continuation of such stereotyping reinforces negative images in the general public's mind and also may generate racist images among those who do not yet harbor them.

3. Children need to associate with their varying cultural roles in order to develop healthy personal identities. Most non-Anglo children are currently not able to have that opportunity within the English-language media.

4. Newspapers and television generally fail to represent minority population segments adequately in their reporting, even in cities with great numbers of minority citizens.

CONCLUSIONS

This review has integrated findings from multiple sources in order to provide as clear and accurate a portrayal as possible about the mass communication orientations of the media and the Hispanic American. Such a portrayal makes it easier to map out directions for future research and to begin to choose from among alternative theoretical postures for such research. This concluding section will draw out highlights from the review.

- English language newspaper usage is low, with Hispanic Americans likely to be around the 50-percent subscriber level.
- Television usage is at least as great as for the general public and is being consumed at the adult rate of about 4 hours per day.
- Radio listening is extensive, at a rate of perhaps 3 to 4 hours per day.
- There is large-scale interest in more Spanish-language mass communication material—in news and entertainment—across all media; this is particularly true for adult Hispanics.
- The broadcast media, particularly television, are more relied on as sources of information than the print media.
- Spanish-language television is dominated by foreign interests; Spanish-language radio stations are primarily owned by non-Hispanics.
- Spanish-language radio and television, where available, are very popular with Hispanic audiences and where unavailable, are desired.
- Public television has been particularly significant in its efforts to create programs for Hispanic-American children and has a fairly impressive record of programming effects, including the following:

    A persistent demonstration of cognitive learning effects

    Perceptions by teachers and parents that self-images of Hispanic children were improved, with some corresponding evidence in the children themselves

    A demonstration that follow-up discussions of program content enhance their impact

    Strong positive reactions to the programs from the child viewers

    Strong favorable reactions from Hispanic parents and their children's teachers

Also, there has been:

- A surfeit of negative news about Hispanic Americans in print media and an underrepresentation overall.
- An absence of positive images in television and a virtual absence of any images

- An emphasis on the portrayal of Hispanics as crooks, cops, and comics
- A positive trend in Hispanic imagery in children's literature, particularly in fiction but less so in texts

These bits and pieces from separate and often disparate research studies provide outlines for significant research questions but do not satisfy the rigor of a comprehensive examination of mass communication orientations. At the least, one would now wish to move to a multimedia examination for both adults and young people of use, content preferences, and attitudes, including both English-language and Spanish-language media. One would wish to isolate Hispanic community leaders and determine their uses of formal and informal information sources in their communities and their relationships to the available Anglo and non-Anglo media opportunities. Current and more comprehensive content analyses across different media in the same locales at the same and different times also seem necessary. Concurrently, these approaches would begin to bring coherence to questions concerning Hispanic Americans and mass communication.

2
INTERPERSONAL COMMUNICATION AND MEXICAN AMERICANS

JUDEE K. BURGOON
ERIC M. EISENBERG
MICHAEL BURGOON
FELIPE KORZENNY
BRADLEY S. GREENBERG

This chapter presents a comprehensive review of the research literature on nonmediated communication behaviors of Hispanic Americans. Included in this review are reports on various topics related to communication. These include Hispanic Americans' *self-image, values,* and *cognitive styles; perceptions* of Hispanic Americans by non-Hispanics; *interpersonal communication,* with emphasis on family communication and social participation; and *language usage* and its relationship to culture. Excluded are reports dealing exclusively with the psychology of Hispanic Americans, their socioeconomic concerns, and other subtopics without a clear relationship to communication behavior.

Only a small percentage of the articles and texts reviewed in this paper could be classified as empirical research. In this review, we have synthesized pertinent empirical studies, books, and reports produced between January 1970 and February 1980. Although some experimental and field studies have been done, much of the work in the area can be classified as anecdotal and editorial. Empirical articles are described in far greater number and detail in this review. In data-based studies, some description of the sample and type of procedures is also provided. Whenever possible, we have deemphasized prescriptive conclusions and have focused on descriptions of existing communication behaviors among Hispanic Americans.

The literature search followed essentially the same process as for the mass communication review in Chapter 1.[1] This review is divided into four major sections: (1) self-image, values, and cognitive styles of Hispanic Americans (HAs); (2) perceptions and stereotypes of HAs by others; (3) interpersonal communication and social participation of HAs; and (4) language usage.

HISPANIC AMERICAN SELF-IMAGE, VALUES AND COGNITIVE STYLES

In examining the nonmediated communication behaviors of Hispanic Americans, one must take into account those sociocultural attitudes and values that can significantly influence communication patterns. Of particular importance here is the degree to which Hispanic beliefs, values, and perceptions parallel or differ from those of the larger Anglo community.

Self-Image

One potentially central consideration is the cultural group with which the Hispanic identifies. Driedger (1976) advanced Lewin's (1948) thesis that individuals need a firm, clear sense of identification with either their ingroup or the host society in order to find a secure basis for a sense of well-being. Sufficient ingroup insecurity may result in self-hatred and ingroup denial. Even when ingroup identity is strong, an individual's self-image may suffer if the reference group represents a small or outcast portion of society. Individual self-images are often tied to the growth in size and importance of a given ethnic group in a particular society (Driedger, 1976).

Hispanics living in the U.S. think of themselves as belonging mainly to the larger and more heterogeneous Anglo culture, while those living in Mexico experience an essentially homogeneous culture. For this reason, the self-images of Hispanics born in Mexico tend to be more positive than those of Hispanics born in the U.S. Hispanics born in the U.S. have higher expectations provided by the society they use as a reference group, while those in Mexico have a different comparison group and may feel quite well-off with respect to their background (Korzenny et al., 1979).

---

[1]The primary sources included the following: several abstracting services (*Psychological, Sociological, Communication, Journalism,* and *Anthropological Abstracts, Topicator*); computer-based bibliographies (*ERIC, Social Science Citation Index*); communication conference listings of delivered papers; and relevant journals (*American Sociological Review, Journal of Cross-Cultural Psychology, Journal of Social Psychology, Agenda, Aztlan, Communication Monographs, El Grito, Journal of Communication, Journal of Ethnic Studies, Journal of Personality, Journalism Quarterly, International Journal of Intercultural Relations,* and *Public Opinion Quarterly*). About 200 of the emergent titles were examined in some detail, and full abstracts were created for approximately 65. These 65 are emphasized in this review.

Hispanic Americans are far from being a homogeneous community. The determinants of the unique characteristics of Hispanic-American culture have been spelled out by Penalosa (1970), who describes four sets of influences that have shaped HAs: (1) the traditional Mexican culture; (2) the majority American culture; (3) generally low social class influences; and (4) the minority status that HAs experience.

Dworkin (1970) studied self-images of Hispanic Americans and was able to identify various components of the HA self-image. In his study, students were asked to think of and write down all the words they felt accurately described the personality, appearance and physical features, mannerisms, family and religious life, intelligence, educational experience, socioeconomic status, ambitions, and activities of Hispanic-American populations.

Dworkin's results showed a wide variability in perceptions of self-image among HAs. Self-images of HAs differ greatly as a function of where the individual was born (U.S. or elsewhere). Native-born HAs characterize themselves as emotional, authoritarian, old-fashioned, poor and of low social class, uneducated or poorly educated, having little care for education, mistrusted and lazy, indifferent, and unambitious. Foreign-born HAs, on the other hand, characterize themselves as proud, religious, gregarious, friendly, happy, racially tolerant, practical, and well adjusted. The differences in self-image resulting from place of birth are striking; at least seven of the self-attributes of HAs born in the U.S. are negative, while none of the self-images of foreign-born Hispanics can be classified as undesirable. Dworkin's research pointed out that it may be inappropriate to lump all HAs into one group, since differences may exist within the group among variables that have not been clearly identified (such as place of birth).

Hispanic American self-esteem is subject to the impact of many variables. Social and cultural status, along with language barriers, impinge on HAs in such a way that many are apprehensive about interacting with the majority reference group. Self-esteem is affected by both apprehension about communicating and about being rejected or ridiculed by members of the majority culture (Korzenny et al., 1979).

The use of Spanish, particularly nonstandard dialects, and the use of accented English may also contribute to a negative self-image. Research by Flores and Hopper (1975) revealed that many HAs negatively evaluate nonstandard Spanish and English. Except for those who labeled themselves Chicanos, the Hispanic respondents in their study assigned more negative personality characteristics to speakers using Tex-Mex (nonstandard Spanish) and accented English speech than to speakers using standard Spanish and English. Those who were less educated, less affluent, and older were least favorable toward nonstandard speech; those who used Spanish more frequently were most favorable toward standard English. Given the generally lower education and income levels among HAs, along with the prevalent use of Spanish, these results suggest that large segments of the HA population may negatively stereotype other HAs based on their language use.

While there is some negative prejudice felt by HAs toward other HAs, there is also evidence of "positive" prejudice. In a study of 309 youths classified as Mexican American based on their parents' ethnic background, Lampe (1975) found that almost all of them preferred their own ethnic group to Anglos, Negroes, Jews, and Asian Americans. Only those labeling themselves Anglo Americans showed a higher preference for Anglos. Moreover, those identifying themselves as Chicanos were more favorable to Blacks than to Anglos (a reversal of the pattern found among the rest of the sample), indicating that these junior high school students had not rejected their ethnic background in favor of the Anglo culture.

Overall, the research and writing related to Hispanic self-image suggests that while many HAs hold a negative view of themselves and their culture, they do not uniformly do so. Factors such as degree of identification with Anglo culture, socioeconomic status, language use, and communication practices influence the holding of a favorable self-image.

Values

Many writers have speculated about the value systems of contemporary Hispanic Americans. In an extensive discussion of Spanish Americans in the southwestern U.S., Christian and Christian (1966) outlined what they believed to be the fundamental difference in values between Anglos and HAs. Anarchism is considered to be the chief attribute of traditional Spanish society, and for this reason many Anglos may perceive HAs as irrational. Anarchism is translated by HAs to indicate extreme personal autonomy, vitality, passion, and freedom. It is sometimes interpreted by Anglos to indicate degree of inefficiency or living in chaos. Many H-A men have problems getting jobs in American businesses because they perceive the model of the salable American executive to be effeminate and weak (Christian and Christian, 1966).

Literature reviewed by Romero (1966) suggests further possible differences between H-A and Anglo values. The groups are expected to differ in (1) time span allowable for delayed gratification; (2) attitudes toward health, sanitation, and medical care; (3) fatalistic views about life and the extent to which the individual can control his or her outcomes; (4) the importance of the family group; (5) the value of education; (6) attitudes toward the profit motive; (7) attitudes toward economic efficiency; (8) interpretation of justice; (9) success orientation; and (10) emphasis on competition as a whole.

In sum, most writers about HAs have pointed out that they are "caught between two cultures." Large differences are expected to occur between HAs and Anglos in terms of their value system. Empirical research has not borne out this intuition. A study by Weigel and Quinn (1977) attempted to find ethnic differences in cooperative language behavior among 148 13-year-old urban males. Whites, Blacks, and Puerto Ricans were included in the study. There were no ethnic differences in regard to cooperation, and self-defeating competitive behaviors dominated for all groups. The results show that ethnic differences, if any, in disposition to cooperate have become negligible by the time individuals reach their teens.

Romero (1966) tested two hypotheses concerning the values of HAs: that (1) Anglo and H-A "culture value concepts" are somewhat in conflict with one another and (2) H-A students are not acculturated—many aspects of the Anglo middle class culture have not as yet been internalized. Data from Romero's acculturation questionnaire yielded few of the differences suggested by his review of the literature. HAs at the secondary school level demonstrated a high degree of acculturation and were in general complying with the Anglo cultural value system. Romero (1966) warned that attempts to adapt to purported H-A cultural values in school systems may bring about personality disorganization in their attempt to solve a problem that does not, in fact, exist.

In an article advocating consumer education for Mexican Americans, Gromatzky's (1968) review of research in economics revealed that Mexican Americans value the same basic things for their family as others do: good health, comfortable homes, attractive and comfortable clothing, time to enjoy friends and family, and extended opportunities for their children.

Research and writing related specifically to the value of familism— the overriding importance of family and collective needs over personal needs— have produced mixed conclusions. A study by Bean et al. (1977) surveyed familism values among 325 Mexican-American couples in Austin, Texas. With few exceptions, results paralleled Anglo samples; there was little evidence that familism is an overridingly important factor in Mexican-American family life, especially as a determinant of marital satisfaction.

A somewhat contrasting view is represented in a study of 7- to 15-year-olds by Goodman and Beman (1968), who concluded that the home and the people at home were central to the H-A child's view of the world. In response to the open-ended question "Whom do you love?" no H-A children included anyone but relatives in their responses, whereas Anglo and Black children included many nonfamily members and friends.

Mirande (1977) presents a comparison of two conflicting views of H-A families. One view depicts a rigid, male-dominated, authoritarian family structure that breeds passivity and dependence. A more realistic perspective (according to Mirande) is that the H-A family is warm, nurturing, and supportive and serves to give individuals a strong sense of security. Both views reflect a high degree of intrafamily dependence. The difference lies in the interpretation and evaluation of these characteristics. While the familistic orientation of HAs is considered well recognized, not everyone agrees on the effects of this orientation. Supporters maintain that it provides for invaluable emotional and material reinforcement, while critics of this structure attack it as being atypical, undemocratic, and impeding social achievement.

This latter perspective is echoed in a research review by Miller (1979). Stereotypically, images of Hispanic families tend to gloss over the disorganizing influences of immigration, economic hardship and poverty, language barriers, and cultural and generational conflict. Miller argues that the lack of upward social mobility among HAs can often be attributed to the exaggerated influence of the family. Specifically, he posits that HAs cannot get ahead because the family takes precedence over the individual. Gains made by the individual are often deemphasized or erased because of the forced necessity to help needy relatives. Thus, according to Miller, HAs are confined to an economic treadmill, with nonachievement the norm, lest the upwardly mobile family member incur the wrath of those who are less fortunate. This view is also expressed by Madson et al. (1966).

Regarding familism, then, one might conclude that while Anglos and HAs both value the family, it has a more pervasive influence in organizing and orienting Hispanic behaviors and attitudes.

Whether or not the family is an overriding influence, it appears not to produce the purported value for nonachievement. Hsia (1973) studied the motivation, communication, and aspirations of 168 Blacks, Chicanos, and low- and high-income Anglos in Texas. Multiple analyses yielded no support for the thesis that Blacks or Chicanos lack motivation or aspirations. The only qualifications on this trend were that Chicanos were less ambitious to attain elected office than Blacks or Anglos and had the lowest aspirations for their children's education; but they still desired that it be higher than their own. No ethnic differences were found in earnings desired or willingness to work.

The degree to which H-A values are moving toward Anglo cultural values also was studied recently by Knight and Kagan (1977). They employed frequency of prosocial and competitive behaviors as indicators of acculturation to either the majority or the barrio model. Subjects were second- and third-generation Mexican-American and Anglo children in the fourth through sixth grades; an equal number of children from both sexes were used. The Mexican-American sample was taken from a traditional community, so that acculturation to the barrio was potentially possible. In all communities, for second- and third-generation Mexican-American children, the study revealed a loss of prosocial values in favor of competitive values through successive generations. The authors suggest that acculturation to the barrio model may hold only for isolated rural communities.

Taken together, the above findings suggest a clear conclusion: The cultural values typically assumed to play a large part in the lives of Hispanic Americans may no longer be applicable. Empirical research suggests instead that

Hispanic Americans are often like Anglos (perhaps even affluent Anglos), and more so than other minotirities in the U.S. The one exception, and it has been challenged, might be the greater centrality of the family; to the extent it exists, it has not produced social and personal values contrary to the majority culture.

Cognitive Styles

Another way in which Hispanics have been posited to differ from Anglos is in cognitive styles. Knudson and Kagan (1977), for example, compared field independence for Mexican American and Anglo children aged 5 to 9. Whereas the Anglos tended to be more field independent—that is, they were better at making analytical discriminations than the Hispanic children—the Hispanics were generally more altruistic and less competitive.

Other research has supported the greater field dependence of H-A children. In a review of research findings designed to aid teachers in becoming more aware of factors to consider in teaching composition to Mexican-American children, Rodrigues (1977) found that nonbilingual Mexican Americans are more teacher dependent and require more support than Anglos. In general, Mexican Americans from traditional homes are more field dependent (i.e., rely more on the direction and interpretations of the instructor) in learning situations than Anglos. Based on these findings, Rodrigues (1977) urged multicultural teaching styles to deal with these differences in learning style, a recommendation echoed by Tyler (1970), who cited differences in learning style, along with the language barrier, as factors placing H-A youth at a distinct disadvantage in school.

These apparent differences in cognitive styles are compounded by other problems encountered by H-A youth in the school system, problems that may partly account for the observed differences in learning styles. In reviewing literature in anthropology, Singleton (1969) discussed the educational processes and problems confronting minority groups in modern society. He maintained that since the school is a "proving ground" for the identity of all adolescents, minority identity crises are compounded by confusion about Hispanic and Anglo values and priorities. This assertion is corroborated by the sociological study of Christian and Christian (1966), who contended that H-A students encounter values at the school in conflict with those they see at home. It is important to note, however, that editorials and sociological studies have reached conclusions not corroborated by systematic study of larger samples. For example, the study by Romero (1966) revealed that there is, in fact, little cultural conflict in schools and that teachers are well aware of the little conflict that does exist. He warns overzealous reformers of the potential dangers of correcting for value differences that may not actually exist.

PERCEPTIONS AND STEREOTYPES
OF HISPANIC AMERICANS

Stereotypes of Hispanics abound. Some have a basis in reality; others do not. To judge which ones are without foundation, one needs to know what characteristics are truly applicable to the Hispanic populace. Some initial insights come from Casavantes' (1970) profile of Mexican Americans. According to him, it is safe to say that they have brought with them many customs from their country of origin; they speak Spanish to some degree, and many have a noticeable accent; they are mostly Catholic; and they are frequently distinguishable from the majority culture due to their darker skin and hair. Casavantes further reports that most MAs reside in the Southwest, have an average educational level of less than eight years, and that 30 to 40 percent of M-A families live below the poverty level. He argues that many of the attitudes attributed to Mexican Americans in particular are poverty related and cut across ethnic lines; for example, fatalism, machismo, and reliance on larger groups of people are all a result of impoverishment rather than ethnicity. Writing from an anthropological perspective, Williams (1975) argues further that family life among the poor has been badly misrepresented. The large families of Chicanos are often labeled by outsiders as "stifling," and women's involvement in them is taken as conservativism and a sign of oppression. In the face of poverty and limited upward mobility, however, these kinship coping strategies take on a different meaning.

As is the case with most sociological groupings, perceptions of Hispanics often vary widely from more objective characteristics. A variety of factors may lead to stereotyping; in addition to ethnicity, occupational roles and social status have strong effects (Corenblum et al., 1976). The societal image of Hispanic Americans available in mass media portrayals (Greenberg and Baptista-Fernandez, 1980) is less than favorable. The use of accented speech also triggers a variety of associations (e.g., Delia, 1972; Giles, 1973; Mulac et al., 1974). Numerous studies have assessed non-Hispanic-American perceptions of HAs. Some of the more informative ones are discussed next.

Baird (1974) surveyed 550 Anglo households in Lubbock, Texas, in an attempt to determine the most common Mexican-American stereotypes. Mexican Americans were, in general, perceived as individuals, which contrasts with past wisdom suggesting that they are seen as monolithic, as part of a large, undifferentiated group. Most Anglos stated that MAs either were or should be treated as equals, and most said that they would vote for MAs if they were otherwise qualified. However, respondents reported that race relations between Anglos and MAs were between average and poor, and most Anglos preferred that MAs join Anglo groups rather than form their own.

In another survey of predominantly Anglo respondents, Funk et al. (1976) used multidimensional scaling to identify stereotypical "clusters" on an "activist" scale. Blacks and MAs clustered together and were perceived as most activist, followed by Anglos and Poles. Chinese and Japanese were perceived as the least activist of the three clusters.

Rich and Ogawa (1972) surveyed 100 Black ghetto residents to determine what stereotypes they held of Anglos, Mexican Americans, and Japanese Americans. Results showed that ghetto Blacks had a strongly negative view of Anglos and of Mexican Americans. Ghetto Blacks described Mexican Americans as emotional, radical, talkative, argumentative, and loud. Japanese Americans were seen more favorably than the other two groups. Rich and Ogawa concluded that Blacks' stereotypes of MAs are remarkably similar to Anglos'.

Stephan (1977) considered the views of Blacks, Anglos, and Hispanics, and attempted to relate stereotyping to attribution theory. Of interest was whether members of an ingroup would make more dispositional attributions (i.e., assuming the behavior was due to personal casuality and responsibility) for *positive* behaviors and fewer situational attributions (i.e., assigning responsibility instead to situational factors) for *negative* behaviors than would members of the two outgroups. The results showed this clearly to be the case for Hispanics—HAs attributed *negative* H-A behavior to situational factors more often than Blacks and Anglos did and attributed *positive* H-A behavior to dispositional factors more often than Blacks did. The Anglos held more favorable attitudes toward the HAs and Blacks than the two minority groups held for each other. The antipathy manifested between Blacks and HAs was assumed to contribute to the negative dispositional attributions. Stephan concluded, "When a member of a disliked outgroup engages in a positive behavior, he is less likely to have that behavior attributed to positive dispositional characteristics than would be the case if an ingroup member engaged in the same behavior [p. 265]." In this manner, negative stereotypes of Hispanic Americans, who are given less credit for positive behavior, may be perpetuated.

As noted earlier, one factor that may trigger negative attributions and stereotypes is language use. Ryan and Carranza (1975) researched evaluative reactions toward speech varieties associated with Mexican Americans. Anglo and Mexican-American adolescents rated the personalities of 16 speakers representing four combinations of interaction context (home vs. school) and language (Spanish vs. English). Congruent with findings reported on language usage in the next section, both groups preferred English in the school context. The effect of the interactional domain on evaluative reactions toward English and Spanish speakers suggests that subjects take into account the appropriateness of the speaker's behavior for the situation in addition to the ethnicity of the speaker. In another related study comparing standard English with accented English speakers, standard English speakers received more favorable evaluations in all cases; contrary to expectations, Mexican-American receivers did not prefer accented English in the home context. A follow-up study performed by the same authors indicated that small increments in accentedness are associated with gradually less favorable impressions of the speaker.

Recent linguistic research conducted by Williams and his associates (Hopper and Williams, 1973; Whitehead et al., 1974; Williams, 1970; Williams et al., 1972; Williams et al., 1971; Williams and Naremore, 1974) also describes some of the attributions made about people with accented speech. This program of research has obtained several consistent findings: (1) teacher attitudes toward taped samples of children's speech are most often judged using two dimensions, confidence-eagerness and ethnicity-nonstandardness; (2) children who use nonstandard English are often perceived to have important academic limitations; and (3) there is a good deal of heterogeneity of language attitudes among teachers, and this heterogeneity is not entirely a function of the ethnicity of the teacher. Regarding the last conclusion, Williams and Naremore (1974) identified through factor analysis five distinct teacher types based on their evaluations of Anglo, Black, and Hispanic-American students. One major type tended to rate H-A children as particularly nonstandard, while another type did not consistently distinguish between Anglo and H-A children in their evaluations. Yet both types included virtually identical distributions of teachers by ethnicity.

Other research has similarly found more negative impressions associated with accented speech. Rodrigues (1977), among others, found that even fluent speakers of English are stereotyped if they speak with an accent.

Finally, Ramirez (1977) investigated the effect of communicator ethnicity on social influence. Using 116 Chicano adults in an apartment-house setting, he found that subjects reacted equally positively toward Anglo and Hispanic-American communicators, but they were more likely to comply with requests for behavior made by the Anglo communicator. Similar results have been reported by Ramirez and Lasater (1977), with the added finding that minority communicator evaluation is dependent upon the self-esteem of the evaluator. Evaluators with high self-esteem reacted more favorably to the Hispanic-American communicator than those with low self-esteem.

Consistent with expectations, most studies suggest that while Hispanic-American values may not be radically different from those of the majority culture and many supposed H-A characteristics are, in fact, a function of poverty and limited upward mobility, negative stereotypes continue to be held, both by Blacks and Anglos. Accented speech, in particular, creates a context in which these stereotypes are evident.

INTERPERSONAL COMMUNICATION

Family Communication

As noted earlier, many stereotypes have been attributed to Hispanic-American families (Peñalosa, 1970; Tijerina, 1977; Miller, 1979). A central one is the importance of the extended family in H-A life. Research has demonstrated that traditional characteristics of H-A families are that they live in the same neighborhood, often for many years; they visit each other frequently; they maintain close contact with their elderly; and they tend to help each other in times of crisis (Bean et al., 1977; Gromatzky, 1968; Clark, 1959; Goodman and Beman, 1968; Sena, 1973; Tijerina, 1977). Williams (1975) suggested that a large extended family is a sensible coping mechanism for families faced with extreme poverty. Even so, Anglo-controlled agencies find it difficult to understand why HAs are leery of outside help and will often share badly needed resources with other family members (Ramos, 1973). That they do so is evidence of the supportive network maintained by the H-A family.

Tijerina (1977) surveyed 163 elderly Mexican Americans in Austin, Texas, in an attempt to identify their major problems in American culture. Results showed that isolation was a major problem facing the elderly, with transportation especially difficult. Even so, elderly MAs were fairly well connected with their families. Twenty-nine percent of them lived with their families. A stable pattern of residence existed, many had immediate relatives in their neighborhoods, and 60 percent visited with their offspring or families at least once a week.

Steward and Steward (1974) investigated social distance and interaction patterns in a study where Anglo and Mexican-American mothers taught games to (1) their own child, (2) a child of the same ethnicity who was not their own, and (3) a child of different ethnicity. A number of comparisons were made to determine the degree to which social class, ethnicity of mother and child, and ethnic match between mother and child affected interaction patterns.

Mothers did not differ in the amount of time spent with each child. Anglo mothers, however, initiated more instructions, while Mexican-American mothers gave more original instructions. Middle-class mothers of both ethnicities initiated more instructional units and used more nonverbal communication than lower-class mothers. Middle-class MAs used more questions of greater specificity than lower-class MAs; however, the reverse was true for Anglos.

Differences in the children's behaviors were also found. Children in general were more accepting when paired with Mexican-American mothers, especially when those mothers were middle class. Also, Mexican-American middle-class children were the most accepting overall. Several interactions were observed. Anglo children with M-A mothers showed higher acceptance behaviors than M-A children with Anglo mothers. Mexican-American mothers, particularly lower class, used more negative reinforcement, and more to their own child than to others. Lower-class mothers were most likely to use information from children as meaningful feedback. Overall, Mexican-American mothers were most successful at gaining compliance. Mexican-American children were less compliant than Anglos when paired with mothers other than their own.

Hsia's (1973) study of 168 Texans of various ethnic backgrounds is relevant here. Chicanos placed more importance on husband-wife communication than did Blacks or Anglos. Chicanos were most similar to affluent Anglos, both in this respect and also in their relatively high communication with friends and neighbors. Blacks tended more toward isolation and communication more with ministers than did Chicanos. Finally, Chicanos were not significantly different in overall frequency of communication from the Blacks and Anglos.

Littlefield (1974) tested the effects of sex, ethnicity, and disclosure target on the amount of self-disclosure for 300 Black, Anglo, and Mexican-American ninth graders. When sexes were pooled, Anglo students reported the most total disclosure, followed next by Blacks. Mexican Americans showed the least total self-disclosure. A significant sex-by-ethnicity interaction was found such that Anglo and Mexican-American females disclosed more than males. Of all the groups, Mexican-American males reported the least total amount of self-disclosure. Anglo and Mexican-American females favored the best female friend as a disclosure target; mother was reported as the preferred disclosure target for Black women and all males.

In sum, it appears that HAs show a high frequency of interpersonal communication in general and with family in particular. The amount of contact with children, the elderly, friends, and neighbors and the value placed on good husband-wife communication parallels or exceeds that of Anglos. There do appear to be differences, however, in styles of communication (at least between mothers and children) and in willingness to self-disclose, with Hispanic males least inclined to disclosure.

Communication with and
Participation in Social Institutions

Research cited earlier has alluded to a tendency among HAs to rely on family rather than social institutions in times of need and to participate less in social/political activities. Few studies have actually addressed these perceptions.

Duran and Monroe (1977) conducted a large exploratory study of the communication behavior, resource utility, and organizational activity of Mexican Americans (MA), Cuban Americans (CA), and Puerto Rican residents of Chicago. Four hundred Latinos (Hispanic Americans, in our terms) were interviewed by trained bilingual interviewers. In general, results showed a pattern of "information poverty" for most Latinos. Most HAs rely on local sources of information exclusively and know very little about social services, employment opportunities, and general news items (Christian and Christian, 1966). In Hsia's study (1973), Chicanos were found to have similar needs to Anglos in most walks of life but lacked awareness of the social agencies that could help them in meeting these needs. In her description of consumer-education programs, Gromatzky (1968) argued that most HAs would like household goods similar to those Anglos like but lack in consumer awareness.

Some studies begin with the premise that participation of Hispanic Americans in various social institutions would be a positive sign of acculturation, and they set out to identify those factors related to social participation (Williams et al., 1973; Clements and Sauer, 1975; Antunes and Gaitz, 1975). Duran and Monroe (1977) reported that reading activity and use of the public library are positively associated with participation in voluntary organizations. Mounting evidence suggests that social participation in voluntary organizations is related to an increased likelihood of voting. In the studies by Antunes and Gaitz (1975) and Williams et al. (1973), ethnicity was a better predictor of social participation than social class or age. However, the expectation that felt discrimination by an ethnic group should lead to increased participation in social and political activities was not borne out. While Blacks were shown to be far and away the most involved, Mexican Americans did not evidence any greater involvement than Anglos. Put differently, while ethnicity has a large effect on sociopolitical participation, it does so in a way that many contravene expectations: MAs tend to be least involved and Blacks most involved.

One final study offers some insight into how communication between HAs and institutions or agencies might be facilitated. Holladay (1971) studied the communication preferences of 130 Mexican-American parents of elementary school children in East Los Angeles, California. Parents were asked about the best and worse ways for them to receive information from school about their children. Results showed that the choice of channel depends on the type of message and the demographics of the parents. Bilingual messages were preferred, and most parents indicated that they should be received by both parents, not only the father. The teacher was generally preferred as the source of this kind of information, and parents had mixed feelings about how they would respond to messages sent by the principal.

The conclusions to be drawn from this limited empirical evidence are that, despite their need for social services and political involvement, HAs are generally less well informed about services or jobs available and less likely to be politically active than other ethnic groups. Parental preferences for bilingual messages from the school system, directed to both parents, and sent by the teacher rather than the principal, underscore the importance of language medium, authority level of the source, and intended receiver of messages in establishing communication channels between HAs and social or political institutions.

LANGUAGE USE

The Spanish language is strongly associated with the Spanish culture for Hispanic Americans. Many Hispanic Americans stress their desire to remain in the U.S. without having to sacrifice their language or their culture. In a sociological study of Southwestern HAs, Christian and Christian (1966) describe the strong relationships between Hispanic-American culture, language, and world view. In their model, the nature of H-A culture is embedded in the Spanish language; language and culture together form a basic, irreducible orientation of HAs to the external world.

The Spanish language serves some very specific purposes for Hispanic Americans. One of the first investigations in this area was done by Mahoney (cited in Patella and Kuvlesky, 1973), who studied the language choices of rural and urban Mexican-American household heads and their children in various contexts. She found that, in general, urban MAs use more English than do rural MAs. She also observed that the degree of English use correlated negatively with age and positively with education level, American birth, income, and occupational level of M-A head of household.

There is strong support for the hypothesis that language choice in a given situation is determined by the nature of the interaction and the gender of the participant (Barker, 1972; Brennan and Ryan, 1973; Kuvlesky, 1973; Laosa, 1975; Patella and Kuvlesky, 1975; Ward, 1972). Furthering Mahoney's work, a program of research was carried out by Patella and Kuvlesky (1973, 1975) to determine the relationships among social context, language use, and social aspirations among HAs in border regions of Texas and Colorado. Mexican-American high school students were used in each of three studies. The major goals of the studies were to determine: (1) what difference gender and situational variables made in language use and (2) whether changes had occurred between 1967 and 1973 in language use.

Almost all the MAs studied by Patella and Kuvlesky in 1967 and in 1973 were able to speak some Spanish, and a shift was noted toward an increased preference for speaking Spanish. Most of the reported use of Spanish was for oral communication, especially with family and friends. The least use of Spanish was always reported to occur at school. English also dominated H-A reading and writing habits.

Many of these findings were complicated by situation and gender differences. Males indicated using Spanish more often in all oral situations (talking to parents, friends) while females indicated using more Spanish in reading (magazines, newspapers, letters). This pattern, which remained the same from 1967 to 1973, may be due to the general tendency for American women to have better verbal skills than males. Reported language usage patterns of parents and friends closely paralleled those reported by respondents for themselves. While both male and female youths perceived their parents as highly Spanish-dominant, females saw their friends as more English-dominant in *oral* situations, and males saw their friends as more English-dominant in *written* contexts. The parallelism may lead one to conclude that these M-A youth see themselves in harmony with their contexts of interaction, using more or less Spanish in accordance with situational norms for language use which they perceive to exist.

Kuvlesky's study (1973) extended the research to include a sample of

Colorado students. Mexican-American Coloradans were found to be remarkably similar to Mexican-American Texans in general patterns of language use. Most youth reported they can speak Spanish; gender differences occurred in reported use of Spanish and were consistent over language situations; the use of Spanish by MAs varied by the channel used; oral communication in Spanish was more common than written communication. The two differences for the Colorado sample were (1) less use of spoken Spanish in general in Colorado and (2) one-third of the Colorado sample read non-English newspapers, which was higher than the Texas groups. In comparing Spanish use with level of social aspirations, Kuvlesky concluded that the bulk of evidence indicates that the use of Spanish over English is not related to level of aspiration.

In an extensive anthropological study attempting to relate language use to social behavior among Mexican Americans in Tucson, Barker (1972) found that the choice of whether to use Spanish or English depends on bilingual ability, type of interpersonal relationship, subject context (identity of the speaker), and social context. Of these, the interaction context is the strongest determinant of language choice among bilinguals. Barker's work supports the hypothesis that when a bilingual minority is undergoing cultural change, the functions originally served by the ancestral language become split between two or more languages, so that each language comes to be identified with specific interaction situations. For example, even when both members of a dyad are HAs, and speak Spanish, certain interactions will be carried out in English.

Brennan and Ryan (1973) studied 36 Mexican-American males in California and found that the "domain" of the listener is the best determinant of language choice and that Spanish is most associated with the home domain, English with the school domain. As an illustration, the intimacy of Spanish makes it rare for native bilinguals to speak it with Anglos in public settings. Regardless of setting or topic of conversation, a Mexican-American adolescent is more likely to use Spanish when conversing with his or her older brother than with a teacher who is equally fluent in English and Spanish. The data of Brennan and Ryan (1973) do not support a relationship between home or school fluency and actual language use in these settings.

Choice of which language is used by bilinguals in a given situation is also addressed in the literature of code-switching. In a study of code-switching among Mexican-American children in Illinois, McClure and Wengz (1975) concluded that the choice of whether to use one language or the other is not random. In less formal conversation style, code-switching occurs more frequently than in more formal narratives. In formal narratives, code-switching is allowed only for specific purposes, such as asides to the audience, openings and closing, puns, and quotations.

Laosa (1975) studied 295 Mexican-American, Puerto Rican, and Cuban-American boys and girls in Texas, New York City, and Florida. The children were equally divided in each city by gender and grade level. Results showed that Spanish is used predominantly in the home by Puerto Ricans and Cubans and much less by MAs (25 percent). Of the three groups, MAs were the only ones to report a mixture of Spanish and English used in the home (40 percent). The number of households where English predominated was greater among MAs (25 percent) than in either of the other groups (less than 10 percent for each). Peer interactions in school (outside of classroom time) were almost exclusively in English for Mexican Americans and predominantly in Spanish for Cuban Americans and Puerto Ricans. It is clear from this study that HAs are not homogeneous with regards to language patterns and that there are wide differences in the language environments to which they belong. Since most of the empirical literature deals with Mexican Americans, there is some question as to whether the results on a variety of dimensions can be applied to HAs in general.

Aguirre (1977) studied the sociolinguistic situation of 75 high school students in a California border town. Family income in each home was less than $5,000 annually. Parts of Aguirre's results conflict with Brennan and Ryan's (1973) discussed above: Language usage and proficiency were found to be positively related. Other results confirmed earlier studies: Among bilinguals, use of one language over another is determined by the nature of the interaction situation; specific situation domains are associated with specific language behaviors. Use of Spanish was found to decrease in situations further away from the home domain.

The Hsia (1973) study described earlier also has implications here. Poor Hispanic Americans are most likely to be monolingual, while upwardly mobile HAs are likely to be bilingual. There exists large variability in degree of bilingualism across different geographic and ethnic groups among Hispanic Americans. Degree of bilingualism is related to overall frequency of interpersonal contact, both with HAs and Anglos; monolingual HAs have the most interpersonal contacts and monolingual Anglos the least (Duran and Monroe, 1977). In general, linguistic systems are good indicators of assimilation and acculturation (Barker, 1947).

The speaking of Spanish by HAs has of late become a matter of linguistic pride. Data collected from Chicanos in Texas by Elias-Olivares (1976) indicate that young Hispanic Americans are speaking more Spanish than ever and claim to be proud of their language. Meanwhile, older HAs still harbor embarrassment (a sense of linguistic inferiority) about their language. The increase in Spanish speaking is primarily due to an increase in ethnic awareness among HAs, along with the recent development of other language preservation movements (Brennan and Ryan, 1973).

Where a person was raised influences whether or not they will speak Spanish; rural Hispanic Americans are more likely to use Spanish than urban HAs (Rodrigues, 1977). Rodrigues reviewed research on language use and classroom perceptions and reached some conclusions about language use of HAs in general. Hispanic-American females were found to speak more English than males but are not necessarily more fluent; language choice is dependent upon peer group, not language dominance; upward mobility leads to a decline in loyalty to the Spanish language; the more traditional the cultural values, the greater the desire to speak Spanish; and, finally, the speaking of Spanish does not interfere with English-language production any more than does the speaking of a nonstandard variety of English.

There appear to be differences in the degree of bilingualism across H-A populations in different regions of the U.S. primarily as a result of variations in economic status and rural-urban differences. Among H-A bilinguals, however, extremely consistent patterns of language choice are identified. The two major variables influencing the choice to speak Spanish or English in a given situation are (1) the nature of the interaction situation and (2) the gender of the speaker. Capability for bilingualism of the listener and conversational topic are not major factors. Finally, there has been an overall increase in the speaking of Spanish among HAs in recent years, which some attribute to a growing cultural and linguistic awareness, especially among younger people.

Bilingual Education

As the number of Hispanic Americans increases and ethnic awareness grows, additional effort is exerted to facilitate effective acculturation. A main method for changing deficiencies among Hispanic Americans in information access and socioeconomic position is the educational system, where much attention has been given to the development of bilingual education programs.

Cohen (1975) assessed the effects of bilingual schooling on 30 Mexican-American kindergarteners advancing into first grade. He concluded that students in the bilingual program developed a more positive attitude toward Spanish and used more Spanish in a variety of settings as a result of the program. Proper English usage was continued along with the addition of Spanish. Family interaction patterns were not significantly affected by the bilingual programs.

The study described earlier by Rodrigues (1977) on first-grade Mexican-American students showed that when students used their native language at school, they were also more likely to use it at home, and in many cases it actually aided them in their learning. In an investigation to determine the relationship between bilingualism and cognitive style, Price-Williams and Ramirez (1977) found that balanced bilingualism (the ability to speak English and Spanish equally well) promoted divergent thinking, which is a measure of fluency and flexibility of thought. Male, balanced bilinguals were found to be better than Anglos monolingual in English at divergent thinking tasks. Comparisons for females were uninterpretable.

CONCLUSIONS

The research cited in this summary has by no means been exhaustive. It has highlighted those aspects of nonmediated communication among Hispanics that complement the research review on mass media behavior and provide a broader framework for interpreting the CASA studies to be presented.

If one overriding conclusion can be drawn from this brief review, it is that many of the purported differences between Hispanics and Anglos do not exist. Nevertheless, the stereotypes persist, among Hispanics and Anglos alike. While Spanish culture understandably has some influence on H-A values and behaviors, many of the characteristics assigned to HAs are more a function of education and income level than of a distinctly different ethnic orientation.

Areas where Hispanic culture appeared to influence communication patterns and orientations tend to center around the following:

1. Cultural self-identification and consequent self-image
2. Organizing and orienting influence of the family (but not the value for the importance of the family, which is shared by other ethnic groups)
3. Field dependence in educational contexts
4. Stereotypes associated with accented speech
5. Styles of communication between parent and child
6. Willingness to self-disclose
7. Social and political participation
8. Contexts for bilingualism and monolingualism in conversation

II
WHAT WAS EXPECTED?

3

HOW COMMUNITY LEADERS, NEWSPAPER EXECUTIVES, AND REPORTERS PERCEIVE MEXICAN AMERICANS AND THE MASS MEDIA

Felipe Korzenny
Betty Ann Griffis
Bradley S. Greenberg
Judee K. Burgoon
Michael Burgoon

Before any original field research was started, focused interviews were sought with two groups of people. One was to be a subset of Hispanic community leaders in each of the study sites. From each leader we wanted background on his or her community, its problems, and its people. The second was to be a subset of key media personnel in the same study sites. We sought their perspectives on the same issues, but also some further insight on media-related issues. This chapter summarizes both sets of interviews. From those interviews, the field studies of Project CASA were born.

Lists of Hispanic-American community leaders from San Bernardino, Visalia, Salinas, and Stockton, California; Tucson, Arizona; and Santa Fe, New Mexico were initially provided by publishers of the local Gannett newspaper in each community. Attempts were made to contact each leader by phone. About 80 percent of those leaders were reached, and they in turn were asked to name other influential individuals in the local H-A community. Individuals who were mentioned repeatedly and those whose occupations or positions of leadership represented different perspectives on the community were invited to an interview session.

Three categories of interviewees were identified, as follow:

1. *Educators and religious leaders:* This category comprised individuals who in one way or another were engaged in the transmission of information regarding cultural norms and other cultural aspects.

2. *Business persons and other professionals* who, from their positions, had access to a large number of Hispanic Americans and who had emerged from lower socioeconomic classes, in most instances. This group usually contained a media representative in each community.

3. *Grass roots leaders:* This category included persons who had distinguished themselves in community work and who closely related to the working class and the most deprived segments of the H-A population.

Group interviews were conducted in homogeneous groups according to the categories outlined above, with one group interview per category in each community. Individual interviews were conducted with a representative of each of the categories, especially when the individual was identified as being extremely important in his or her community and would have been unavailable to participate in a group session.

Fifteen interviews were scheduled for each city, with three four-person groups and three individuals. Actual totals were 15 participants in San Bernardino, 14 in Visalia, 14 in Salinas, 18 in Stockton, 14 in Tucson, and 13 in Santa Fe, for a total of 88 H-A community leaders interviewed in the winter and spring of 1980.

The average group session lasted about two hours; individual interviews lasted about one and a half hours. Interviewers were two social scientists, one male and one female, with multicultural backgrounds and knowledge of the Hispanic culture and language.

The following question areas were used as guides in the interviews:

1. *Community description:* H-A groups; other population segments; H-A organizations, their functions and interrelationships; leadership patterns in respect to politics, economics, and social issues

2. *Community relationships and mutual perceptions:* between Anglos and HAs, among H-A subgroups, between other subgroups and HAs

3. *Issues and problems over the past 4 or 5 years:* those concerning the H-A community exclusively; those between segments of the Anglo and H-A communities

4. *Media relations with the H-A community:* newspapers, radio, television; adequacy of coverage and of overall representation in respect to content and personnel; perceptions of credibility, trust, and competence of media; adequacy of communication channels between media and the H-A community.

5. *Media availability:* Are there Hispanic media?; what are they?; adequacy of service; how can they be improved?; any improvement of service over the past 4 or 5 years?; perceptions of power of the media; are the interests of

HAs represented across content areas within the media?; are sources and reporters representative of the H-A community?

6. *Media habits of HAs regarding Anglo and Hispanic media:* Who reads, watches, listens?; how much?; when?; why?; functions, motivations, reasons?; specific complaints against the media?

These six areas were collapsed into three for the purpose of detailed description and analysis:

1. Community description and community relations
2. Current problems and issues
3. Relationship of Hispanic Americans to the media, including their patterns of media exposure

In February and March 1980, the four principal investigators of this project met with the publishers of the Gannett newspapers from each locality to obtain the publishers' perspectives on the same subjects. Each publisher brought staff members to the session, including a Hispanic staff member. First, we will detail the results obtained for the Hispanic community leaders and then the results of the interviews with the newspaper executives and staff.

INTERVIEWS WITH HISPANIC COMMUNITY LEADERS

This study phase provided in-depth information about the social complexities and communication environments of Hispanic-American communities in the western U.S.

With the ultimate goal of investigating specific mass communication behaviors of Hispanic Americans and the media content available to them, it was decided that:

1. Firsthand knowledge of the overall social structure and mass-media-related issues of selected Hispanic communities should be obtained.
2. A conceptual frame of reference would be necessary to orient the generation of research questions.
3. For communication research to be socially meaningful, it ought be based on firsthand accounts of problems perceived by members of the communities studied.

To accomplish these goals, field research in the form of interviews with community leaders was undertaken. The responses were considered to be the accounts of informants well acquainted with the communities in which they lived and exerted influence.

The basic questions assessed were:

1. To what degree are H-A population segments in the western U.S. similar in their *problem sets, media relationships, media perceptions,* and *media usage?*
2. How are media-related behaviors associated with overall social structures and concerns?
3. What questions and issues need to be investigated to advance an understanding of H-A media behaviors and to improve the information environment of H-A communities?

Community Description and Relations

Because 1970 Census figures might not have reflected the current population profiles of the study communities, community leaders were asked to estimate total and Hispanic-American (H-A) populations:

Community	Total Population	Percent HA
San Bernardino	125,000	15
Visalia	46,000	30
Salinas	75,000	20–30
Stockton	120,000	30
Tucson	500,000	25–35
Santa Fe	45,000	55

Hispanic-Americans' population proportions range from 15 percent in San Bernardino to 55 percent (a majority) in Santa Fe. The estimates for Salinas and Tucson vary because relatively large numbers of legal or illegal HAs inhabit those areas during specific seasons of temporary work.

Principal employment opportunities in the six communities vary. Agriculture is primary in Visalia, Salinas, and Stockton. The main types of employment in San Bernardino, Tucson, and Santa Fe are government jobs at all levels, education, and various industries. Santa Fe is characteristically dedicated to the tourism industry.

Relative wealth and upward mobility across the six communities was delineated as follows: Tucson and Stockton contained the poorest HAs, with about 50 percent of the Hispanic populations living in conditions of poverty ranging from what was called "notch people" (who can hardly sustain themselves) to those on welfare. Their relative deprivation was compounded by the problems associated with urban settings. Visalia was described as the third poorest community of the six, with about half its Hispanic population in agricultural jobs, plus those individuals on welfare and other social-aid programs.

Salinas followed with about 60 percent of Hispanics earning between $14,000 to $20,000 per year. San Bernardino was fifth in order of ascending well-being, with about 75 percent of its Hispanic population in a mixture of white- and blue-collar positions. Santa Fe was said to exceed by far the other communities, with 60 to 70 percent of HAs employed in middle-class jobs.

Economic and political power were said to reside with the following groups in each community: San Bernardino—"WASPs and Mormons"; Visalia—the "farmers," who are Anglo, Armenian, Portuguese and Japanese; Salinas—the Anglo landlords; Stockton—the Anglo majority; Tucson—the Anglo population and the incoming retirees; and Santa Fe—the Anglo population and the "privileged Hispanics"—long-time residents and perpetuators of a relatively rigid class structure. Even in Santa Fe, where some of the highest political offices are held by HAs, sources cited evidence that the real economic power was held by Anglos.

Except in Santa Fe, there is a trend to perceive a negative relationship between the length of generational permanence of Hispanics and their concept of self, educational aspirations, and achievement. Individuals whose families had been in a given location for a generation or more were said to be less proud, more confused about their identity, and more fatalistic. The successful ones were integrating upward in the larger community, while disadvantaged individuals were experiencing a growing sense of alienation in the barrio.

All communities were experiencing the impact of waves of legal and illegal immigration. With the exception of Tucson, some rivalry was reported between Hispanic newcomers and long-established residents. Overall community integration was reported to be strongest in Visalia and Tucson. San Bernardino, Stockton, Salinas, and Santa Fe were identified as communities where the H-A community was not unified.

Perceived political activity among Hispanics was said to be strongest in Stockton; moderate in San Bernardino, Salinas, Tucson, and Santa Fe; and weak in Visalia.

Cultural identity was a main factor described as affecting community integration and the well-being of individuals. Cultural identity was variously conceptualized as consisting of self-designation and/or awareness of one's cultural roots. Overall, the following labels seemed to be accepted by most interviewees: *Americans*, who conform to the norms of the Anglo society and aspire to it; *Mexican Americans,* who perceive themselves to be in a position of equilibrium between the two cultures without a clear-cut definition; *Chicanos,* more militant segments of Hispanic-American communities, who express pride in their bilingualism and biculturalism; and the *Mexican* or *Mexicano,* who still has his or her roots in Mexico and who longs for it.

Santa Fe was the most atypical community. Given its long historical tradition, about 65 percent of the HAs there call themselves Hispanics or Spanish Americans when interacting in English. (When conversing in Spanish, however, they call themselves Mexican American.) The most easily recognized segment across communities was that of Chicanos, with the following distribution: San Bernardino, 50 percent; Visalia, 40 percent; Salinas and Stockton, about 30 percent each; Santa Fe, 15 percent; and Tucson, 10 percent. This variability seems to be a function of the social prestige associated with the label *Chicano*. In Tucson, for example, the term Chicano is more likely one of scorn. In Santa Fe, a H-A woman said she would leave the room if she were called a Chicano.

The label *Mexican American* was widely prevalent: Salinas, 50 to 60 percent; Stockton, 30 percent; Tucson and Santa Fe, 20 percent each; Visalia, 10 percent; and San Bernardino with an undetermined percentage. Choice of the label *American* was as infrequent as the label *Mexican* or *Mexicano,* with estimates varying from 5 to 10 percent across communities, except for Tucson and Visalia. In Tucson, 60 percent were reported to identify themselves as Mexicanos, in Visalia about 50 percent.

H-A organizations were abundant. Their objectives and procedures varied within each community. The most powerful organizations were more frequently said to be those national in scope with some political and/or educational goals. One of these was the G.I. Forum, the most common across communities. The G.I. Forum is composed of war veterans who organize youth activities, offer scholarship funds, and arrange celebrations. The League of United Latin American Citizens (LULAC) is another of the national political/ educational type organizations. LULAC's programs include training, housing for the elderly, education, affirmative action, and relationships with the news media. In Salinas, for example, LULAC brought an action before the Federal Communications Commission (FCC) against a local television station, claiming that its coverage of Hispanics was abrasive and racist. As a result, the station's license was held back temporarily by the FCC. Another organization is the Consejo para Pueblos Unidos (CPU), a national organization of workers, professionals, clergy, campesinos, students, businesspeople, and other segments of the Hispanic community working together for the promotion of social change and justice through unified action. According to its leader, Dr. Armando Navarro, of San Bernardino:

> Hispanics are in a state of crisis. Politically, the Hispanic finds himself underrepresented, powerless and alienated from the political process. Economically, the Hispanic is at the bottom of the totem pole, where he is victimized by increasing impoverishment and inflation. Socially, the poverty syndrome, coupled with racism, is transforming the barrios into concrete jungles where violence and self-destruction prevail. With our human condition deteriorating, Hispanics must begin to confront these crises with unified action and the power of organization.

In Tucson, a Hispanic priest voiced an opinion that seems to reflect a general truism. The Tucson priest said that the umbrella organization of H-A organizations is the Catholic Church. In fact, most Hispanic-American organizations have some kind of religious affiliation or set of activities incorporated in their constitutions. This religious concern emerged as an underlying cultural trait.

Santa Fe was distinct in that its best-known organizations were those with cultural goals, such as preserving the cultural heritage of the community.

In general, educators, students, and government employees tended to be the ones best organized to address H-A problems. However, a common complaint was voiced: They felt they were not unified enough, that they needed more consciousness-raising activities, and that the occasion of the interview was one of the first chances they had had to discuss these issues among themselves.

In summary, within a wide range of community sizes, economic activity, and organizational patterns, H-A leaders described their communities as having only marginal power but determined to acquire more. Communities were said to lack unity, and the relationship between generational length of residence and cultural identity were described as contributing factors. Marginal participation in political activity was the overriding factor. Concerted organizational efforts were cited as initial steps to give impulse to H-A concerns.

Current Community Problems and Issues

The set of social problems in the communities presented common patterns and unexpected uniformity. Racism was the constant theme, and it related to these main problems across communities:

1. Education
2. Employment
3. Politics
4. Housing
5. Health
6. Crime

Other problems less frequently mentioned were status quo conformity or passivity, divorce, cultural preservation, women's issues, and an in-group resentment of HAs against their illegal-immigrant counterparts.

The issue of racism underscored all other issues and was the most vociferously expressed complaint. The perceptions of racism were most strongly raised in Stockton, San Bernardino, and Salinas: There were claims of "shrewdness" in discrimination and the allegation that "racism is rampant." In Visalia, racism in employment practices was mentioned most. Santa Fe leaders were less likely to mention racism as a problem except for the grass-roots individuals who mentioned it as a most serious problem.

Racism was perceived in each of the major community problem areas identified:

Education. The most frequently mentioned community problem was education. The counseling services available in high schools were said to be somewhat biased and far from adequate. Except in Santa Fe, the counselors tended to be Anglo and were unaware of the needs and potential of Hispanic children. Teachers and counselors had low expectations for Hispanic students, which tended to become self-fulfilling prophecies. Counselors were said to advise H-A children to become beauticians or mechanics, expecting them to achieve no more than that.

Little education and lack of fluency in English prevented many Hispanic-American parents from communicating with teachers and school administrators. Cultural norms endorsing submission to authority deterred parents from working to achieve a better education for their children. The general belief seemed to be that "the teacher knows best."

Dropout or "pushout" rates were disproportionately higher among Hispanic children. Bilingual education was far from uniform across schools and communities. Well-trained bilingual teachers were in short supply. Bilingual education, mandated by law, was perceived to create animosity against HAs. Anglos resented paying for it, and other minorities, e.g., Asians, wanted bilingual education programs as well. Stockton H-A leaders were proud of having the only completely bilingual school in the U.S. Leaders in Santa Fe expressed concern that loss of federal funds might curtail bilingual educational programs. In Santa Fe, Anglos more actively encouraged bilingual education, and local Hispanics were losing interest in it.

In some communities, Anglo children were accused of prejudice against H-A children, reflecting attitudes presumably learned at home. In-school fighting between Anglos and HAs ("cowboys" vs. Chicanos), and fights among Hispanics (Chicanos vs. Mexicans) detracted from educational goals. Visalia H-A children were prohibited from gathering together in groups at times of school fighting, while Anglo children were not so restricted. Further, H-A children of long-established U.S. backgrounds tended to discriminate against or make fun of the children of recent immigrants from Mexico. Local colleges were said to lack Hispanic personnel despite growing numbers of Hispanic students. The rising cost of higher education was expected to increase the education gap between the rich and the poor and, more specifically, between Anglos and Hispanics. It was believed that scholarships were less available to Hispanics than to Anglos.

Another education-related issue is the impact of educational practices on the self-concept of children. A system of education that expects little of Hispanics and that excludes them at higher levels tends to promote feelings of anomie and lack of self-confidence. The lack of successful models to emulate in the educational system and in the media was said to contribute to identity crises in Hispanic-American children.

Children of recent arrivals from Mexico were described as doing better in school than children of families long established in the U.S. It was speculated that values, morality, and family ties were stronger for recent immigrants: "Unoccupied youth, without respect for family or religion, are hard to control."

Employment. This was the second most frequently mentioned area of concern. Prejudice was particularly evident in employment practices; affirmative action was said not to be enforced. Given equal qualifications, Anglos were believed to be selected for positions of responsibility; Stockton, Tucson, and Visalia were said to be notorious for this.

All H-A leaders cited employment as a community problem, although the emphasis differed in each community. In Salinas, Stockton, Visalia, and Santa Fe, there was Anglo opposition to large-scale industry because it was expected to drive wages up. Stockton leaders emphasized that mechanization in farm work was displacing people. Farm-labor strife was the harshest in Salinas. In Visalia, farmer groups discouraged unionization to keep wages low.

Along with educational issues, employment for youth was perceived as most important. Unemployed youngsters tended to resort to crime and vandalism. They lacked ties to the social institutions that enforce social norms, except for the legal system, which is dominated by the Anglo majority. Many criminals from Los Angeles were sent to prison in Stockton and then released in that area. Ex-convicts were believed to become the instructors of the youth in the area, intensifying the problem.

Politics. In general, the concern was that Hispanics were not proportionally represented in political positions; decisions were continually being made *for* HAs. Political participation as well as representation of Hispanics was said to be low overall, except for Santa Fe. In the larger cities (San Bernardino, Tucson, and Stockton) political representation of Hispanics on school boards and government bodies had recently begun to increase. Santa Fe had perhaps the fullest range and scope of political representation because of its long established Hispanic population. However, it was emphasized that to make it in politics in Santa Fe, one must look like an Anglo, have an Anglo or anglicized surname, and speak without an accent. Visalia and Salinas had the least Hispanic political representation.

Housing. The poor in the Hispanic areas of the six cities were said to live in substandard conditions. Waiting lists for housing were extremely long, especially in Tucson, where families were said to wait their turn in unsanitary hotels. Property values in Tucson and Santa Fe have been driven up by retirees and other Anglos moving in from the northern and eastern U.S., driving HAs out of their living areas and discouraging desegregation.

Disadvantaged housing predominated. Visalia leaders and those in Stockton, Tucson, and Santa Fe indicated this as an important issue. There were general complaints of manipulation of the housing market to drive prices up, and it was emphasized that HAs were not represented in the housing industry.

Health. A pressing problem was health, especially in Stockton and Tucson. Individuals without health insurance were hit hard by rising medical costs. In Tucson, physicians were said to have moved to the areas where more affluent segments of the population live. Local public clinics lack the capacity to meet public needs. "People have to wait until they are hospitalized," a health worker said.

Crime. Perceived to be a joint product of educational and employment patterns, crime was cited, with drug usage a contributing factor. In nonagricultural months, a period of lower employment, crime increased. Youth crime was especially important; most communities mentioned attempts to keep youth "out of trouble." It was argued that Anglo teenagers were not as severely criticized as Hispanic-American teenagers for engaging in disapproved activities. This was cited as a further manifestation of discrimination.

Overall, a growing sense of militancy and a desire for preservation of cultural identity and pride were detected across communities. Lack of unity to deal with these issues seemed to be the main obstacle to effective social action. Racism as inferred from lack of equal participation and opportunity in the mainstream of society was a constant theme.

Hispanic American Media Relations
And Patterns of Media Exposure

Lack of Hispanic media personnel was a primary issue mentioned across communities. There was concern about the general lack of media education and the small number of HAs who pursue media studies. The virtual absence of H-A media personnel is a composite of traditional hiring practices and availability. Related to this was the complaint that H-A media personnel were seldom in decision-making capacities. Further, Hispanic media personnel tended to be hired from places other than the local community and consequently failed to identify and focus on those issues perceived by the Hispanic constituency as important. In San Bernardino, a Mexican, not a Mexican American, was hired to write for the local paper; in Santa Fe the owner of a radio station said that he would not hire someone who had not been a long-time resident of the community.

Employment patterns and traditional stereotypes were said to cause an overemphasis on negative news and an underemphasis on positive H-A news.

There was a prevalent feeling that the H-A communities strongly resented the heavy reporting of H-A crime-related events without a counterbalance of positive event reporting. In Visalia, a local activist with political aspirations wrote a weekly column, "Counterbalance," to counteract this trend.

All media were considered unsupportive of attempts to strengthen community unity and the H-A self-concept. Exceptions were the Hispanic radio stations in Tucson and Santa Fe. The general feeling was that Hispanics had to plead for coverage while other segments of the population obtained it more readily. Not only were image-enhancing community activities ignored, but common reports of births, weddings, sports, and deaths were underemphasized or ignored in the media, according to these community leaders. Even in locations where Hispanics were more evident in the media, their coverage and portrayals were characterized as poor.

Radio station managers, including those in San Bernardino, Tucson, and Santa Fe, said that radio is more responsive to community needs due to federal regulation of their activities.

In most communities, television coverage and service to the Hispanic community was said to be nonexistent. Whatever there was, was said to be imported from other cities and in turn imported from Latin America, especially Mexico, through SIN (Spanish International Network). Stations carrying SIN's signal were available through cable in all communities except Tucson. SIN was reported to be the most popular entertainment channel wherever it was available.

The media were blamed not only for polarizing Anglos and Hispanics, but for polarizing Hispanics among themselves, e.g., for spotlighting one gang over another. Media attention drawn by local gang activities tended to reinforce those activities.

Television and radio were reported to be the most popular media in all the communities. Radio was overwhelmingly mentioned as the most prominent medium for Hispanics; all communities had either a full- or part-time Spanish-language station. Radio's popularity did not necessarily redeem the complaints voiced above.

H-A community leaders complained especially about newspapers. A common complaint was that the newspaper was insensitive because of ignorance. Leaders attributed this insensitivity to the facts that their major local newspapers had absentee owners and their editors and publishers were not familiar with community problems. Reactions to newspaper coverage ranged from hatred to belief that newspapers were "trying to improve."

Selective reporting to reinforce bias against Hispanics was a continuous issue across cities. In Santa Fe, a grass-roots leader presented a box with newspaper clippings purporting to document biased and selective coverage. Plaintiffs were said to be commonly turned into defendants. Editorials and letters to the editor were said to be published in a highly selective fashion and with strong biases against HAs. Recent newspaper hiring of Hispanic reporters was said to be window dressing. Even when local newspapers were doing something positive in trying to cover H-A issues, the suspicion persisted that the policy was only to appease the H-A community. In respect to a positive article about the President of the Hispanic Chamber of Commerce in Stockton, the belief was expressed that the picture of the President in mechanic's work clothes would not have been used if he had been an Anglo. There was a perceived imbalance in crime coverage, including subtle discriminatory practices such as publishing the picture of the criminal and/or identifying him or her as Hispanic and not identifying by ethnicity or picture other criminals.

Other coverage issues frequently mentioned were location of articles in the paper, emphasis on ethnicity, length of article, paternalistic and condescending attitudes reflected in language, and selective reporting of stereotyped events.

Despite the wealth of criticism against their local papers, not one leader said that he or she did not read the local paper. One aspect of H-A leaders' sensitivity to the media was a realization of its impact. In San Bernardino, leaders active with volatile youth groups in the barrios said that gang members bought the local paper to see write-ups of their activities. The leaders who worked in programs to promote positive activities expressed frustration at the power of this reinforcement of negative activities. An influential businessman in San Bernardino displayed an article in that day's paper correcting what he felt was an inaccurate and demeaning article from the previous day. He said that HAs believed that the paper, which portrays them negatively, was the voice of the Anglos, and was not representative. He felt that the paper stirred up factionalism between HAs and Anglos because of the strength of its position as the only home-town paper, even though its negative attitude toward Hispanics was not representative of the majority of Anglos in the community.

Newspaper readership for news, sports, and advertising was said to be widespread; estimates ranged from limited readership to about 60 percent of the Hispanics. In Visalia, for example, it was said that newspaper readership was highest on Monday to find out sports scores and weekend news, and on Wednesday to read store advertisements. Spanish newspapers from out of town were said to be popular, such as *La Opinion* from Los Angeles.

San Bernardino, Salinas, Stockton, and Tucson all had a Spanish-language newspaper of some kind, usually a weekly. Only Stockton seemed to be proud of its local Spanish paper, which is fully bilingual.

It was said that HAs like to read in Spanish and that they would welcome Spanish-language columns or sections in the local paper. The items that H-A leaders believed HAs would read in Spanish in the local papers included community news, job listings (especially those requiring bilingual skills), coverage of social activities, tax information, sports, and advertising. Some community leaders argued that occasionally the local paper had published some Spanish-language content and that it had failed because the paper made no attempt to discover what really interests the community.

CONCLUSIONS

Here, we will synthesize responses to the questions asked of the community leaders.

  1. To what degree are H-A populations in the western U.S. similar in their problem sets, media relations, media perceptions, and media usage?

Across the six communities, opinion leaders had very similar perceptions of existing problems and their importance. Racism was the overall concern voiced, a feeling that Anglos and other holders of power believed that HAs are not worthy and treated them as inferiors. Problems with education were most frequently mentioned, partly attributed to discriminatory practices. Employment patterns were said to reflect prejudice and a very strong resistance to change on the part of those who control the status quo. Employment and educational issues were said to converge and lead to other social problems, such as a lack of adequate political representation, inadequate housing and health care, and increased crime. The lack of a stable and uniform cultural identity and a weak self-concept were identified as resulting from, and at the same time aggravating, the problems identified.

Media relations with the Hispanic communities were said to be uniformly bad. Lack of accessibility with respect to employment and coverage were at the top of the list of complaints. Negative portrayals of HAs in the media were blamed for perpetuating a poor self-concept and lack of cultural pride. Almost complete focus on crime and racism in coverage were said to be the norm. Lack of Spanish-language media was a prevalent concern.

No major medium was perceived to be oriented toward Hispanics. Radio was the closest in terms of fulfilling H-A expectations and needs. A Spanish-language radio station was available in most communities. Television was perceived to fulfill entertainment needs, especially where SIN was available. The local paper, the major news medium, was not considered to be a vehicle of actual service to Hispanics. Overall, the media were perceived to provide entertainment but to do little in respect to news. The media are needed, and yet they do not fulfill expectations.

Newspaper readership levels were described as low, due to lack of appropriate content, relevance, and language accessibility. A preference for non-print media was said to exist, a cultural aspect of the heritage of an oral society, a trend compounded by the element of poverty. Less literate individuals prefer media that require fewer literary skills. Television and radio were most popular for entertainment and newspaper for local news.

  2. How are media-related behaviors of HAs associated with overall social structures and concerns?

Older segments of the Hispanic populations were said to prefer more traditional content in the media and to be more likely to conform to the demands of the status quo. At the community level, specific differences were found in respect to possibilities for upward mobility, militancy, and organizational unity of H-A community members. The more united and more socially and politically active community leaders voiced strong complaints against the media. Lack of print coverage of relevant H-A issues appeared to be accompanied by cynicism and distrust.

The H-A communities were perceived by their leaders to be relatively weak organizationally. As the overarching unit that influences organizations in each locality the Catholic church had the potential for unifying communities and promoting cultural pride and a sense of identity. The church and secular segments of the H-A communities have been working to influence the media. Growing organizational strength, a trend toward increased political participation, and the growing H-A population, which is attracting commercial and political attention, will likely result in greater media efforts to serve H-A constituencies.

    3. What questions and issues need to be investigated to further advance our understanding of H-A media behaviors and to improve the information environment of H-A communities in the western U.S.?

This is perhaps the most crucial question explored. Figure 3.1 graphically represents the interrelated perceptions of H-A leaders.

No directionality or causality is implied in the relationships in Figure 3.1. The lines indicate associations among sets of factors. H-A communication is expected to be related to H-A culture, social psychology, larger social structure, media institutions, and media content. Indirectly, H-A communication patterns are thought to be affected by the larger culture, and Anglo or majority psychosocial factors.

Some questions can be derived from this model:

1. What specific media content do H-A audiences need?
2. What functions do the media serve for different H-A audiences?
3. How do cultural identity and socioeconomic status relate to content needs and functions served by the different media?
4. How do media exposure patterns vary with cultural identity, socioeconomic status, media evaluations, content needs, preferences, and functions?
5. How are H-A children socialized to use and understand the media?
6. How is language preference and/or proficiency associated with media evaluations, functions, content preferences, socioeconomic status, and cultural identity?

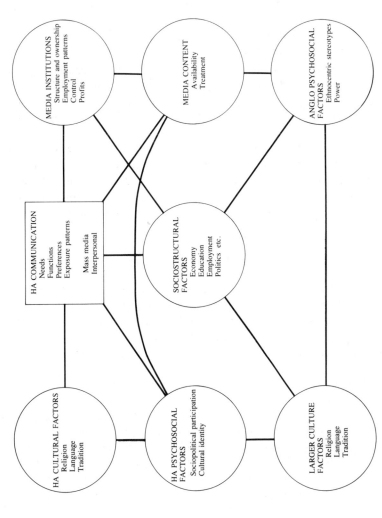

FIGURE 3.1 Interrelated factors affecting Hispanic-American (HA) communication behaviors

7. How are media portrayals associated with the cultural identity and self-concept of HAs?

8. Are media portrayals of Hispanic Americans biased?

9. Are HAs underrepresented by the news media in the areas of sports, cultural events, and social activities?

10. Could the news media have more penetration in H-A communities if the Spanish language were used?

11. Could the news media gain better penetration in H-A communities by providing the content perceived as needed by community members?

12. Could media editorial policies promote more harmonious relationships between the Anglo majority and the H-A community, and among Hispanics?

The questions could continue indefinitely; the answers are more problematic. However, questions such as these based on the factors represented in Figure 3.1 guided the field studies of adults and children and the media studies of content and style, to be detailed in the next several chapters of this book. First, however, we will add the local newspaper's perceptions of these same issues.

MEETINGS WITH NEWSPAPER EXECUTIVES

In January 1980, the four principal investigators of Project CASA met with publishers and staff members of the Gannett newspapers from each of the six cities studied. These meetings, held in San Francisco, provided the opportunity to determine the newspapers perceptions of Hispanic-American issues in their respective communities. Three focal areas were discussed:

1. Community descriptions were elicited first; then groups were asked to identify major issues related to the H-A community.

2. The groups were asked to describe H-A perceptions of their newspapers and to identify specific complaints they had received from the Hispanic community. The publishers were asked what changes they had made in response to the complaints received regarding the quality of coverage of H-A affairs and what employment practices there were with regard to H-A staff.

3. Finally, the groups were asked to describe the communication environments of their communities, including the availability of Spanish-language media.

This summary highlights key perceptions and concerns expressed by the newspaper personnel interviewed.

Community Descriptions and Issues

The publishers identified specific Hispanic subgroups in their communities. In Salinas, a lower-income subgroup, a mainstream middle-class element, and a small upper-income group comprise the H-A community. Also significant in number are the migrant farm-laborers, estimated to be from 4,000 to 6,000 people, and the undocumented Hispanic population, estimated at 3,000.

San Bernardino was described as the most urban of the six locations, located on the edge of the Los Angeles basin. Three subgroups of Mexican Americans were identified: American-born Hispanics; undocumented illegal aliens; and Mexican-born Hispanics who had become permanent, legal residents of the United States.

Santa Fe was described as an integrated community, both historically and socially. Its major H-A subgroups included: a significant element of older, elitist families who had been in Santa Fe for several generations; the barrio neighborhood groups who focused on social-service activities and were not in favor of community expansion; and the Mexican undocumented nationals who generally comprised the unskilled labor group.

The publishers in Stockton classified the permanent H-A subgroups in economic terms, as primarily lower class (about 70 percent), with the remainder middle class. In addition, a transient migrant group of about 15,000 people was identified. Although several social-service and cultural groups existed, no particular political or social organizational system among the Hispanics could be identified in Stockton, and a generally high level of community apathy was indicated.

Many HAs in Tucson were said to have been there for about three generations. The H-A subgroup was divided into four units: upper-middle class citizens; the middle class; the poor; and illegal aliens. In general, the newspaper people viewed this community as well integrated and without large political divisions.

In Visalia, a small, rural community, there was reported a large influx of undocumented Mexican nationals into the community. This trend was expected to continue because of the agricultural base of the community.

The issue of concern mentioned most frequently in five of the six cities was crime and the lack of police response to escalating crime. The publishers reported widespread concern about the level of violent crime in both Hispanic and non-Hispanic communities. For example, the Tucson group reported that one in every ten Tucson residents was the victim of some type of crime in 1979. The Visalia newspaper group expressed a particular concern about crime against minorities gang/youth violence. In San Bernardino, "the paper does not attempt to deliver in specific areas because of the threat of violent crime to carriers." The level of criminal activity in these cities was judged to have an equivalent impact on both Hispanic and non-Hispanic sectors alike.

Much dissatisfaction was expressed regarding the response of local police forces to criminal activity in these cities. The San Bernardino newspaper group reported that Hispanics "feel that the police are apathetic about violence and victims, especially when such crime occurs in Hispanic areas." In Stockton, the dissatisfaction with the local police is manifested through a general distrust of the Anglo-dominated police force; this distrust becomes heightened the longer the police take to respond to calls in the Hispanic sections of the community. The Tucson newspaper group mentioned abuse by police and other authorities as a major concern in the community.

A second major concern was the potential for greater racial unrest. For example, in San Bernardino, there had been reports of increasing racial tension among Blacks, Hispanics and "rednecks." In Stockton, it appeared that school desegregation, in effect through a court order, was the basis for concern about racism. In Tucson, desegregation in the schools was also a widely contested issue, producing high levels of discontent in the Hispanic community.

A third issue mentioned by the newspaper groups was bilingual education and the extent to which bilingual education might stigmatize some students. In Santa Fe, bilingual education was available at the K through 4 levels; in Salinas, bilingual education was described as "mandated for K through 12." In Visalia, the concern was primarily with cutbacks to education in general and especially to bilingual education.

Other issues discussed as prevalent by the newspaper groups were unemployment, housing shortages, the influx of illegal aliens, exploitation of Mexican nationals, legal rights, political representation for Hispanics, problems connected with urban development, and farm mechanization and farm labor.

Publisher Perceptions of
Hispanic Responses to the Local Paper

The publishers varied markedly in their views on how they believed their papers were perceived by the local communities. In general, the publishers expressed an awareness of the growing dissatisfaction with their coverage of Hispanic-related events; in Santa Fe, the publishers felt that the Hispanics would say that the paper "is a daily disappointment" but that "the paper is generally doing a good job."

Specific complaints against the newspapers ranged from excessive emphasis on crime within the Hispanic community to a lack of knowledge and sensitivity displayed by reporters in covering Mexican-American affairs. Particularly noteworthy were the complaints about the newspapers' perpetuation of negative stereotypes of Hispanics. In Salinas, there was concern about the excessive identification of Spanish surnames associated with criminal activity. In San Bernardino, the paper had a reputation for being somewhat racist; specific complaints charged that the paper published too many negative stories about Hispanics and not enough "upbeat" stories. In Stockton, reports indicated that excessive coverage was given to crime-related stories about Hispanics. The Visalia newspaper group also indicated that complaints had been received regarding the paper's overemphasis on crime and the use of stereotypic art. The

Chicano community in Visalia was described as feeling that the paper had been insensitive through its "bad publicity" of the Chicano community. Overall, the publishers perceived that communities held attitudes toward their local newspapers ranging from mild discontent to outright distrust.

All the newspapers have begun to implement changes so as to become more responsive to Hispanic communities. The publishers think that by employing local Hispanic Americans on the newspaper staff, they are encouraging representation of Hispanic concerns. Each newspaper currently employs Hispanics on its staff. In San Bernardino, three to five reporters deal exclusively with Hispanic news items; in Santa Fe, six of 23 reporters are Hispanic; in Stockton, three of 16 persons are Hispanic; in Tucson, five of 100 persons employed by the newspaper are Hispanic; and in Visalia, three of 21 newsroom staff persons are Hispanic. The Salinas publisher group articulated the need for more staff to respond to Hispanic affairs.

A second major need expressed by the publishers was increased coverage of local Hispanic concerns, as well as of news from Latin America, South America, and Mexico. In Santa Fe, plans to initiate community meetings were seen as a favorable "grass-roots" approach to gathering news. In Stockton, there existed the desire to obtain a Hispanic byline from Washington or Sacramento. In Visalia there had been some support for the idea of covering more human-interest aspects of life in the Chicano community.

One idea frequently mentioned to increase readership within the Hispanic communities was to introduce a Spanish-language section in the newspaper. This idea has met with mixed reaction. In Salinas, the publishers feared possibly alienating the Anglo readers if a Spanish-language section was introduced. Also, agreement could not be reached regarding which Spanish dialect to use or which level of Spanish would be acceptable for the community. In Tucson, there was staff interest in doing parts of the paper in Spanish, particularly basic news items, sports, and advertisements. Santa Fe, the only city with some Spanish-language sections, appears to have considered that step an improvement. Specifically, they have tried a Spanish columnist, the comic strip "Peanuts" in Spanish, and some briefs in Spanish.

A few communities have implemented changes to increase community accessibility to the newspaper. In San Bernardino, the newspaper has opened a branch office on the west side of the city; in Visalia, the publisher has met with community leaders and has visited schools in an effort to improve the quality of coverage of H-A affairs.

In general, it appears that newspaper groups are becoming increasingly sensitive to Hispanic problems and concerns within their communities. Through more Hispanic representation on their staffs, more Hispanic-related news coverage, and increased accessibility, the publishers believe that they may reduce distrust and improve the image of their newspapers among Hispanics.

The Availability of Spanish-Language Media

Print and electronic media available in Spanish or with key Spanish emphasis differed from city to city.

In some cities, Spanish-language newspapers were available to the H-A community. Salinas had a weekly Spanish newspaper, *El Sol*. In San Bernardino, two Chicano magazines and one Spanish-language newspaper published in Los Angeles were available. In Santa Fe, the local Gannett newspaper had provided Spanish-language sections in the past, but there was no report of any other Spanish newspaper circulating in the area. In Stockton, a new weekly Spanish newspaper (*Portavoz*) became available in February 1980. In Tucson, a number of English-language options were available: a University weekly school-year newspaper (*El Independiente*) concerned itself with Mexican-American affairs; and *The Citizen* published a weekly insert in tabloid format, "Old Pueblo," that frequently featured human-interest stories from the Hispanic community. In Visalia, there was no report of additional print media available to HAs.

Spanish-language news and feature stories were available to HAs through the electronic media. In every city, Spanish-language radio and/or television was accessible.

In Salinas, two local radio stations broadcast in Spanish and a third radio station carried about four hours a week of Spanish broadcasting. No Spanish-language TV station was reported; however, Salinas was described as having considerable community service news broadcast coverage, particularly in the form of consumer information. Although two or three radio stations reach San Bernardino, the publishers reported very little local enterprise on KCAL, the radio station closest to that area. The only Spanish-language radio stations with even minor penetration in the area originated from Los Angeles. There was no report of Spanish-language TV in San Bernardino. Santa Fe, however, was served by one Spanish-language television channel on the cable system, as well as one Hispanic-oriented radio station. These media primarily provide meeting announcements but were judged to be inadequate in their news coverage of the local community.

In Stockton, the Hispanic-oriented broadcast media were said to consist of one FM radio station from a nearby town, some valley area news from Modesto, and one show on an ABC affiliate. The newspaper group from Tucson identified one radio station in the area that primarily featured musical programming and a second radio station, perceived as the more modern and popular one, that broadcast community news and reports from Latin America. In addition to those Spanish-language radio broadcasts, three television channels provided minimal Spanish segments. Finally, in Visalia, one television station broadcast in Spanish. A radio station that provided some job information was also available.

In summary, publishers and their staffs emphasized that they were trying to improve coverage of the Hispanic Americans in their communities and that the communities had taken note of those developments. Publishers seemed aware of the existence of racism in most communities and that their image in H-A communities was not good.

Complaints of unfair or unbalanced coverage emphasizing crime were also acknowledged by publishers. However, the publishers tended to endorse the belief that crime *was* prevalent in the Hispanic-American sections of town and that in covering those events they were doing their job.

Overall, the perceptions of the H-A leaders and the newspaper publishers were basically in agreement. The newspapers had been taking steps to improve their service to the Hispanic community, but there was still discontent, of which the papers were aware. Community leaders, however, tended to be unaware of the relatively accurate perceptions of issues and complaints held by the newspaper publishers, and cynicism was voiced about positive newspaper intentions.

III
WHAT DID WE FIND?

4

MASS MEDIA USE, PREFERENCES, AND ATTITUDES AMONG ADULTS

JUDEE K. BURGOON
MICHAEL BURGOON
BRADLEY S. GREENBERG
FELIPE KORZENNY

A review of research on the mass media and communication attitudes and behaviors of Hispanic-American adults, summarized in chapters 1 and 2, indicates that little systematic evidence has been accumulated. Much of what has been written in academic and professional journals has been anecdotal and speculative. Moreover, what empirical research has been done has often reported conflicting or confusing conclusions. As a result, several assumptions and stereotypes have emerged concerning the media access, usage patterns, media attitudes, sources of information, and interpersonal styles of Hispanic Americans. Moreover, media policy makers and community leaders have tended to reinforce these assumptions in their perceptions of the communication behaviors of Hispanics. The adult survey was undertaken to determine the validity of these conclusions and to explore in a more systematic way the differences and/or similarities in the communication behaviors and attitudes of Anglos and Hispanics in the U.S.

We ourselves had certain expectations going into the adult survey. First, we expected Hispanics to have low access to such print media as newspapers and magazines and to have a low likelihood, on any given day, to expose themselves to such media. Evidence for this conclusion came not only from prior research but also from the circulation patterns of print media in cities with large Hispanic-American populations. Similarly, some research suggested that Hispanics spend less time with print media, particularly newspapers, when they do use them.

Second, fragmentary research claimed that the Hispanic-American population in the U.S. depends on and trusts broadcast media more than print media. In particular, Hispanics were said to believe TV and radio over newspapers and to be much more likely than their Anglo counterparts to depend on the broadcast media as their primary sources of information about a variety of topics. Speculation based upon little empirical evidence had been advanced that Hispanics have a stronger oral tradition than Anglos, leading to greater broadcast dependence as well as greater dependence on interpersonal contacts in the family and the community for useful information. It had similarly been reported that the Hispanic community depends heavily on both radio and television, especially Spanish-language broadcasts, for much of their day-to-day news. It has been contended that large segments of the Hispanic population (especially older people) are simply unable to use English-language print or broadcast media because of their inability to read or understand English and that they prefer to get news and other information from Spanish-language media.

Third, prior research and interviews with media managers and Hispanic community leaders paint a picture of the typical Hispanic American as relatively uninvolved with English-language media for news. It has been claimed that the low usage of such media is highly correlated with negative evaluations of both print and broadcast media. Reasons advanced for such low involvement include assertions that these media do not present the content most desired by Hispanic Americans so that this minority group simply turns to other sources of information. Others suggest that many Hispanic Americans view their local English-language media as very biased and racist sources of information. Specific complaints about the way local media cover Hispanic stories suggest the existence of a generally negative attitude in the Hispanic community toward the local media, causing the avoidance of reading, watching, or listening to anything presented. It has been charged that the local media avoid covering the Hispanic community and what coverage exists portrays Hispanic Americans in a very negative way.

Fourth, Hispanics are said to want broader news and entertainment content from the local media. Again, based upon very little empirical evidence, much of the literature suggests that cultural differences between Anglos and Hispanics lead to very different content demands on the media. It is alleged that the local media, in their efforts to satisfy the majority community, neglect the needs of the Hispanic community. Such neglect is seen as the basis for the alleged negative attitudes of Hispanics toward the English-language media.

Finally, others suggested that Hispanics consume media for different uses and gratifications than do Anglos. Some newspaper publishers believe that Hispanics primarily view the newspaper as a "use paper" and rely on newspapers for nonbreaking news, features, and advertisements, while Anglos have a greater interest in hard news, a conclusion supported by limited research. Others believe that Hispanics use both the print and broadcast media for entertainment, relaxation, and escape more than Anglos, who use the media for information and news. Where Hispanics show an interest in hard news, it is supposedly directed toward local news and crime.

Many of these speculations and assumptions have clearly been inferred from incomplete and inadequate data. Yet media policy makers and community leaders make decisions based upon such notions. To obtain more comprehensive and objective data on the media attitudes and behaviors of adult Anglos and Hispanics, we addressed several different areas in our survey:

- Ethnic identity and language use
- General media use and access
- Spanish-language media use and preferences
- Media evaluations
- Media functions
- Sources of information
- Media content preferences
- Demographics and other classification variables

METHOD

The adult survey was conducted during the months of May, June, and July 1980 in seven southwestern cities: Salinas, San Bernardino, Stockton, and Visalia, California; Santa Fe, New Mexico; Tucson, Arizona; and El Paso, Texas. Altogether, 1,703 people were surveyed, including 765 Anglos and 820 Hispanics.

Sample

A number of considerations governed selection of sites for the study. First, communities were chosen from those with one or more local Gannett newspapers. Selection was confined to the southwest because of the large concentration of Hispanics there. Because southwestern Hispanics are largely of Mexican descent, the results of this investigation should most appropriately be generalized to this subgroup and to this region of the country. Communities were selected for which there was an estimate of at least a 20- to 25-percent Hispanic population. Additionally, sites were selected for the variability in size of the Hispanic community, ranging from minority (21 percent in Visalia) to majority (65 percent in Santa Fe) status; variability in the occupational and economic base of the community; diversity on other demographic characteristics; availability of a range of print and broadcast media; and diversity in the circulation size, publication cycle (morning or afternoon-evening), and reach of the local paper.

The original sample plan called for a quota sample in each community of a minimum of 100 Anglos and 100 Hispanics; El Paso, where 150 Hispanics were to be interviewed, was the exception. To achieve a representative sample within ethnic groups, a system of random-digit dialing was used initially. This procedure called for the selection of six-digit telephone prefixes from current telephone directories in proportion to the number of households in each municipal unit within each site. A seventh random digit was then added to the prefixes to complete the number. This procedure has the advantage of confining calls to working telephone banks while insuring that those who have unlisted or not-yet-listed numers are included in the sample. In communities where mobility is high or the minority population is large, the number of numbers not listed may reach as high as 40 percent. A random-digit dialing procedure is therefore essential to achieve a representative sample with proper demographic balance.

In this survey, this procedure was followed until the quota of at least one ethnic group was filled (usually Anglos). Up to that point, all respondents were interviewed, including those falling in the "other" ethnic identity category (e.g., Blacks, Orientals, native Americans). Beyond that point, only the target ethnic group was interviewed; others were screened out. To improve the likelihood of reaching the target group, calls were then confined to those telephone prefixes that had already yielded target group interviews and the last two digits randomized. Finally, when this approach produced diminishing returns, Hispanic quotas were completed by identifying Hispanic surnames in the telephone directory and using a skip interval to select every nth name to call. The Census Bureau's list of Hispanic surnames was used to determine which names qualified.

As a further measure to insure proper demographic balance, interviewers initially asked to speak to an adult male in the household, if one was available; if not, a female was interviewed. This procedure consistently produces a male-female proportion consistent with Census Bureau estimates. In this survey, it yielded 49 percent males and 51 percent females. Only adults 18 years of age or older were interviewed.

The final sample in each community, broken down by ethnic identity, was as follows:

Location	Anglos	Hispanics	Other	Total
Salinas	102	118	20	240
San Bernardino	101	110	14	225
Stockton	117	98	31	246
Visalia	111	118	11	240
Santa Fe	106	104	6	216
Tucson	119	108	15	242
El Paso	109	164	21	294
Total	765	820	118	1,703

In all cases except San Bernardino, the geographic area sampled constituted the newspaper's city zone; in San Bernardino, it was the newspaper's primary market area.

Interview Procedure

All interviews were conducted by telephone from centralized facilities at Michigan State University, East Lansing. Calls usually were made between 5:00 P.M. and 10:00 P.M. (in each community) during the week, and between 11:00 A.M. and 3:00 P.M. on weekends.

Twenty-nine completely bilingual interviewers, who received extensive training, conducted all interviews. Constant supervision and frequent monitoring insured uniformity in procedures and timely retrieval of any missing information.

To complete this study, interviewers used a system of three callbacks and reached individuals at 4,039 telephone numbers. The number of ineligible respondents (under 18 years of age, answering from a business or other institution, or hard of hearing) was 506. Additionally, another 435 were screened out of the full survey because the ethnicity quota was filled; these respondents were given an abbreviated interview (six questions) instead. Additionally, 1,170 people refused to be interviewed, and an additional 119 terminated the interview before it was completed. Out of all eligible respondents (including those who were assigned the short version), the completion rate was 64 percent, with 33 percent refusals and 3 percent terminations. Of the 1,703 interviews completed, 15 percent were conducted in Spanish (55 percent of those were with females, 45 percent with males).

The Questionnaire

Because of the number of issues to be addressed, the questionnaire was modularized and divided into two forms, with any respondent answering 96 to 98 questions. The topics addressed are discussed, by category, below.

Ethnic Identity and Language Use. The opening question on the survey asked for the subject's ethnic identity and was worded as follows:

> Because we want to gain a better understanding of how people of different cultural origins in the [*location*] area view the media, we would like to know by what term you prefer to identify yourself—as Mexican, Mexican American, Chicano, Hispano, Black, Anglo, White, native American or another term?

Respondents were classified as Anglo, Hispanic, or Other. Two additional questions asked respondents what language they speak and read. Half the sample was asked what languages are spoken in the home most often.

Media Use and Access. All respondents were asked (1) what daily newspapers they had read in the last week; (2) how many days out of seven they had read them; (3) how much time they had spent reading the paper "yesterday"; (4) how many people in the household read the newspaper; and (5) how it was obtained. Television use was assessed by asking respondents how much time they had spent "yesterday" watching (1) national news programs on television (including programs like *Veinte y Cuatro Horas*), (2) local news shows, television entertainment (3) before noon, (4) before supper, and (5) "last night" and (6) how many television sets were in the home. Radio use was assessed by asking how much time the person had spent listening (1) to radio news and (2) to other things on the radio "yesterday," as well as (3) how many working radios there were in the person's home and in the cars of the people living there. Magazine use was determined by asking how much time the person spent reading magazines in the previous week.

Additionally, a series of questions probed use of Spanish media. Respondents were asked how many hours or minutes they had spent in the last week (1) reading Spanish-language newspapers; (2) watching Spanish-language television; (3) listening to Spanish-language radio; (4) reading other things written in Spanish, such as magazines; and (5) listening to Spanish records and tapes. Half the sample was further asked (1) if there were people in the household who do not read the local daily newspaper because it is written in English, (2) if they would prefer to have all, part, or none of the daily newspaper printed in Spanish; and (3) if they would prefer to have all, part, or none of current English-language local television shows broadcast in Spanish.

Media Evaluations. This sequence of questions, asked of half the sample, began by asking respondents to rate their overall satisfaction with (1) local newspapers, (2) local television news and community issues shows, and (3) local radio news and community issues shows, on a scale of 1 (extremely dissatisfied) to 5 (extremely satisfied). Respondents were then asked their respective satisfaction with television, newspaper, and radio coverage of four topics. Anglos were asked about coverage of local people and their accomplishments; social news such as social activities, weddings and deaths; local cultural activities; and treatment of crime. Hispanics were asked the parallel topics of local Hispanics and their accomplishments; social news in the Hispanic community, such as social activities, weddings, and deaths; local cultural activities within the Hispanic community; and treatment of crime in the Hispanic community.

Anglos and Hispanics alike were then asked (1) how fair they thought the local media's coverage is of the Hispanic community; (2) given a local news event reported differently by TV, radio, and the newspaper, which medium they would be most likely to believe; and (3) what topics they want to receive greater media coverage.

Media Functions. A series of 30 questions addressed the importance of the media in performing various functions, including timeliness and thoroughness of news coverage, providing relaxation and arousal, offering vicarious knowledge, and serving as a means of improving language ability. One-fourth of the sample supplied ratings of the importance of these functions being performed by newspaper, and one-fourth rated television news shows, in each case using a scale of 1 (extremely unimportant) to 5 (extremely important). All those who completed these questions were then asked to rate on a scale of 1 to 5 how well the functions most important for them were being satisfied respectively by local newspapers, local television shows, local radio shows, and the magazines they read.

Sources of Information. Half the sample indicated for each of four types of information they might need what source they would be most likely to turn to first—TV, radio, newspapers, people in organizations like the church or social agencies, or family and friends. The four information categories were job possibilities, local political activities, community events, and making major purchases such as a car or stove.

Media Content Preferences. Half the sample was asked to specify on a scale of 1 to 5 their degree of interest in 37 different topics that generally appear in the media (radio, television, and newspapers). Topics included such things as stories about national politics; news and features on business; news of Mexico and Latin America; health and medical advice; stories about discrimination, problems in the schools, and professional sports; and comics and cartoons. Additionally, they indicated how much they liked to watch eight types of TV entertainment programs (e.g., soap operas and situation comedies). One final content-related question was a follow-up to the questions on satisfaction with the media. It asked respondents what topics, if any, they would like to see receive increased coverage by the media.

Newspaper and Television Image. One-fourth of the sample rated TV, and one-fourth newspapers on 17 adjective pairs designed to measure image. The ratings covered such aspects of image as expertise, trustworthiness, objectivity, and power; it included such items as "competent–incompetent," "not racist–racist" and "courageous–not courageous."

Demographics and Other Classification Variables. Four variables were simply recorded by the interviewer: (1) gender of respondent, (2) location, (3) day of interview, and (4) date of interview. Beyond those and (5) ethnic self-identity, respondents were asked (6) how long they had lived in the commu-

nity, (7) age, (8) education, (9) income, (10) size of household, (11) first generation in the family to live in the U.S., (12) evaluation of the community's quality
of life (better, worse, or the same as 5 years ago), and (13) likelihood of moving
from the community. Additionally, respondents were classified as regular, occasional, or nonreaders of newspapers and as users or nonusers for each of the
media variables covered in the survey.

All questionnaires were printed in both English and Spanish. Respondents who reported they were bilingual were given a choice of language in
which to be questioned. The questionnaire was first constructed in English, then
translated into Spanish, and then retranslated into English to check for consistency in interpretation and to control for connotative as well as denotative meaning.

Table 4.1 sets out demographic comparisons between Anglo and
Hispanic-American respondents.

TABLE 4.1 Demographic comparisons for Hispanics and Anglos

	Total Sample	Among Hispanics	Among Anglos	Significance
Education				*
Less than high school	25%	41%	10%	
High school graduate	29	30	28	
Some collete	26	22	30	
Collete graduate/postgrad.	20	8	32	
Income				*
Under $10,000	20%	27%	13%	
$10–15,000	22	28	17	
$15–20,000	19	19	18	
$20–30,000	23	19	29	
Over $30,000	15	7	23	
Age				*
18–24	23%	28%	19%	
23–34	30	33	27	
35–44	15	14	15	
45–54	14	13	15	
55–64	10	8	12	
65 and over	8	4	12	
Length of Residence				*
Less than 2 years	11%	8%	15%	
2–5 years	13	13	13	
6–10 years	16	15	16	
Over 10 years	60	64	57	
Likelihood of Moving				
Very likely	20%	18%	22%	
Somewhat likely	15	16	15	
Not sure	5	6	3	
Somewhat unlikely	16	18	14	
Very unlikely	44	42	46	

TABLE 4.1. (continued)

	Total Sample	Among Hispanics	Among Anglos	Significance
First Generation in U.S.				*
Self	10%	15%	3%	
Parents	21	31	11	
Grandparents	27	29	26	
Earlier generations	41	23	59	
Not sure	1	1	1	
Quality of life in the Community				*
Better than 5 years ago	37%	40%	33%	
About the same	30	25	35	
Worse	33	35	32	
Language(s) Spoken				*
English only	40%	6%	73%	
Spanish only	7	14	0	
Both equally	22	43	2	
Mostly Spanish	8	16	0	
Mostly English	17	21	14	
Other combinations	7	1	11	
Language(s) read				*
English only	47%	16%	78%	
Spanish only	8	16	0	
Both equally	18	36	2	
Mostly Spanish	5	11	0	
Mostly English	15	20	11	
Other combinations	7	1	10	
Sex				
Male	49%	47%	51%	
Female	51	53	49	

*Significant differences across groups ($p < .05$).

Note that four out of every 10 Hispanic respondents have less than a high school education, and another three out of 10 have only a high school degree. Moreover, a full 55 percent of Hispanics earn $15,000 or less, compared to 30 percent of the Anglos. These figures are significant, for many of the differences in media habits and evaluations to be discussed may be more attributable to socioeconomic differences than to ethnic differences per se. Additionally, the high proportion of young people—61 percent of the Hispanics in the sample are under age 35—may account for some of the observed ethnic differences.

Despite the large percentage of young people, Hispanics show a pattern of long-term residence in their communities, with 64 percent having lived there in excess of 10 years, and only 8 percent having moved there very recently. Consistent with this picture of stability, 60 percent of the Hispanics say they are somewhat or very unlikely to move from the community, the same percentage as among Anglos. And while the Anglo families tend to have immigrated to the U.S. earlier than the Hispanics, over one-half the Hispanics report that their grandparents or earlier generations were the first to arrive; only 15 percent report that they were the first, in contrast to the stereotypic picture of the Hispanic as recent immigrant or migrant.

As further evidence of the typical Hispanic's integration into the U.S. culture, 80 percent are bilingual speakers, and only 14 percent report speaking Spanish only. A similar pattern holds for use of written language, with 72 percent reporting good proficiency in reading English and only 16 percent reporting that they read only Spanish (a small figure relative to expectations). As for language spoken in the home, over one-third of the Hispanics report using mostly or only Spanish and another one-third mostly or only English.

General Media Use and Access

Newspapers. Consistent with past research, Anglos are significantly more likely to be newspaper readers than are Hispanics. Among Hispanics, 70 percent read a local daily newspaper, while 30 percent are nonreaders; by contrast, 88 percent of the Anglos are readers, 12 percent nonreaders. Not only is there a difference in whether a paper is read or not, there is also a difference in the *regularity* with which papers are read among those who read. This is true whether one considered readership of the local Gannett paper specifically or other available local papers generally. To illustrate this difference, respondents were classified as regular newspaper readers (reading five or more issues of local daily papers in the last 7 days), occasional newspaper readers (reading one to four issues in the last 7 days) or nonreaders (reading no issues in the last 7 days). Further, readership of the local Gannett paper was similarly classified (regular readers were those who read five or more issues of a 7-day Gannett paper, four or more issues of a 6-day paper; occasional readers were those who read one to four issues of a 7-day paper, one to three issues of a 6-day paper; competition-only readers were those who read no issues of the Gannett paper but at least one issue of another paper; and nonreaders were again those who had read no daily newspaper in the last 7 days). When considered according to these classifications, the data presented in Table 4.2 show more regularity in readership among Anglos.

TABLE 4.2. Percent of readership among Hispanics and Anglos, by reader classification.

Reader Classification	Total Sample	Among Hispanics	Among Anglos	Significance
Regular newspaper reader	57%	45%	68%	*
Occasional newspaper reader	22	25	20	
Nonreader	21	30	12	
Regular Gannett reader	36%	28%	44%	*
Occasional Gannett reader	29	28	30	
Reader of competing papers only	14	14	14	
Nonreader	21	30	12	

*Significant difference between groups ($p < .05$).

Another measure of frequency of readership—average number of issues of daily newspapers read in a week's time—similarly shows a significant difference. Among Hispanics who read a paper, the average is 6.0, compared to 7.1 for Anglo readers. When averaged across all respondents in each ethnic subgroup, the results are even more pronounced, Hispanics averaging 4.2 issues and Anglos 6.3.

While Hispanics differ from Anglos on their likelihood of reading daily papers and the regularity with which they read them, those who do read spend as much time as Anglos with the paper on a given day, a finding contrary to previous research and assumptions. The summary in Table 4.3 on average time spent reading the newspaper per day reveals that whether or not Sunday is included in the average, Hispanic and Anglo readers alike spend about 40 minutes or more a day reading the paper. Only when nonreaders are included in the average is there a difference between the two groups.

TABLE 4.3. Mean minutes spent reading the newspaper "yesterday"

Base	Total	Hispanics	Anglos	Significance
Among readers, across seven days	43.6	41.3	45.1	
Among readers, Sunday excluded	41.7	39.1	43.4	
Among all respondents	29.5	23.9	34.9	*

*Significant difference across groups ($p < .05$).

Two other measures of newspaper use suggest that Hispanics have less access to local daily newspapers than do Anglos. The percentage of households who read a newspaper is only 59 percent for Hispanics compared to 80 percent for Anglos. This means there is less reinforcement available in Hispanic households from others reading a paper. More importantly, fewer Hispanics subscribe to a daily newspaper: Only 50 percent of those who read a paper reported subscribing; another 44 percent purchase their paper from a store or newsstand; and 6 percent obtain their paper as a pass-along from someone else. By contrast, 77 percent of the Anglo newspaper readers subscribed; 19 percent purchase their paper at a store or newsstand; and 4 percent have their paper passed on to them.

While the results on newspaper use suggest marked differences in reading habits of Hispanics versus Anglos, to focus exclusively on ethnicity or to assume it is the primary determinant of differences can be misleading. To better assess what factors actually influence newspaper habits and what role ethnicity plays in the broader picture, multiple-regression analyses were conducted. Multiple regression statistically determines which subset of variables out of a large set of potentially influential variables best predicts the criterion variable. In this case, the two criterion variables to be predicted were frequency of readership and amount of time spent reading. For each criterion variable, 25 predictor variables were identified that were thought possibly to influence newspaper reading. They included demographics, use of other media, and some attitudinal (evaluative) variables, as follows:

1. Ethnicity
2. Age
3. Sex
4. Size of household
5. Length of residence in the community
6. Education
7. First generation in family to live in U.S.
8. Income
9. Language spoken (predominantly English, predominantly Spanish, or both equally)
10. Likelihood of moving from the community
11. Judgment of quality of life in the community (compared to past)
12. Proportion of newspaper readers in the household
13. Method of obtaining the paper (subscriber versus nonsubscriber)
14. Time spent reading the newspaper per day/Frequency of reading the newspaper (time was the predictor when frequency was the criterion and vice versa)
15. Satisfaction with the newspaper
16. Number of TV sets in the household
17. Time spent watching TV news
18. Time spent watching TV entertainment
19. Satisfaction with local TV news coverage
20. Number of radios in the household
21. Time spent listening to radio news
22. Time spent listening to radio entertainment
23. Satisfaction with radio news coverage
24. Time spent reading magazines in last week
25. Location[1]

Both analyses were confined to newspaper readers. For frequency of readership, 11 variables emerged as significant predictors and accounted for 35 percent of the variance. They are listed in order of importance, given the constraints on entry into the model, in Table 4.4.

The results indicate that while ethnicity and related language use are

---

[1]Because some of these variables were thought possibly to influence some of the others, the order of entry into the analysis was constrained such that items 1 through 4 were allowed to enter first (if significant), following by items 5 through 8, followed by item 9, item 10, and item 11, and then all the media-use variables, and finally item 25. Location was entered last to see if the preceding variables better accounted for observed differences across markets.

TABLE 4.4. Predictors of frequency of readership among newspaper readers.

Predictors	Description of Relationship
1. Age	As age *increases,* readership *increases.*
2. Ethnicity	Anglos are *more frequent* readers than Hispanics.
3. Sex	Males are *more frequent* readers than females.
4. Income	As income *increases,* readership *increases.*
5. Education	As education *increases,* readership *increases.*
6. Length of residence	As years in the community *increase,* readership *increases.*
7. Language spoken	Predominantly Spanish speakers are *less frequent* readers than predominantly English or equal Spanish and English speakers.
8. Time spent reading the newspaper	As time reading *increases,* frequency of reading *increases.*
9. Size of household	As the number of people in the household *increases,* readership *increases.* [This is after controlling for the previous variables. Otherwise, the relationship is the reverse: More people # less reading.]
10. Proportion who read the newspaper	As proportion of household who read a newspaper *increases,* readership *increases.*
11. Location	Highest frequency is in Santa Fe, followed by San Bernardino and Stockton, followed by El Paso and Visalia, and finally by Salinas and Tucson.

$R^2 = 35\%$

indeed important determinants of the regularity of readership (as noted earlier), an even bigger predictor is age. Younger readers are more occasional in their reading habit. Given the large numbers of young people in the Hispanic subgroup, this relationship with age partly accounts for the weaker reading habit. From a policy standpoint, this finding suggests that the concern about lower readership among Hispanics should not be seen just as an ethnicity problem but also as a young reader problem, and efforts to better reach the Hispanic newspaper audience must take into account the interests and needs of young people in general.

Consistent with a number of other newspaper readership studies, the results above also reveal that frequency of readership generally increases with education, income, length of residence in the community, and amount of time spent reading the newspaper. By contrast, the finding that males read more frequently than females does not occur with regularity in other research. An analysis of sex differences by location showed that this difference was typically too slight to be significant; only when cumulated across seven sites did it become sizable enough to make a difference. Another interesting finding is the relationship with size of household. While the simple relationship between household size and readership is an inverse one—that is, the larger the household, the less frequent the reading—this analysis reveals that if one adjusts for such other factors as ethnicity, age, and length of residence, then the pattern reverses itself and readership increases as households become larger. Finally, the location differences reveal that there are geographic differences in readership above and beyond those due to such demographic factors as income, education, stability of the community, and size of the Hispanic population. While some of those differences can be accounted for by the presence or absence of a local Sunday edition, this analysis was conducted on each person's total amount of newspaper readership across a week's time, not just readership of the local Gannett paper.

A similar analysis was conducted using the amount of time spent reading as the criterion variable. The results, summarized in Table 4.5, show that demographics are far less effective in predicting how long a person will read the newspaper in an average day. Ethnicity is not even a factor. Only age and gender again influence reading: Young people and women spend less time with the paper. Instead, other media habits better predict how much time a person will spend. It should be noted that contrary to the popular view, newspaper reading *increases* as TV viewing and magazine readership increase. The relationship among media is therefore complementary rather than competitive. Although, only 14 percent of the variance in time spent reading is accounted for, signalling that other factors not included in this analysis explain the preponderance of a person's reading habit.

TABLE 4.5. Predictors of time spent reading the newspaper "yesterday" among readers.

Predictors	*Description of Relationship*
1. Age	As age *increases,* reading time *increases.*
2. Sex	Males spend *more* time than females.
3. Frequency of newpaper readership	As frequency *increases,* reading time *increases.*
4. Time spent reading magazines	As magazine time *increases,* newspaper time *increases.*
5. Time spent watching TV news	As TV time *increases,* newspaper time *increases.*
6. Time spent watching entertainment	As TV watching *increases,* newspaper time *increases.*

$R^2 = 14\%$

In sum, the ramifications of the regression analyses for understanding the role of ethnicity in newspaper use are that many other factors impinge on newspaper habits, some more powerfully than ethnic identification, and that once Hispanics elect to read the newspaper, they spend as much time with it daily as do Anglos. If increased access to print media among Hispanics is a goal, key areas where efforts can be targeted are increasing the regularity of readership and increasing home subscription rates.

Television. Television news consumption "yesterday" was split into two questions, one addressing local news viewing and one national news viewing (including programs like "Veinte y Cuatro Horas"). The results, summarized in Table 4.6, counter the perceptions of the Hispanic as either less news oriented or more dependent on broadcast media. They indicate that the percentage of Hispanics who watch the news daily does not differ from the percentage of Anglos, nor do the number of minutes each group spends watching. Only when the results for nonusers are averaged in with those for users do Hispanics as a subgroup show less time watching national news than Anglos. The average "news watcher" in both groups reports spending approximately 1.5 hours per day watching news on TV, compared with 0.75 hours reading the newspaper.

TABLE 4.6. Percentage and frequency of watching television local and national news "yesterday"

	Total	Hispanics	Anglos
Percentage watching national news	67%	65%	70%
Percentage watching local news	66%	64%	68%
Mean minutes watching national news			
Among users	54.2	51.9	55.9
Among all respondents	37.4	33.5	40.9
Mean minutes watching local news			
Among users	37.3	37.1	37.6
Among all respondents	24.6	23.7	25.4

*Significant differences between groups ($p < .05$).

Television entertainment viewing was assessed by means of three questions that split viewing into the hours (1) before noon, (2) afternoon before supper, and (3) evening. The percentage of viewers and the average minutes of daily viewing for each of those time periods are summarized in Table 4.7.

As the percentage comparisons show, the numbers of Hispanics who watch morning and evening entertainment programming are no different than the numbers of Anglos; it is only in the afternoon that Hispanics showed a greater proportion of viewers. As for the average amount of time spent watching TV entertainment in a day, Hispanics average more time than Anglos, both in the morning and the afternoon. As a result of both the higher percentage of afternoon viewers and the average amount of daytime viewing time, Hispanics as a group show greater overall TV entertainment viewing than Anglos: Among all His-

TABLE 4.7. Percentage and frequency of watching morning, afternoon, and evening television entertainment "yesterday"

	Total	Hispanics	Anglos	Significance
Percentage watching morning TV entertainment	24%	26%	23%	
Percentage watching afternoon TV entertainment	39%	48%	30%	*
Percentage watching evening TV entertainment	66%	65%	66%	
Mean minutes of morning viewing				
Among users	94.3	98.5	84.5	*
Among all respondents	23.1	26.0	19.1	
Mean minutes of afternoon viewing				
Among users	104.0	108.0	94.7	*
Among all respondents	41.0	52.6	28.6	*
Mean minutes of evening viewing				
Among users	129.9	128.2	128.2	
Among all respondents	87.9	85.6	86.4	

*Significant difference between groups ($p < .05$).

panics, the average viewing time per day is approximately 2.75 hours, compared with 2.25 hours for Anglos. When news time is also added in, the averages become 3.66 hours for Hispanics and 3.33 hours for Anglos.

The difference in TV viewing time cannot be explained by the number of TV sets in the household. Hispanics average 1.7 sets, Anglos average 1.8.

As with newspaper use, multiple-regression analyses were conducted to identify the most important predictors of TV news and entertainment viewing. Local and national news viewing times were summed to measure overall news viewing. Morning, afternoon, and evening entertainment viewing were similarly summed to yield one entertainment time total per respondent. The same predictor variables were used, with both frequency of reading the newspaper and time spent reading the paper included as potential predictors. The analyses were again confined to those who actually watched television.

Table 4.8 reports the predictors of news viewing; Table 4.9 reports predictors of entertainment viewing.

The degree to which one watches the news is not significantly influenced by ethnicity. Rather, a person's demographic characteristics better determine how much viewing takes place. Surprisingly, females report more news viewing, as do lower-income respondents, older people, and newcomers to the community. (It should be noted, however, that when local TV news watching is analyzed separately from national TV news, length of residence makes no difference in the amount of time spent watching local news. Moreover, while national news viewing is highest among those aged 25 through 34 and 45 and

TABLE 4.8. Predictors of amount of time spent watching television news "yesterday" among viewers

Predictors	Description of Relationship
1. Sex	Females watch *more* often than males.
2. Income	As income *increases*, news viewing *decreases*.
3. TV entertainmnet viewing	As entertainment time *increases*, news viewing *increases*.
4. Age	As age *increases*, news viewing *increases*.
5. Length of residence	As number of years in the community *increases*, news viewing *decreases*.
6. Number of TV sets	The *more* TV sets in the home, the *greater* the viewing.
7. Time reading magazines	As reading time *increases*, news viewing *increases*.

$R^2 = 10\%$

older, local news viewing is highest among those aged 18 through 24 and 55 and older. Thus, there is a curvilinear relationship between age and each type of newscast, but the curves are not the same. The main consistency is that those 55 and older watch longer.) The other determinants of news viewing are media-related. Those who consume more entertainment programming are also more likely to watch the news. Similarly, those who read more magazines are more inclined to watch TV news. It will be recalled that both these variables also predicted spending more time with the newspaper. Finally, when the analysis is limited to those who actually watch the news, the number of TV sets in the household becomes relevant.

As the previous analyses revealed, ethnicity makes a difference in amount of time spent with TV entertainment. It is, in fact, the single most important predictor. Other demographic determinants are sex, age, income, and

TABLE 4.9. Predictors of amount of time spent watching television entertainment "yesterday," among viewers.

Predictors	Description of Relationship
1. Ethnicity	Hispanics spend *more* time watching than do Anglos.
2. Sex	Females spend *more* time watching than do males.
3. Income	As income *increases*, viewing time *decreases*.
4. Education	As education *increases*, viewing time *decreases*.
5. TV news viewing	As news viewing time *increases*, entertainment viewing *increases*.
6. Age	As age *increases*, viewing time *decreases*.
7. Time reading the newspaper	As reading time *increases*, viewing time *increases*.

$R^2 = 15\%$

education. In the case of the first two, the relationship is the same as for news viewing: Women and the less affluent watch longer. However, with age the pattern is reversed: Older viewers spend less time than younger viewers. Education, like income, shows declines in viewing time as it increases. Finally, both newspaper reading and TV news viewing correlate with entertainment viewing; again, greater consumption of one medium or content form is accompanied by greater consumption of another. The emerging pattern is that greater media use in one area promotes greater use in others.

Radio. Contrary to expectations, Hispanics do not differ from Anglos in their dependence on radio, either for news or for entertainment. The only difference between the two groups is that Hispanics have access to slightly fewer radios. All the radio results are summarized in Table 4.10.

TABLE 4.10. Use and access to radio news and entertainment.

	Total	Hispanics	Anglos	Significance
Percentage listening to news	40%	43%	43%	
Mean news time "yesterday"				
Among users	32.6 min.	33.3 min.	30.6 min.	
Among all respondents	19.4	18.9	20.0	
Percentage listening to entertainment	60%	62%	60%	
Mean entertainment time "yesterday"				
Among users	174.2 min.	176.3 min.	174.1 min.	
Among all respondents	106.8	111.1	105.8	
Number of radios	3.8	3.5	4.1	*

*Significant differences between groups ($p < .05$).

The lack of ethnicity differences in Table 4.10 is confirmed by multiple-regression analyses for radio news listening and entertainment listening. In the former analysis (not tabled), only one predictor emerged—entertainment listening—and it only accounted for 2 percent of the variance. In the latter analysis, reported in Table 4.11, ethnicity is again not directly relevant, although language spoken is: Those who speak primarily English listen less often than those who speak primarily Spanish or those who speak both languages equally. Additionally, three other demographics (household size, location, and education) and two media variables (radio news listening and magazine reading) affect entertainment listening.

TABLE 4.11. Predictors of amount of time spent listening to radio entertainment "yesterday," among listeners.

Predictors	Description of Relationship
1. Size of household	As number of people *increases*, radio listening *decreases*.
2. Education	As education *increases*, listening *decreases*.
3. Language spoken	Predominantly English speakers listen *less* often.
4. Radio news listening	As radio news listening time *increases*, entertainment listening time *increases*.
5. Number of radios in home and car	As number of radios *increases*, listening *increases*.
6. Magazine reading time	As reading time *increases*, listening *increases*.
7. Location	Listening time is *lowest* in Salinas and Visalia.

$R^2 = 10\%$

Magazines. When asked how much time they have spent reading magazines during the last week, fewer Hispanics report such reading than do Anglos. However, among those who do read, there are no differences by ethnicity in amount of time spent. These results are summarized in Table 4.12.

TABLE 4.12. Time spent reading magazines in last week.

	Total	Hispanics	Anglos	Significance
Percentage who read magazines in last week	67%	60%	73%	*
Mean minutes reading/week				
Among users	161.8 min.	161.8 min.	159.4 min.	
Among all respondents	109.9	98.0	118.2	*

*Significant differences between groups ($p < .05$).

Spanish-Language Media: Use, Access, and Preferences

All respondents were asked how much time they had spent in the previous week reading or listening to Spanish-language (1) newspapers, (2) other print media, (3) TV, (4) radio, and (5) tapes and records. The averages, reported in Table 4.13, show that radio has the heaviest usage among Hispanics, who typically spend about 9.3 hours per week listening to broadcasts in Spanish. (Computed on a daily basis, Hispanics average over 1.3 hours with Spanish-language radio alone, indicating that much of their total radio listening is to Spanish-language broadcasts.) Total time with print media among Hispanics is not particularly high. Predictably, Anglos show almost no use of Spanish-language media.

TABLE 4.13. Time spent with Spanish-language media in last week.

	Total	Hispanics	Anglos	Significance
Mean minutes reading Spanish-language newspaper/week	14.2 min.	29.2 min.	.3 min.	*
Mean minutes reading Spanish-language magazines, other print/week	21.4	43.4	1.4	*
Mean minutes watching Spanish-language TV/week	199.6	391.1	21.1	*
Mean minutes listening to Spanish-Language radio/week	276.7	557.3	14.6	*
Mean minutes listening to Spanish tapes and records/week	55.7	108.1	5.8	*

*Significant differences between groups ($p < .05$).

Among those who use Spanish-language media (primarily Hispanics), multiple regression analyses were conducted to asses what factors contribute to greater or lesser usage. In these analyses, 26 variables were entered as possible predictors. These included the demographics and media use variables used earlier, plus use of other Spanish-language media beyond the one being predicted. Additionally, variables that did not emerge as significant predictors but still had a moderate correlation with the criterion variable were also identified so as to provide a more complete picture of what factors promote use of the various Spanish-language media. The results appear in Tables 4.14 through 4.18.

As one might expect, those who speak predominantly Spanish are heavier users of Spanish-language newspapers. Males also read them more often, as do residents of El Paso and Salinas and newer residents in all seven communities. Beyond these demographics, newspaper use is heavily influenced by other media habits. Specifically, those who spend more time with English-language print media and those who spend more time with other Spanish-language media generally also spend more time reading Spanish-language newspapers in a week. However, one exception to this pattern is that those who *subscribe* to English-language newspapers are less likely to spend much time with Spanish-language papers.

TABLE 4.14. Predictors and correlates of time spent reading Spanish-language newspapers, among users.

Predictors	Description of Relationship
1. Language spoken	Predominantly Spanish speakers are the *most* frequent and predominantly English speakers the *least* frequent readers.
2. Sex	Males read Spanish newspapers *more* often than do females.
3. Time spent reading magazines	As magazine time *increases*, Spanish newspaper reading time *increases*.
4. Time spent reading other Spanish print media	As other Spanish print media time *increases*, Spanish newspaper reading time *increases*.
5. Newspaper subscription (local daily newspaper)	Nonsubscribers read Spanish newspapers *more* than do subscribers.
location	*Highest* in El Paso and Salinas, *lowest* in Visalia and Santa Fe.

$R^2 = 30\%$

Other Significant Correlations

1. Time spent listening to Spanish radio	As Spanish radio listening *increases*, time spent reading Spanish newspapers *increases*.
2. Time spent listening to Spanish music	As Spanish music listening *increases*, time spent reading Spanish newspapers *increases*.
3. Time spent reading the local daily newspaper	As time reading newspapers *increases*, time spent reading Spanish papers also *increases*.
4. Years in the community	As years living in the community *increases*, time spent reading Spanish newspapers *decreases*.

With Spanish-language magazines and other publications, the only demographic determinants of reading time were language spoken and location. Again, greater use of spoken Spanish corresponded with greater reading of publications in Spanish. Otherwise, reading time increased as consumption of other entertainment media, and especially Spanish-language media, increased.

Interestingly, TV viewing is most strongly associated with one's education. As was true with English-language TV entertainment, the more educated viewers watch less. Language spoken and location are again relevant, with Santa Fe remaining at the low end on Spanish-language media use. While time spent with certain broadcast media is positively related to use of Spanish-language TV, in this case use of newspapers is negatively related. Households

TABLE 4.15. Predictors and correlates of time spent reading other Spanish print media, among users.

Predictors	Description of Relationship
1. Language spoken	Predominantly English speakers are *less* frequent readers than predominantly Spanish speakers or bilinguals.
2. Time spent reading magazines	As magazine time *increases,* time spent reading print media *increases.*
3. Time spent watching TV entertainment	As TV watching *increases,* time spent reading Spanish print media increases.
4. Time spent reading Spanish newspaper	As Spanish newspaper reading *increases,* time spent reading other Spanish print media *increases.*

$R^2 = 18\%$

Other Significant Correlations

1. Time spent watching Spanish TV	As Spanish TV watching *increases,* time spent reading Spanish print media *increases.*
2. Time spent listening to Spanish music	As Spanish radio listening *increases,* time spent reading Spanish print media *increases.*
3. Time spent listening to Spanish music	As Spanish music listening *increases,* time spent reading Spanish print media *increases.*
4. Time spent watching TV entertainment	As TV watching *increases,* time spent reading other Spanish print media *increases.*
5. Location	*Highest* is in Visalia and El Paso, *lowest* in Santa Fe.

and individuals with a strong newspaper habit are less likely to be heavy consumers of Spanish-language TV.

In contrast to the pattern shown with Spanish-language TV viewing, Spanish-language radio use *increases* with education. In other ways, the results are similar to those for TV. Language spoken and location again make a difference, usage increases with greater use of broadcast media and Spanish-language media, and it decreases with readership of and subscription to English-language newspapers. Interestingly, radio listening also decreases the more TV sets there are in the home.

As with Spanish-language TV, Spanish tapes and records are more popular with the less educated. By location, Santa Fe again shows least usage. As for the influence of other media use, record and tape playing consistently increases with greater use of other Spanish-language media, as well as with the number of radios in the house and the proportion of newspaper readers.

Three additional questions probed the relationship between language and media use. The first two asked respondents if (1) they would prefer to have all, part, or none of the local daily newspaper printed in Spanish and (2) all, part, or none of the currently English-language local TV news broadcasts done in Spanish. The results, reported in Table 4.19, are broken down by ethnicity and location. They reveal that two-thirds of the Hispanics prefer to have part or all of the newspaper printed in Spanish, while three-quarters prefer to have local TV

TABLE 4.16. Predictors and correlates of time spent watching Spanish-language television, among users.

Predictors	Description of Relationship
1. Education	As education *increases*, Spanish TV use *decreases*.
2. Language spoken	Predominantly Spanish speakers spend the *most* time, predominantly English speakers, the *least*.
3. Time spent with Spanish radio	As radio listening *increases*, TV viewing *increases*.
4. Proportion who read the newspaper	As the proportion of household who read a newspaper *increases*, Spanish TV viewing *decreases*.
5. Time spent watching TV entertainment	As TV time *increases*, Spanish TV time *increases*.
6. Location	*Highest* viewing is in Salinas, *lowest* in Santa Fe.
7. Quality-of-life judgments	As a person's view of the quality of life in the community becomes more *positive*, Spanish TV viewing *increases*.

$R^2 = 24\%$

Other Significant Correlations

1. Frequency of newspaper readership	As frequency *increases*, Spanish TV use *decreases*.
2. Newspaper subscription	Nonsubscribers watch *more* Spanish TV.

news broadcast in Spanish. By comparison, 69 percent of the Anglos prefer to have none of the paper and none of the local TV broadcasts in Spanish. Greatest preference for predominantly Spanish newspapers and broadcasts appears in Salinas. Tucson and Santa Fe Hispanics, in comparison, show a greater preference for a bilingual approach. Among Anglos, greatest receptivity to having part of the newspaper in Spanish occurs in Tucson and San Bernardino, while greatest receptivity to TV news broadcasts using some Spanish appears in those same two locales plus El Paso.

The final question that sheds some light on the issue of language and media use asked Hispanics if there were any people in their household who do not read the local daily newspaper because it is written in English. The percentages replying ''yes'' in each market are as follows:

Salinas	44%
San Bernardino	19%
Stockton	32%
Visalia	12%
El Paso	32%
Santa Fe	7%
Tucson	18%
Overall	24%

TABLE 4.17. Predictors and correlates of time spent listening to Spanish-language radio, among users.

Predictors	Description of Relationship
1. Education	As education *increases,* Spanish radio listening *increases.*
2. Language spoken	Predominantly English speakers are *less* frequent listenters than predominantly Spanish speakers or bilinguals.
3. Time spent with Spanish TV	As Spanish TV viewing *increases,* Spanish radio use *increases.*
4. Time wpent with radio entertainment	As radio entertainment time *increases,* Spanish radio use *increases.*
5. Time spent with Spanish print media (other than newspaper)	As Spanish print media time *increases,* Spanish radio use *increases.*
6. Number of TV sets	The *more* TVs in the home, the *less* amount of time spent listening to Spanish radio.
7. Location	*Highest* listening time is in Salinas, *lowest* in San Bernardino, Visalia and El Paso.

$R^2 = 25\%$

1. Time spent reading Spanish newspapers	As time reading *increases,* Spanish radio use *increases.*
2. Time spent reading the regular daily newspaper	As time reading *increases,* Spanish radio use *decreases.*
3. Newspaper subscription to daily newspaper	Nonsubscribers listen to *more* Spanish radio.

TABLE 4.18. Predictors and correlates of time spent listening to Spanish records and tapes,, among users.

Predictors	Description of Relationship
1. Education	As education *increases,* listening *decreases.*
2. Research of Spanish newspapers	As readership *increases,* listen *increases.*
3. Number of radios in household	The *more* radios, the *greater* the amount of listening to records and tapes.
4. Time watching Spanish TV	As TV viewing *increases,* listening *increases.*
5. Location	Listening is *highest* in Salinas and Tucson, *lowest* in Santa Fe.
6. Proportion of household who read the newspaper	The *greater* the proportion of newspaper readers, the *greater* the amount of listening.

$R^2 = 9\%$

TABLE 4.18. (continued)

Predictors	Description of Relationship
Other Significant Correlations	
1. Spanish writing	As readership *increases,* listening *increases.*
2. Spanish radio	As radio listening *increases,* tape and record listening increases.

TABLE 4.19. Preferences for printing newspapers and broadcasting local television news in Spanish.

	Location							
	Total	Sal	San B	Sttn	Visa	El P	SF	Tuc
Preference for newspapers printed in Spanish								
Among Hispanics								
a. All	12%	30%	11%	10%	13%	11%	2%	9%
b. Part	54	39	54	57	41	57	63	65
b. Part	54	39	54	47	41	57	63	65
c. None	34	30	35	33	46	32	35	26
Among Anglos								
a. All	1%	0%	0%	0%	$%	5%	0%	0%
b. Part	30	25	42	10	10	27	32	50
c. None	69	75	58	90	90	68	69	50
Preference for Local TV News in Spanish								
Among Hispanics								
a. All	15%	34%	11%	13%	17%	11%	2%	13%
b. Part	60	46	51	60	53	61	76	72
c. None	25	20	38	27	29	28	22	15
Among Anglos								
a. All	1%	0%	0%	0%	0%	5%	0%	0%
b. Part	30	26	39	11	23	32	32	39
c. None	69	74	61	89	77	63	68	61

Nearly a quarter of the Hispanic households report having at least one person in their home who does not read the newspaper because it is in English. While the dramatically different results across locations suggested a differential need for use of Spanish in newspapers, these findings must be juxtaposed with those from the earlier preference question. For instance, in Santa Fe, only 7 percent of the Hispanic households appear to have a need for greater use of Spanish in the newspaper, yet a full 65 percent express a preference for having at least part of the paper in Spanish. By contrast, Visalia shows a similarly low amount of apparent "need" and a more even split on whether any of the newspaper should be printed in Spanish. Any policy decisions on a bilingual approach to the newspaper would therefore undoubtedly have to take both sets of responses into account.

Media Evaluations and Image

As a global assessment of their satisfaction with the media, respondents rated local newspapers, local television news and community issues shows, and local radio news and community issues shows. The comparison of ratings between Anglos and Hispanics produced some unexpected results: Hispanics are more satisfied than Anglos with both newspapers and television news. The results, shown in Table 4.20, reveal that the greater satisfaction with newspapers is true for the Hispanic sample as a whole, as well as for Hispanic newspaper readers alone. However, it should be recognized that the overall satisfaction scores for newspapers across all respondents are somewhat low (just above the midpoint of the scale) and below those for TV and radio.

TABLE 4.20. Mean satisfaction ratings for newspapers, television news, and radio news.

	Total	Hispanics	Anglos	Significance
Overall satisfaction with local newspapers				
Among all respondnets	3.29	3.40	3.22	*
Among users	3.33	3.46	3.24	*
Overall satisfaction with local TV news and community issues shows	3.70	3.85	3.61	*
Overall satisfaction with local radio news and community issues shows	3.53	3.62	3.44	

*Significant difference between groups ($p < .05$).

As had been done with media use, multiple-regression analyses were conducted to determine what factors are most responsible for satisfaction with each of the media. The analyses included essentially the same set of variables used to predict general media use and were again confined to users. Interestingly, as the summaries in Tables 4.21, 4.22, and 4.23 indicate, ethnicity is not a significant predictor in any of the analyses, despite the fact that significant differences were found between Anglos and Hispanics on newspaper and TV satisfaction. It appears that the ethnicity difference is better explained by other demographic characteristics of the two subgroups, such as differences in size of household, education, and language use. When these are taken into account, ethnicity per se becomes less relevant.

TABLE 4.21. Predictors of satisfaction with the local daily newspaper, among users.

Predictors	Description of Relationship
1. Size of household	As number of people in the household *increases*, satisfaction *increases*.
2. Education	As education *increases*, satisfaction *decreases*.
3. Satisfacation with local TV news	As TV satisfaction *increases*, newspaper satisfaction *increases*.
4. Quality-of-life judgment	As a person's view of the quality of life in the community becomes *more* positive, newspaper satisfaction *increases*.
5. Satisfaction with radio news	As satisfaction with radio news *increases*, newspaper satisfaction *increases*.
6. Proportion who read the newspaper	As proportion of household who read the newpaper *increases*, satisfaction *increases*.
7. Location	Stockton and Santa Fe are *least* satisfied.

$R^2 = 31\%$

The results on satisfaction with the newspaper show that people from large households, the less educated, those who are more satisfied with broadcast news, those who have a more favorable view of the quality of life in the community, and those who come from households with a strong newspaper habit are more satisfied with the newspaper.

TABLE 4.22. Predictors of satisfaction with local television new coverage, among viewers.

Predictors	Description of Relationship
1. Size of household	As number of people in the household *increases*, satisfaction *increases*.
2. Education	As education *increases*, satisfaction *decreases*.
3. Income	As income *increases*, satisfaction *decreases*.
4. Language spoken	Predominantly Spanish speakers are *more* satisfied than predominantly English or bilingual speakers.
5. Satisfaction with the newspaper	As satisfaction with the newspaper *increases*, satisfaction with TV news coverage *increases*.
6. Satisfaction with radio news	As satisfaction with radio news *increases*, satisfaction with TV news coverages *increases*.
7. Length of residence	Long-term residents are *more* satisfied.
8. TV entertainment viewing	As TV entertainment viewing *increases*, satisfaction with TV news *increases*.

$R^2 = 31\%$

The results on satisfaction with TV news coverage closely parallel those for newspapers. People from larger households, the less educated (and in this case, the less affluent), and those who are more satisfied with news coverage by other media are more satisfied with TV coverage. The satisfaction across media deserves notice, since it conflicts with the sometimes-held notion that greater *dissatisfaction* with other media is responsible for satisfaction with and use of a particular medium. These results instead imply that greater satisfaction with one medium may promote greater satisfaction with other media. The three other predictors of TV satisfaction show that those who speak predominantly Spanish, longer-term residents, and entertainment viewers are more satisfied with news coverage.

TABLE 4.23. Predictors of satisfaction with local radio news coverage, among users.

Predictors	Description of Relationship
1. Income	As income *increases*, satisfaction *decreases*.
2. Language spoken	Predominantly Spanish speakers are *more* satisfied than predominantly English speakers or bilingual speakers.
3. First generation in U.S.	The *longer* the family has been in the U.S., the *greater* the satisfaction.
4. Satisfaction with TV news	As satisfaction with TV news *increases*, satisfaction with radio news *increases*.
5. Sex	Males are *more* satisfied than females.
6. Location	Satisfaction is *lowest* in El Paso, *highest* in Tucson.

$R^2 = 19\%$

Like the results of newspapers and TV news, satisfaction with radio news is influenced by socioeconomic status: Those who are more affluent are less satisfied. Similarly, satisfaction with other media—in this case, TV news coverage—corresponds with radio satisfaction. As in the case of TV satisfaction, those who speak predominantly Spanish, too, are more satisfied. The factors of gender and familial longevity in the U.S., however, are unique to radio satisfaction. Those who are first- or second-generation U.S. residents are less satisfied with radio news coverage, as are women. Finally, there are again location differences, El Paso having the least satisfaction and Tucson the greatest.

Although Hispanics show a generally more favorable attitude toward newspapers than do Anglos, this favorability does not hold when respondents are asked about coverage of specific topics. The comparison by media between Hispanic ratings of coverage of specific topics within the Hispanic community and comparable ratings by Anglos, shown in Table 4.24, reveal that there are

TABLE 4.24. Satisfaction ratings for coverage of specific topics by newspapers, radio, and television.

	Total	Hispanics	Anglos	Significance
Newspaper coverage ov Local Hispanics and their accomplishments/Locals and their accomplishments†	3.29	3.06	3.54	*
Social news in the Hispanic community/Social news	3.31	3.08	3.54	*
Local cultural activities within the Hispanic community/Local cultural activities	3.34	3.14	3.55	*
Treatment of crime in the Hispanic community/ Treatment of crime	3.14	2.96	3.31	*
Local TV coverage of Local Hispanics and their accomplishments/Locals and their accomplishments	2.93	2.94	2.92	
Social news in the Hispanic community/Social news	2.70	2.83	2.54	*
Local cultural activities within the Hispanic community/Local cultural activities	2.99	2.98	3.02	
Treatment of crime in the Hispanic community/ Treatment of crime	2.93	2.86	3.00	
Local radio coverage of Local Hispanics and their accomplishments/Locals and their accomplishments	3.13	3.20	3.02	
Social news in the Hispanic community/Social news	2.94	3.06	2.81	*
Local cultural activities within the Hispanic community'Local cultural activities	3.12	3.22	3.10	*
Treatment of crime in the Hispanic community/ Treatment of crime	2.98	2.98	3.04	*

*Significant differences between groups ($p < .05$).

†Wording of questions differed for the two groups. The Hispanic version is listed first, followed by the version used with Anglos and others.

areas of dissatisfaction for Hispanics. Regarding newspaper coverage, Hispanics are consistently less satisfied than Anglos with how local people and their accomplishments, social news, local cultural activities, and crime are covered in their community. By contrast, Hispanics are *more* satisfied than Anglos with TV and radio coverage of social news within their community and radio coverage of local cultural activities. Only in the area of radio coverage of crime do Hispanics show less satisfaction with the broadcast media. It is important to note, however, that the overall levels of the broadcast ratings are rather low, compared to the newspaper ratings. In fact, most of the TV ratings are below the midpoint of the scale, as are several of the radio ratings. The newspaper ratings are uniformly higher.

Two additional questions that assessed general evaluations of the media asked respondents about the fairness of coverage given the Hispanic community by the local media and which of the media they would be most likely to believe if reports differed across them. Table 4.25 summarizes the results. Anglos see the media as being more fair than do Hispanics. Both groups award greater believability to TV than to newspapers or radio, but Hispanics are considerably more inclined to trust TV over the other two media, while a good percentage of Anglos express greater faith in newspapers.

TABLE 4.25. Fairness and believability evaluations.

	Total	Hispanics	Anglos	Significance
Fairness of coverage of Hispanic community by local media				
Very fair	22%	10%	36%	*
Somewhat fair	48	52	43	
Not sure	8	7	8	
Somewhat unfair	16	21	11	
Very unfair	6	10	2	
Mean	3.40	3.20	3.76	
Which version most likely to believe in news reported differently across three media				
TV	53%	61%	45%	*
Radio	12	13	11	
Newspaper	21	14	28	
Not sure	14	12	16	

*Significant difference between groups ($p < .05$).

As a final measure of evaluation of the media, ratings of TV and newspaper image were gathered. These often supply a more sensitive measure of satisfaction than do general satisfaction ratings. The results, reported in Table 4.26, are consistent with the general satisfaction findings in showing a favorable attitude toward the media among Hispanics.

TABLE 4.26. Image ratings† for television and newspapers.

	Television				Newspaper				Newspaper Users Only			
	Hispanic	Anglo	Total	Significance	Hispanic	Anglo	Total	Significance	Hispanic	Anglo	Total	Significance
1. Competent/Incompetent	4.07†	3.73	3.90		4.00	3.39	3.68	*	4.02	3.39	3.65	*
2. Trusted/Can't be trusted	3.68	3.60	3.64		3.66	3.43	3.54		3.57	3.42	3.49	
3. Personal/Impersonal	3.29	3.27	3.28		3.32	3.05	3.18		3.35	3.06	3.18	
4. Unbiased/Biased	3.19	3.26	3.25		3.22	3.01	3.10		3.21	3.03	3.10	
5. Lively/Dull	3.53	3.19	3.64	*	3.53	2.90	3.22	*	3.40	2.90	3.14	*
6. Receptive/Unreceptive	3.53	3.42	3.48		3.50	3.26	3.38		3.49	3.24	3.36	
7. Not racist/Racist	3.45	3.68	3.56		3.49	3.53	3.51		3.54	3.62	3.57	
8. Community watchdog/Not	3.65	3.38	3.53		3.69	3.40	3.54		3.70	3.43	3.54	
9. Accurate/Inaccurate	3.69	3.53	3.59		3.57	3.39	3.46		3.56	3.37	3.43	
10. Latest news/Not the latest	4.08	4.10	4.04		4.13	3.84	3.97	*	4.15	3.81	3.95	*
11. Doesn't sensationalize/Does	3.04	3.21	3.13		3.12	3.16	3.12		3.19	3.16	3.15	
12. Cares what you think/Doesn't care	3.71	3.50	3.58		3.54	3.31	3.42		3.49	3.35	3.40	
13. Powerful/Weak	3.69	3.51	3.59		3.61	3.13	3.36	*	3.62	3.18	3.37	*
14. Concerned about community well being/Not concerned	3.97	3.87	3.91		3.96	3.77	3.85		3.96	3.80	3.86	
15. Influential/Not influential	3.70	3.73	3.71		3.76	3.46	3.59	*	3.71	3.44	3.55	
16. Represents whole community/Doesn't	3.38	3.34	3.36		3.31	3.14	3.22		3.28	3.12	3.18	
17. Courageous/Not courageous	3.51	3.29	3.39		3.50	3.11	3.28	*	3.47	3.10	3.23	*

*Significant difference between groups ($p < .05$)

†Scale 5 (best) to 1 (worst)

On every image comparison, Hispanics are equal to or more favorable than Anglos. The few significant differences are confined to competence (Hispanics award greater competence to both TV and newspapers than do Anglos), liveliness (Hispanics are again more favorable for both TV and newspapers), immediacy of the news, power, influence and courage (Hispanics hold a more favorable image of the newspaper on the latter four items). The results for newspapers are essentially the same whether they include all respondents or just newspaper readers, indicating that familiarity with the paper was not the cause of greater or lesser credibility. These findings are in stark contrast to the expectations derived from past literature and from media and community leader perceptions.

To achieve a better understanding of how Hispanics and Anglos might differ in their ways of evaluating the media, the image ratings were also factor analyzed. The results, presented in Tables 4.27 and 4.28, show the overall factor structure for Hispanics and Anglos combined on the left side of the tables. In the center and right columns are the results for each subgroup when their ratings are analyzed separately.

In the combined analysis for newspaper image, three dimensions emerged. The first, *Local involvement and concern,* represents the degree to which the newspaper is perceived as a vigilant, influential, active, and caring institution in the community. The second dimension, *Credibility*, includes those elements traditionally associated with source credibility: competence, trust, character, and dynamism. The newspaper is apparently judged much as people are. The third dimension, *Objectivity and fairness,* combines the elements of sensationalism, bias, and racism and clearly represents a separate assessment that is made of newspapers. These results closely conform with those from other studies of newspaper image.

When separate analyses were conducted for Anglos and Hispanics, the same structure did not hold for both groups. Specifically, Anglos make four rather than three types of judgments. They split *Local involvement and concern* into two parts: *Power and courage* and *Local surveillance and concern.* For them, vigilance and community concern are two different types of evaluations they make of the newspaper. Otherwise, the Anglo and Hispanic factor analyses are nearly identical, demonstrating that Anglos and Hispanics generally evaluate newspapers along the same dimensions.

As for the dimensions of TV image, the overall factor analysis has three factors that share some similarities with the newspaper dimensions. Taken together, the first and third factors, *Local surveillance and concern* and *Power and courage,* are equivalent to the first newspaper image factor. The second TV dimension, *Credibility,* is also a diluted version of the newspaper dimension. What is missing from TV image is a dimension related to objectivity and fair-

TABLE 4.27. Dimensions of newspaper image.†

Factors and Isolates Among Total Sample, in Order of Importance	Factor Placement Among Hispanics	Among Anglos
I. Local involvement and concern		
a. Influential	1	2
b. Concerned about community	1	3
c. Courageous	1	2
d. Powerful	1	2
e. Acts as watchdog	1	3
f. Has latest news	1	1
g. (Cares what reader thinks)	1	(1)
h. (Accurate)	(1)	(3)
II. Credibility		
a. Compenent	2	1
b. Can be trusted	2	1
c. Personal	2	1
d. Receptive	2	1
e. Lively	(1), (2)	1
III. Objectivity and Fairness		
a. Doesn't sensationalize	3	4
b. Not racist	3	1
c. (Unbiased)	I	I
Isolates		
a. Represents whole community	1	I
Variance accounted for: 53%	50%	61%

	Factor 1 = *Local involvement and concern*	Factor 1 = *Credibility*
		Factor 2 = *Power and courage*
	Factor 2 = *Credibility*	Factor 3 = *Local surveillance and concern*
	Factor 3 = *Objectivity and fairness*	Factor 4 = *Objectivity and fairness*

†Items in parentheses had moderately strong relationships with more than one factor. In the Hispanic and Anglo columns the numbers designate on what factor the item loaded within that subgroup. For example, all items with numeral 1 formed the first factor. Isolates are designated with an *I*.

TABLE 4.28. Dimensions of television image.†

Factors and Isolates Among Total Sample, in Order of Importance	Factor Placement Among Hispanics	Among Anglos
I. Local surveillance and concern		
a. Concern about community	1	3
b. Acts as watchdog	(1)	3
c. Represents whole community	1	3
d. Accurate	(3)	1
e. (Unbiased)	3	I
II. Credibility		
a. Competent	2	(1)
b. Lively	2	(1)
c. (Can be trusted)	2	1
III.Power and courage		
a. Powerful	1	2
b. Influential	1	2
c. Courageous	1	2
Isolates		
a. Personal	3	1
b. Receptive	I	1
c. Not racist	4	4
d. Has latest news	I	1
e. Doesn't sensationalize	4	4
f. Cares what reader thinks	1	(3)
Variance accounted for: 49%	53%	60%

	Among Hispanics	Among Anglos
	Factor 1 = *Local involvement and concern*	Factor 1 = *Credibility*
		Factor 2 = *Power and courage*
	Factor 2 = *Credibility*	Factor 3 = *Local surveillance and concern*
	Factor 3 = *Personalism and bias*	
	Factor 4 = *Fairness*	Factor 4 = *Fairness*

†Items in parentheses had moderately strong relationships with more than one factor. In the Hispanic and Anglo columns the numbers designate on what factor the item loaded within that subgroup. For example, all items with a numeral 1 formed the first factor. Isolates are designated with an *I*.

ness. The large number of isolates implies that a combined factor solution does not adequately represent the views of the Anglo and Hispanic subgroups. This is supported by the small number of isolates that appear when the two groups are analyzed separately, as well as the emergence of four rather than three dimensions in each case. For Anglos, their four dimensions closely parallel those they recognize for newspaper image. The main differences are that the TV credibility dimension includes accuracy and timeliness of the news and the TV local surveillance and concern dimension includes the community representation and caring items. For Hispanics, three of the dimensions are similar to the three for newspaper image but a fourth that is unique, *Personalism and bias,* emerges. Rather than seeing this as part of one large credibility dimension, Hispanics separated competence, trust, and dynamism from personalism, accuracy, and bias. Additionally, the most important dimensions of image differ for the two groups. For Anglos, general credibility is the most important. For Hispanics, local involvement and concern is preeminent.

Overall, if the image ratings for the newspaper are compared to those for TV along the commonly occurring dimensions, the ratings for both media are nearly identical on community concern and acting as a watchdog, with ratings for concern being better than for vigilance. Television earns higher ratings on power and influence but not courage, the latter being one of the lower-rated items for both media. In the area of general credibility, TV is seen as more competent and lively than newspapers but not more trustworthy, receptive, or personal. Of those elements, personalism generally receives the lowest ratings. In the area of objectivity and fairness, both media again are given the same ratings on sensationalism, bias, and racism, with the most favorable ratings occurring on not being racist. Finally, on such other key judgments as accuracy and timeliness of the news, TV ratings parallel those for newspapers, with both media being rated highest on having the latest news.

Media Functions

Previous research and writing had led to the expectation that Hispanics might use the media for different purposes than Anglos and might be especially dependent on the media for certain functions. Accordingly, respondents who completed the functions module of questions were given a list of 30 "reasons other people have given for (watching television news shows/reading newspapers)" and asked to rate how important the given medium is to them for each purpose. The ratings, on a 1 (extremely unimportant) to 5 (extremely important) scale, are reported in Table 4.29.

A number of significant differences are apparent. In all cases, Hispanics rate the function as more important than do Anglos for TV and newspapers. In particular, Hispanics report that TV and newspapers are more important to them for keeping informed about local events through selectivity, depth, variety, and analysis in reporting; for local vigilance and publicity; for arousal, relaxation, pleasure, and escapism; for redundancy; for cultural information, cultural pride, and language acquisition; for helpful information; and for conversation topics.

If one looks at the relative rank ordering of functions within each

TABLE 4.29. Media functions and satisfaction with them.

Importance of Medium for Following Purposes	Television				Newspaper				Newpaper Users Only			
	Total	Hispanic	Anglo	Significance	Total	Hispanic	Anglo	Significance	Total	Hispanic	Anglo	Significance
1. *Immediate* knowledge of major local news events	4.14	4.47	4.10		3.39	4.02	3.82		3.97	4.12	3.85	
2. *Immediate* knowledge of national and international news events	4.30	4.33	4.13		3.94	3.95	3.96		3.98	3.99	3.99	
3. Helpful information (e.g., consumers)	3.66	4.21	3.46	*	3.55	3.85	3.21	*	3.53	3.86	3.22	*
4. Advice on entertainment	3.04	3.69	2.81	*	3.54	3.61	3.46		3.57	3.66	3.47	
5. For excitement and arousal	2.76	3.25	2.56	*	2.75	3.02	2.49	*	2.76	3.07	2.52	*
6. Relaxation	3.25	2.78	3.12	*	3.08	3.20	2.87	*	3.05	3.27	2.89	*
7. To uncover wrongdoings, scandals, potential problems	3.61	4.09	3.51	*	3.41	3.56	3.31	*	3.43	3.58	3.36	
8. To tell you about places you can't experience personally	3.60	3.90	3.52		3.33	3.39	3.27		3.36	3.47	3.29	
9. Feeling of cultural pride and identity	3.38	4.07	3.10	*	3.14	3.44	2.84	*	3.10	3.47	2.81	*
10. To learn more about other cultures in your community	3.54	4.16	3.32	*	3.38	3.62	3.15	*	3.34	3.58	3.16	*
11. *Full* detail on major local news events	4.04	4.38	4.92	*	3.97	4.11	3.84	*	4.01	4.19	3.88	*
12. *Full* details on major national and international news events	4.16	4.38	4.10		3.89	3.96	3.86		3.94	4.07	3.88	*

Item												
13. To *select* most important local news stories	3.76	4.33	3.57	*	3.61	3.75	3.52	*	3.61	3.77	3.52	*
14. To *select* most important national and international news stories	3.87	4.17	3.76	*	3.65	3.78	3.58	*	3.65	3.80	3.58	*
15. To escape problems	2.70	3.50	2.43	*	2.47	2.86	2.05	*	2.37	2.81	1.98	*
16. More knowledge of how other people live and think	3.49	3.69	3.37	*	3.22	3.30	3.16		3.21	3.34	3.15	
17. To cheer you up	3.31	3.74	3.17	*	3.08	3.36	2.86	*	3.06	3.39	2.84	*
18. To keep you informed about local events	3.89	4.41	3.73	*	3.96	4.05	3.94	*	4.03	4.15	4.01	*
19. To explain how important issues and events relate to you and your community	3.73	4.10	3.56	*	3.73	3.90	3.61	*	3.76	3.97	3.65	*
20. The day's headlines	4.03	4.14	4.00	*	4.06	4.07	4.10		4.14	4.19	4.16	
21. Different points of view on issues	3.72	4.03	3.64		3.72	3.83	3.66	*	3.77	3.93	3.70	*
22. Publicity to newsworthy locals	3.58	4.09	3.35	*	3.69	3.77	3.69	*	3.73	3.84	3.72	*
23. Interesting or unusual stories for conversation	3.50	4.02	3.36	*	3.59	3.71	3.54	*	3.61	3.74	3.57	*
24. Details of news read or heard elsehwere	3.48	3.83	3.40	*	3.53	3.66	3.46	*	3.57	3.71	3.52	*
25. More information and viewpoints on things already experienced	3.36	3.79	3.19	*	3.28	3.35	3.21		3.31	3.42	3.24	
26. *Wide variety* of local news	3.82	4.34	3.66		3.77	3.90	3.72	*	3.85	4.00	3.79	*
27. *Wide variety* of national and international news	4.03	4.29	3.96	*	3.85	3.89	3.88	*	3.91	3.99	3.92	*
28. Information to help form opinions	3.78	4.10	3.68		3.67	3.72	3.66		3.72	3.80	3.69	
29. Improve your knowledge of English	3.22	3.93	2.87	*	3.10	3.54	2.64	*	3.00	3.47	2.61	*
30. Improve your knowledge of Spanish	2.71	3.72	2.18	*	2.47	3.15	1.75	*	2.33	3.10	1.67	*

TABLE 4.29. (continued)

Satisfaction with Media Fulfillment of Important Function	Anglo	Hispanic	Total
Local newspapers	3.40	3.54	3.44*
Local newspapers/users only	3.38	3.47	3.41
Local TV shows	3.35	3.75	3.55*
Local radio shows	3.36	3.61	3.50*
Magazines you read	3.76	3.58	3.68*

*Significant difference between groups ($p < .05$).

medium, some additional subtle differences between Hispanics and Anglos become apparent. For Hispanics, the most important eight functions that newspapers perform are, in order:

1. Providing immediate knowledge of major local news events
2. Giving the day's headlines
3. Keeping the individual informed about what's happening in the local community
4. Providing immediate knowledge for major local news events
5. Providing full details on major national and international news events
6. Providing immediate knowledge of national and international news events
7. Offering a wide variety of local news
8. Offering a wide variety of national and international news

These functions, which received ratings of almost 4.0 and above from Hispanic newspaper users, reflect a heavy news orientation (as opposed to treating the newspaper as a "use" paper), with somewhat greater priority given to local rather than to national and international interests. For Anglos, the same eight functions are the most important, but the rank ordering is different: Greatest priority is given to the headlines, followed by information about local happenings, immediate knowledge of national and world events, and variety in national and international news coverage. Thus, Anglos show a little more interest in nonlocal stories. However, the importance ratings on all eight of these functions are lower for Anglos than for Hispanics, suggesting greater dependence on newspapers by Hispanics for this kind of information. As an additional indicator of differences, Hispanics rated only one newspaper function below 3.00 (escaping problems), whereas Anglos rate six functions below the midpoint of the scale, indicating those functions are somewhat to extremely unimportant for them.

As for the rank order of television functions, Hispanics see the following as the most important, in order:

1. Providing immediate knowledge of major local news events
2. Keeping the individual informed about what's happening in the community

3. Providing full details on major local news events

4. Providing full details on major national and international news events

5. Providing a wide variety of local news

6. Selecting from all the possible stories, the most important local news stories

7. Providing immediate knowledge of major national and international news events

8. Providing a wide variety of national and international news

Again, Hispanics show a strong orientation toward using the media for news. All eight functions have importance ratings exceeding 4.25. For Anglos, six of the top eight functions are the same, but in place of selectivity and wide variety in local news coverage, Anglos give priority to selectivity and wide variety in national and international news coverage. Moreover, the greater emphasis placed on nonlocal news among Anglos is evident in their top ranked item, immediate knowledge of national and international news. As before, the ratings given these functions by Anglos show lesser dependence on them than that implied by the Hispanic ratings. Additionally, not a single television function receives an importance rating below 3.00 among Hispanics (the lowest, at 3.25, is excitement and arousal), whereas Anglos rate five TV functions as somewhat to extremely unimportant. Overall, television appears to be somewhat more important than newspapers in serving these purposes for Hispanics, but both media must be regarded as important sources of news and information for Hispanics.

Significantly, this dependence on the media is coupled with relative satisfaction in how the media are fulfilling those functions that Hispanics regard as most important. The satisfaction ratings shown at the bottom of Table 4.29 reveal that Hispanics are generally more satisfied than Anglos with how newspapers and broadcast media are fulfilling key functions; only with magazines are they less satisfied than Anglos. While the overall levels of satisfaction among members of both subgroups are not exceptional, they do counter the popular belief that Hispanics are alienated from the media.

To further tease out differences in how Hispanics and Anglos view newspapers and television, the importance ratings of each subgroup were factor analyzed, as well as combined for an overall analysis for each medium. Shown in Tables 4.30 and 4.31, the factor structures on the left side of tables represent the overall results for Hispanics and Anglos combined, while the center and right columns present the factor configurations within the separate subgroups.

In the case of newspaper functions, the combined analysis yielded fewer factors than did the separate subgroup analyses. Four factors emerged in the combined analysis: (1) a rather comprehensive factor encompassing local news functions, surrogate and supplementary social functions, and perspective-broadening functions, labeled *Local awareness, social extensions, and new perspectives;* (2) a combination of *Cultural learning and escapism* functions; (3)

TABLE 4.30. Dimensions of newspapers functions.†

Factors and Isolates Among Total Sample, in Order of Importance	Factor Placement	
	Among Hispanics	Among Anglos
I. Local awareness, social extension and new perspectives		
a. To keep you informed about what's happening in your local community	1	(1), (4)
b. To give you a *wide variety* of local new stories	1	1
c. To provide information you can use to form your own opinion	1	1
d. To provide you different points of view on issues in the news	1	1
e. To add details to news you've read or heard elsewhere	1	1
f. To explain how important issues and events related to you and your community	1	1
g. To give personal publicity to people in your community who do something newsworthy	1	1
h. To provide interesting or unusual stories you can talk about with others	1	1
i. To give you more information and viewpoints on things you've already experienced	1	1
j. (To give you a *wide variety* of national and international new stories)	1	(1), (2)
k. (To give you the day's headlines)	1	I
l. (To give you *full details* of major local news events)	(4)	(1)

TABLE 4.30. (continued)

Factors and Isolates Among Total Sample, in Order of Importance	Factor Placement	
	Among Hispanics	Among Anglos
II. Cultural learning and ecapism		
a. To help you improve your knowledge of Spanish	3	3
b. To help you improve your knowledge of English	3	3
c. To give you a feeling of cultural pride and identity	(2), (3)	(3), (4)
d. To learn more about other cultures in your community	(3)	(4)
e. To allow you to escape problems	I	3
f. To give you stories that cheer you up	I	3
III. Breadth, depth, and selectivity in news coverage		
a. Out of all the possible news stories to *select for you* the most important national and international news stories	4	2
b. To give you *full details* of major national and international news events	(4)	2
c. Out of all the possible news stories, to *select for you* the most important local news stories	4	2
d. To give you *immediate* knowledge of major national and international news events	2	2

TABLE 4.30. (continued)

Factors and Isolates Among Total Sample, in Order of Importance	Factor Placement	
	Among Hispanics	Among Anglos
e. (To give you a *wide variety* of national and international news stories)	1	(1), (2)
f. (To give you *full details* of major local news events)	(4)	(1)
IV. Diversion and simulation		
a. To give you advice on things to do for entertainment	5	5
b. For excitement and arousal	5	5
c. For relaxation	(5)	5
Isolates		
a. To give you *immediate* knowledge of major local news events	2	(1)
b. To give you helpful information such as consumer advice or where to get help to solve problems	1	I
c. To uncover wrong-doings, scandals, potential problems— i.e., to act as a watchdog for the public	(2)	I
d. To tell you about places and events you can't experience personally	2	(4)
e. To give you more knowledge of how other people think and live	I	I
Variance accounted for: 59%	62%	62%
	Factor 1 = *Local awareness, and social extension, and new perspectives*	Factor 1 = *Local awareness, social extension, and new perspectives*

120

TABLE 4.30. (continued)

Factors and Isolates Among Total Sample, in Order of Importance	Factor Placement Among Hispanics	Among Anglos
	Factor 2 = *Immediacy and vicarious experience*	Factor 2 = *Depth, breadth, and selectivity*
	Factor 3 = *Cultural learning*	Factor 3 = *Learning and escapism*
	Factor 4 = *Depth and selectivity*	Factor 4 = *Cultural awareness*
	Factor 5 = *Diversion and stimulation*	Factor 5 = *Diversion and stimulation*

†Items in parentheses had a moderately strong relationship with more than one factor. Numbers designate on what factor an item loaded within the Anglo and Hispanic subgroups. Isolates are designated with an *I*.

a factor reflecting the traditional roles of *Breadth, depth, and selectivity in news coverage;* and (4) a *Diversion and stimulation* factor. Among Hispanics, this factor structure was modified somewhat and a fifth factor added: The first factor, *Local awareness, social extension, and new perspectives,* remained relatively intact; a new second factor related to *immediacy and vicarious experience* (such as learning about other people and places) emerged; the third factor lost the escapism component, leaving only the *cultural learning* functions; the fourth factor lost the breadth element, leaving *Depth and selectivity in news coverage;* and the fifth factor, *Diversion and stimulation,* remained the same as in the combined analysis. Beyond these five factors, four other isolated functions that newspapers may serve for Hispanics are providing helpful information, extending knowledge of how others behave, promoting cheer, and affording opportunities to escape problems.

For Anglos, newspapers serve similar but not identical functions. The first and fifth factors are essentially the same as for Hispanics. But for Anglos, the second most recognized role of newspapers is to supply depth, breadth, and selectivity in news coverage. The third and fourth factors are variations on cultural learning and escapism. Specifically, the third factor is mainly the language *learning and escapism/cheer* functions, while the fourth factor reflects *cultural awareness.* Additionally, there are four isolated functions that Anglos did not see fitting any of the other clusters: extending knowledge of how others behave, providing helpful information, acting as a public watchdog, and providing headlines. By comparison, Anglos make as many distinctions as His-

TABLE 4.31. Dimensions of television functions.†

Factors and Isolates among Total Sample, in Order of Importance	Factor Placement	
	Among Hispanics	Among Anglos
I. Social extension and new perspectives		
a. To provide information you can use to form your own opinions	(2), (3)	1
b. To give you more knowledge of how other people think and life	(2)	1
c. To provide interesting or unusual stories you can talk about with others	(2)	1
d. To add details to news you've read or heard elsewhere	I	1
e. To explain how important issues and events relate to you and your community	2	1
f. To provide you with different points of view on issues in the news	2	I
g. To give you more imfonation and viewpoints on things you've already experienced	3	1
h. To tell you about places and events you can't experience personally	I	I
i. (To keep you informed about what's happening in your local community)	(2)	(1)
j. (To learn more about other cultures in your community)	2	1
II. Breadth, depth, and selectivity in news coverage		
a. To give you *full details* of major national and international news coverage	1	2

TABLE 4.31. (continued)

Factors and Isolates Among Total Sample, in Order of Importance	Factor Placement	
	Among Hispanics	Among Anglos
b. To give you *immediate* knowledge of major national and international news events	1	2
c. To give you a *wide variety* of national and international news stories	1	2
d. Out of all the possible news stories, to *select for you* the most important national and international news stories	1	(3)
e. To give you *full details* of major local news events	1	(2)
f. To give you *immediate* knowledge of major local news events	1	2
g. (Out of all the possible news stories *to select for you* the most important local news stories)	1	I
h. (To give you the day's headlines)	(2)	2
i. (To give you a *wide variety* of local news stories)	(1)	(2)
III. Cultural learning		
a. To help you improve your knowledge of Spanish	3	1
b. To help you improve your knowledge of English	3	1
c. (Out of all possible news stories, *to select for you* the most important local news stories)	1	I
d. (To give you a feeling of cultural pride and identity)	2	1

TABLE 4.31. (continued)

Factors and Isolates Among Total Sample, in Order of Importance	Factor Placement	
	Among Hispanics	Among Anglos
IV. Diversion and stimulation		
a. For excitement and arousal	4	3
b. For relaxation	4	I
c. To give you advice on things to do for entertainment	4	3
d. (To allow you to escape problems)	(3)	3
Isolates		
a. To give you helpful information, such as consumer advice or where to get help to solve problems	2	(1)
b. To uncover wrong-doings, scandal, potential problems— i.e., to act as a watchdog for public	I	I
c. To give you stories that cheer you up	I	(1)
d. To give personal publicity to people in your community who do something newsworthy	2	1
Variance accounted for: 59%	63%	49%

	Factor 1 = Breadth, depth, and selectivity	Factor 1 = Social extension and new perspectives
	Factor 2 = Social extension and new perspectives	Factor 2 = Breadth and depth in news coverage
	Factor 3 = Learning and escapism	Factor 3 = Diversion and stimulation
	Factor 4 = Diversion and stimulation	

†Items in parentheses had moderately strong relationships with more than one factor. In the Hispanic and Anglo columns, the numbers designate on what factor the item loaded within that subgroup. For example, all items with the numeral 1 formed the first factor. Isolates are designated with an *I*.

panics as to what broad roles newspapers play for them; only their composition varies slightly.

As for television functions, the overall analysis shows four factors: (1) a first factor similar to that for newspapers, but focusing primarily on the *social extension and new perspectives* elements; (2) a *Breadth, depth, and selectivity in news coverage* factor that corresponds well with the third newspaper factor; (3) a *Cultural learning* factor, again similar to the newspaper factor except that it omits the escapism component; and (4) a *Diversion and stimulation* factor that incorporates escapism. Among Hispanics, the four factors remain essentially the same, except that the *Breadth, depth, and selectivity* becomes the strongest, emerging first, and escapism returns to the cultural learning factor. The functions that appear as isolates differ a little; they include redundancy, vicarious experience, acting as a public watchdog, and promoting cheer. Among Anglos, television functions fall into only three clusters: (1) a *Social extension and new perspectives* function that includes the items found in the Hispanic analysis and adds the cultural learning functions; (2) a *Breadth and depth* factor that omits the selectivity component found in the Hispanic analysis; and (3) a *Diversion and stimulation* factor that omits the relaxation function. For Anglos, the isolates also differ somewhat; they include vicarious experience, selectivity, differing viewpoints, and acting as a public watchdog. By comparison, then, Anglos evaluate TV functions along fewer dimensions than do Hispanics, and the clusters of functions they do recognize are somewhat different in composition than those used by Hispanics.

Content Preferences

Respondents who completed the content preferences module rated their interest in 37 news topics typically appearing in newspapers, on TV, and on the radio, including 20 that represent a range of "hard news" topics, 14 that represent facets of "soft news," and three that are sports items, on a scale of 1 (not interested at all) to 5 (extremely interested). They also indicated how much they like to watch eight types of TV entertainment programming.

The comparative ratings, presented in Table 4.32, show that Hispanics consistently have the same or higher interest than Anglos on all topics, with the exceptions of local and national political coverage, business coverage, editorials, and humorous stories. They also like to watch six of the eight types of TV entertainment more than do Anglos. These results underscore the receptivity of Hispanics toward the media, a finding that has surfaced throughout this report, and signal an eclecticism in their interests. Among Hispanics, the news content categories that have the greatest appeal are as follows, in order:

TABLE 4.32. Interest in media news content and television entertainment programming.

	Total	Hispanic	Anglo	Significance
Media Hard News Content				
1. National politics and the president	3.31	3.11	3.46	*
2. Local politics and government	3.05	2.95	3.15	*
3. Crime	3.10	3.24	2.94	*
4. Accidents and disasters	3.08	3.37	2.81	*
5. Editorials	2.92	2.74	3.06	*
6. News of Mexico and Latin America	2.90	3.49	2.34	*
7. News of local economy	3.88	3.84	3.93	*
8. Job opportunities	3.12	3.56	2.66	*
9. Agricultural news	2.81	2.81	2.75	*
10. News and features on business	2.93	2.73	3.11	*
11. Real estate and housing	2.85	2.81	2.85	
12. Ads and commercials	2.32	2.65	2.02	*
13. Immigration	2.94	3.15	2.67	*
14. Stories about discrimination	2.43	3.69	3.14	*
15. Drug and alcohol problems	3.46	3.62	3.26	*
16. Bilingual education	3.16	3.76	2.55	*
17. Problems in schools	3.74	3.90	3.57	*
18. Union activities	2.74	2.90	2.58	*
19. Youth gangs	2.99	3.16	2.81	*
20. Women's changing roles	3.31	3.40	3.24	
Media Sports Content				
1. Professional sports	3.13	3.25	2.97	*
2. Local sports and high school	2.84	3.10	2.56	*
3. Sports from Latin America	2.16	2.53	1.75	*
Media Soft News Content				
1. Churches and religion	2.96	3.29	2.64	*
2. Food/recipies/nutrition	3.15	3.31	2.96	*
3. Personal problems	2.89	3.29	2.51	*
4. Health and medical advice	3.52	3.76	3.27	*
5. Consumer information	3.38	3.36	3.36	*
6. How-to advice	3.42	3.57	3.24	*
7. TV and TV personalities	2.71	3.05	2.39	*
8. Movie reviews	2.64	2.90	2.39	*
9. Art, dance, theater, and music	2.98	3.14	2.85	*
10. Retirement and retirement living	2.83	2.99	2.67	*
11. Good Samaritan stories	3.68	3.74	3.60	*
12. Humorous stories and features	3.47	3.34	3.57	*
13. Comics	2.58	2.74	2.43	*
14. Things to do and see in area	3.49	3.47	3.51	
TV Entertainment Programming				
1. Situation comedies	3.38	3.51	3.25	*
2. Soap operas	2.26	2.67	1.85	*
3. Police and detective shows	3.11	3.32	2.92	*

TABLE 4.32. (continued

	Total	Hispanic	Anglo	Significance
4. Movies	3.94	4.09	3.82	*
5. Cartoons	2.31	2.64	1.96	*
6. Game shows	2.54	2.84	2.25	*
7. Nature and outdoor shors	3.63	3.56	3.72	
8. Musical variety shows	3.29	3.35	3.23	

*Significant differences between groups ($p < .05$).

1. Problems in schools
2. News of the local economy
3. Health and medical advice
4. Bilingual education
5. Good Samaritan stories
6. Stories about discrimination
7. Drug and alcohol problems
8. How-to advice on such things as home repair, car care, hobbies, and gardening
9. Job opportunities
10. News of Mexico and Latin America

As is evident from this ranking, social problems and issues are of great interest to Hispanics and exceed interest in the more traditional hard news topics of government and politics, crime, accidents, and disasters. Seven of the top 10 news categories would normally be classified as hard news.

Among Anglos, the top-rated topics differ in their order and their composition, with only four being hard news topics:

1. News of the local economy
2. Good Samaritan stories
3. Humorous stories and features
4. Problems in schools
5. Things to see and do in the area
6. National politics and the president
7. Consumer stories and information
8. Health and medical advice
9. Drug and alcohol problems
10. Women's changing roles
11. How-to advice

Anglos and Hispanics similarly differ somewhat on the topics of least interest. For Hispanics, sports from Latin America, ads and commercials, news and features on business, editorials, and comics hold the least across-the-board appeal (the sports rating is partly accounted for by the low interest among females), whereas for Anglos, sports from Latin America, ads and commercials, news of Mexico and Latin America, features about TV and TV personalities, and movie reviews are the lowest-rated categories.

While Anglos and Hispanics show somewhat different interests in news content, their preferences for TV entertainment are nearly identical. Both groups most prefer movies, nature and outdoors stories, and situation comedies (in that order) and least prefer soap operas and cartoons. However, Hispanics enjoy watching all those types of programming more than do Anglos, except for nature and outdoors shows.

The content preferences in these ratings can be compared to the results from the one open-ended question that asked respondents what topics, if any, they would like to see receive increased coverage from the media. Inasmuch as this question preceded the content interest ratings in the questionnaire, the replies can be considered unprompted. Moreover, since the content questions followed the sequence of questions on satisfaction, they can be inferred to signal some degree of dissatisfaction with current coverage of these topics.

In rank order, the following general categories were mentioned most often as areas for increased media coverage:

1. News related to education
2. News and stories with cultural and ethnic foci (including social news, local events)
3. Stories concerning local people and their accomplishments
4. International news
5. Sports
6. Local news about families and youth
7. National news and documentaries
8. Crime
9. Political issues and news (including military and government activities)
10. Religion
11. Topics related to ecology, nature, animals, etc.
12. Health

To a large extent, these topics parallel those rated high in interest. The fact that respondents expressed a desire for increased coverage of them indicates that the interest ratings are not the result of certain topics such as crime being given excessive coverage currently; or at least respondents do not consider the current level of coverage excessive. The results also underscore the interest in local news, though not necessarily local politics, in social issues such as education, and in hard news topics generally.

As had been done with image and function ratings, content preferences were factor analyzed, in this case to identify what clusters of content represent separate interest areas among Hispanics and Anglos. The combined and separate subgroup analyses of media news content are reported in Table 4.33; the results for TV entertainment appear in Table 4.34.

In the combined analysis, content clusters into five interest areas. The first, *Features,* represents the content that has elsewhere formed three separate factors related to lifestyles, people, and entertainment. That such topics collapsed into one in this study is no doubt due to the much smaller pool of topics included here. The cluster does reveal that those who are interested in one facet of features—say, consumer and medical advice—are likely to be interested in other facets as well—such as features on people and news about the arts. Content in this factor received interest ratings ranging from a low of 2.64 (movie reviews) to a high of 3.68 (Good Samaritan stories—people helping people), with most of the ratings in the moderate to moderately high range. Of special interest are topics related to advice (e.g., leisure activities, how-to, health and medicine) and humor.

The second factor, *Social problems,* includes such breaking news as crimes, accidents, and disasters, and longer-term social issues such as discrimination, drugs, and educational problems. Interest in these topics range from a low of 2.99 (stories about youth gangs) to a highof 3.73 (problems in the schools). As a group, these topics have considerable appeal, with ratings demonstrating moderate to high interest. The fact that this content clusters together has interesting implications for the packaging and segmenting of the news, inasmuch as such topics are not traditionally grouped together.

The third factor, *Politics, business, and economics,* is a traditional cluster that typically includes topics related to local, state, and national politics and government; local and national business trends; financial and stock market news; economic news and issues; and editorials and letters to the editor. The clustering together of business, economics, and government signals the commonality of interest among these three general areas. Those who are interested in one show similar interest in the others; conversely, those who have little interest in one are typically not interested in the others, either. Interest ratings for the topics included in this survey range from lows of 2.92 and 2.93 (for editorials and business news) to a high of 3.88 (for news of the local economy), indicating wide variability in the interest levels. Typically, government, politics, and economics attract high interest whereas business, finance, and editorial opinion appeal only to selective audiences.

The fourth factor, here labeled *Hispanic interests* because of its inclusion of such topics as news of Mexico and Latin America, bilingual educa-

TABLE 4.33. Dimensions of media news content.†

Factors and Isolates Among Total Sample, in Order Of Importance	Factor Placement	
	Among Hispanics	Among Anglos
I. Features (lifestyles, people, entertainment)		
a. Food, recipes, nutritional information	1	1
b. Health and medical advice	1	1
c. Advice on personal problems	1	1
d. Consumer stories and information	(1)	1
e. Stories on things to see and do in the area	I	1
f. How-to advice (e.g., home repairs, cars, hobbies)	1	I
g. Humorous stories and features	(5)	1
h. Good Samaritan stories	1	1
i. News about TV and TV personalities	6	(5)
j. features on art, dance, movies, music	6	I
k. (Movie reviews)	6	5
II. Social problems		
a. Stories about youth gangs	4	(2), (4)
b. Stories on drug and alcohol problems	(4)	(2)
c. Crime news	4	4
d. Accidents and disasters	4	4
e. Stories about discrimination	(4)	2
f. Problems in the schools	5	2
III. Politics, business, and economics		
a. Stories about national politics and the President	2	3
b. News about local politics and government	2	3
c. News and features on business	2	3
d. News of the local and national economy	2	3
e. Editorials and letters to the editor	(2)	I

130

TABLE 4.33. (continued)

Factors and Isolates Among Total Sample, in Order Of Importance	Factor Placement	
	Among Hispanics	Among Anglos
IV. Hispanic interests		
a. News of Mexico and Latin America	1	(2)
b. Churches and religion	I	1
c. (Sports from Latin America)	3	6
d. (Bilingual education)	1	2
V. Sports		
a. Professional sports	3	6
b. Local sports (e.g., high school sports, leagues)	3	6
c. (Sports from Latin America)	3	6
Isolates		
a. Job opportunities	I	I
b. Agricultural news	I	3
c. Real estate and housing	I	3
d. Ads and commercials	I	5
e. Immigration	I	(2)
f. Stories about union activities	I	I
g. Stories about the changing role of women	5	2
h. Retirement and retirement living	1	I
i. Comics and cartoons	6	I
Variance accounted for: 46%	48%	51%

Factor 1 = *Lifestyles and features*	Factor 1 = *Lifestyles and people features*
Factor 2 = *Politics, business, and economics*	Factor 2 = *Hispanic social problems*
Factor 3 = *Sports*	Factor 3 = *Politics, business, and economics*
Factor 4 = *Social problems*	
Factor 5 = *People topics*	Factor 4 = *Accidents and crime*
Factor 6 = *Entertainment*	Factor 5 = *Television and movies*
	Factor 6 = *Sports*

†Items in parentheses had moderately strong relationships with more than one factor. In the Hispanic and Anglo columns the numbers designate on what factor the item loaded within that subgroup. For example, all items with a numeral 1 formed the first factor. Isolates are designated with an *I*.

tion, and sports from Latin America, has lower interest ratings, signaling that its appeal lies with a smaller audience segment. All four topics have ratings around the midpoint of the interest scale.

The fifth factor, *Sports,* is here represented by only a small sample of sports topics but demonstrates that sports represent a separate interest area. In other analyses, professional sports have often been a separate factor from local and participatory sports. Consistent with past results, professional sports attract greater interest than do local sports, with ratings for both being somewhat depressed by the lower interest expressed among many women.

Beyond these five factors, there are nine isolates, topics that did not fit any of the other five clusters. Isolates may appear because they have a relationship, albeit a weak one, with several factors; because they are totally unrelated to the other factors; or because no other topics with which they would naturally cluster were included in the survey. In this case, the latter explanation partly applies. Regardless of why they are isolates, such topics must be regarded almost as additional clusters, since one canot predict how interest in these topics might be related, if at all, to the other topics. While the ratings for these news and features categories tend to be somewhat low (the highest being for changing roles of women, 3.31, and the lowest for ads and commercials, 2.31), because they may appeal to yet separate interest groups who have intense interest in them, their importance should not be discounted.

The factor analysis results for the combined sample have several implications for the segmenting and packaging of the news. They imply first that journalists should attempt to cover all the clusters and isolates on a regular basis so that the full range of audiences is served. Second, they imply that within factors, topics can be substituted and rotated while still satisfying the given interest area. Substitution across clusters and isolates, however, means temporarily sacrificing the interests of a potentially unique or important audience segment, and is therefore an unwise strategy. Third, they imply that ratings within factors may provide some guidance on the relative apportionment of space or time to specific facets of the given interest area, whereas aggregate ratings for a factor may provide rough guidance on space and time apportionment to entire interest areas. Finally, the clusters offer organizational guidance: content within clusters can be profitably grouped together spatially or temporally to heighten continuity and ease in identifying related news and features.

While the overall results of the factor analysis offer one perspective on the public's perceptual organization of news topics, as well as guidance to journalists in how to cover such topics, more precise information comes from the separate factor analyses conducted for the Hispanic and Anglo subgroups. Among Hispanics, six rather than five factors emerged. The main divergences from the combined factor analysis are that Hispanics split the features content into two clusters, one related to *lifestyles* and one to *entertainment;* a factor labeled *People topics* that is predominantly of interest to women appears (it includes changing roles of women, school problems, and humor); and the *Hispanic interests* factor disintegrates, leaving in its place three isolates that represent yet finer differentiations in interest. Otherwise, the factors and isolates are very similar to the combined analysis.

For Anglos, six factors also emerged. Similar to Hispanics, Anglos split the features content into two parts, one related to *lifestyles and people* and one to *entertainment*. However, the entertainment content is more narrowly focused on movies and TV, whereas the *Lifestyles* content is more broadly defined, encompassing humor, things to see and do in the area, and churches and religion. Like Hispanics, Anglos have separate interest clusters for *sports* and *politics, business, and economics*. A primary difference between the two subgroups is that Anglos split social problems into two categories, one covering *accidents and crime* and one that goes beyond the social problems topics in the combined analysis to include news of Mexico and Latin America, bilingual education, immigration, and the changing role of women. It is therefore more descriptive to label the latter *Hispanic social problems and issues*, because the topics parallel those identified by community leaders as of special concern to the Hispanic community.

If one were to use this analysis to better tailor news coverage to both the Hispanic and Anglo communities, the results would argue for further differentiation beyond the five clusters and nine isolates identified in the combined analysis. Specifically, features content would be recognized as being comprised of at least two different content clusters and as many as five—lifestyles, entertainment, people, the arts, and leisure activities. Breaking news such as crimes, accidents, and disasters would be treated as appealing to separate interests from such social issues and problems as discrimination, immigration, drug and alcohol problems. Educational issues and problems would be further recognized as potentially appealing to a different audience segment, one interested in women's issues as well. If any content were to be clustered around a Hispanic theme, it would need to encompass several topics to adequately represent the diverse interest groups within the Hispanic community (since those Hispanic-related topics that Anglos grouped together as one cluster were primarily isolates among Hispanics). Topics and features such as job opportunities, churches and religion, agriculture, real estate and housing, union activities, and comics would be recognized as additional interest areas. Finally, the separate factor analyses could be used to highlight the commonalities between the two ethnic groups. Since Anglos and Hispanics show the same patterns of interest in lifestyles, sports, and political/economic content, the opportunity exists to organize and cover such content in ways that appeal to both groups.

Table 4.34 presents the same analysis on TV entertainment content. Overall, two factors emerge, one related to *regular, continuing* types of programs and one that is perhaps best labeled *Specials* because it includes the kinds of programs that usually appear irregularly. *Regular* programming may be con-

TABLE 4.34. Dimensions of television entertainment content.†

Factors and Isolates Among Total Sample in Order of Importance	Factor Placement Among Hispanics	Among Anglos
I. Regular, continuing programs		
a. Soap operas	1	1
b. Game shows	1	1
c. Police and detective shows	1	1
d. Cartoons	1	I
e. Situation comedies	I	1
f. (Movies)	(1)	1
II. Specials		
a. Nature and outdoor shows	2	2
b. Musical variety shows	2	2
Isolates		
(None)		
Variance accounted for: 46%	44%	45%
	Factor 1 = *Continuing programs*	Factor 1 = *continuing programs*
	Factor 2 = *Specials*	Factor 2 = *Specials*

†Items in parentheses had moderately strong relationships with more than one factor. In the Hispanic and Anglo columns, the numbers designate on what factor the item loaded within that subgroup. For example, all items with a numeral 1 formed the first factor. Isolates are designated with an *I*.

sidered generally less sophisticated than *Specials* programming. For both Anglos and Hispanics, the same configuration of factors appears, the only differences being that Anglos see sitcoms as a third, isolated category, while Hispanics see cartoons as a third, isolated category.

One final analysis that reveals how interest in specific news content and entertainment programming relates to overall media consumption patterns is presented in Tables 4.35 through 4.38. Multiple regression analyses were again used, this time to see how content interests predict frequency of newspaper readership, amount of time spent reading the newspaper, time spent watching TV news, and time spent watching TV entertainment. Additionally, those topics that failed to emerge as significant predictors but still had a moderate and significant correlation with media use are reported.

The results for frequency of newspaper reading show that there are 12 topics, accounting for 18 percent of the variance, that predict how many issues a newspaper reader will read in a week. Where greater interest lead to greater readership, it means the topic is currently of greater interest to *regular* newspaper readers. Where greater interest is associated with less readership, it

TABLE 4.35. Content predictors of frequency of newspaper readership.

Predictors	Description of Relationship
1. Stories about national politics and the president	As interest *increases*, readership *increases*.
2. Job opportunities	As interest *increases*, readership *decreases*.
3. Editorials and letters to the editor	As interest *increases*, readershp *increases*.
4. Professional sports	As interest *increases*, readership *increases*.
5. News about TV and TV personalities	As interest *increases*, readership *decreases*.
6. Real estate and housing	As interest *increases*, readership *increases*.
7. News of Mexico and Latin America	As interest *increases*, readership *decreases*.
8. Cartoons on TV	As liking *increases*, readership *decreases*.
9. TV musical variety shows	As liking *increases*, readership *increases*.
10. Churches and religion	As interest *increases*, readership *decreases*.
11. Stories about discrimination	As interest *increases*, readership *increases*.
12. News about local politics and government	As interest *increases*, readership *increases*.

$R^2 = 18\%$

Other Significant Correlates

1. Accidents and disasters	As interest *increases*, readership *decreases*.
2. News of the local and national economy	As interest *increases*, readership *increases*.
3. News and beatures on business	As interest *increases*, readership *increases*.
4. Ads and commercials	As interest *increases*, readership *decreases*.
5. Bilingual education	As interest *increases*, readership *decreases*.
6. Advice on personal problems	As interest *increases*, readership *decreases*.
7. Health and medical advice	As interest *increases*, readership *decreases*.
8. How-to advice (e.g., home repair, car care, hobbies)	As interest *increases*, readership *decreases*.
9. Movie reviews	As interest *increases*, readership *decreases*.
10. TV soap operas	As liking *increases*, readership *decreases*.
11. TV movies	As liking *increases*, readership *decreases*.
12. TV game shows	As liking *increases*, readership *decreases*.

TABLE 4.36. Content predictors of time spent reading the newspaper.

Predictors	Description of Relationship
1. TV movies	As liking *increases*, time spent reading *decreases*.
2. Editorials and letters to the editor	As interest *increases*, time spent reading *increases*.
3. Ads and commercials	As interest *increases*, time spent reading *decreases*.
4. Professional sports	As interest *increases*, time spent reading *increases*.
5. Problems in the schools	As interest *increases*, time spent reading *decreases*.
6. News about local politics and government	As interest *increases*, time spent reading *increases*.

$R^2 = 6\%$

Other Significant Correlates

1. National politics and the president	As interest *increases*, time spent reading *increases*.
2. News about TV and TV personalities	As interest *increases*, time spent reading *decreases*.
3. Movie reviews	As interest *increases*, time spent reading *decreases*.
4. TV police and detective shows	As liking *increases*, time spent reading *decreases*.

means the topic is currently of greater interest to *occasional* newspaper readers. Thus, national politics, editorials, letters to the editor, professional sports, real estate and housing, stories about discrimination, local politics, and TV musical variety shows are key areas of interest for regular readers, whereas job opportunities, news about TV and TV personalities, news of Mexico and Latin America, TV cartoons, and churches and religion hold special interest for occasional readers. Inasmuch as Hispanics are less frequent readers, the latter topics could be considered more likely to appeal to Hispanics than the former categories. Additionally, almost all the topics that showed moderate correlations with readership are ones with greater appeal to occasional readers, which should include many Hispanics.

As Table 4.37 shows, topics and programming most likely to appeal to the newspaper "skimmer" are TV movies, ads and commercials, and problems in the schools, whereas areas of greatest attraction for those who spend a great deal of time with the paper are editorials and letters to the editor, professional sports, and local politics and government.

TABLE 4.37. Content predictors of time spent watching local and national television news.

Predictors	Description of Relationship
1. Advice on personal problems	As interest *increases*, time spent reading *increases*.
2. TV cartoons	As liking *increases*, time spent reading *increases*.
3. Job opportunities	As interest *increases*, time spent reading *decreases*.
4. Editorials and letters to the editor	As interest *increases*, time spent reading *increases*.

$R^2 = 4\%$

Other significant correlates

1. Comics and cartoons	As interest *increases*, time spent reading *increases*.
2. TV situation comedies	As liking *increases*, time spent reading *increases*.

Regarding TV news viewing, very few types of programming and news content show a strong relationship with it. The only interest areas that predict greater news viewing are advice on personal problems, cartoons, and editorials/letters to the editor. It appears that those who seek opinions, advice, or diversions are more inclined to be heavy consumers of TV news. Conversely, the only topic that shows a negative relationship with TV news viewing is job opportunities. Finally, as Table 4.38 reveals, time spent watching TV entertainment programming is largely related to preferences for TV soap operas, police and detective shows, TV movies, cartoons, and professional sports. Those who are interested in local sports, however, and those who are interested in churches and religion are least likely to watch a lot of TV entertainment.

TABLE 4.38. Content predictors of time spent watching television entertainment.

Predictors	Description of Relationship
1. TV soap operas	As liking *increases*, time spent reading *increases*.
2. TV police and detective shows	As liking *increases*, time spent reading *increases*.
3. TV movies	As liking *increases*, time spent reading *increases*.
4. Professional sports	As interest *increases*, time spent reading *increases*.
5. Local sports (e.g., high school, leagues)	As interest *increases*, time spent reading *decreases*.

TABLE 4.38. (continued)

Predictors	Description of Relationship
6. TV cartoons	As interest *increases*, time spent reading *increases*.
7. Churches and religion	As interest *increases*, time spent reading *decreases*.

$R^2 = 13\%$

Other Significant Correlates

1. National politics and the the president	As interest *increases*, time spent reading *increases*.
2. Crime news	As interest *increases*, time spent reading *increases*.
3. Accidents and disasters	As interest *increases*, time spent reading *increases*.
4. Job opportunities	As interest *increases*, time spent reading *increases*.
5. Stories on drug and alcohol problems	As interest *increases*, time spent reading *increases*.
6. Problems in the schools	As interest *increases*, time spent reading *increases*.
7. News about TV and TV personalities	As interest *increases*, time spent reading *increases*.
8. Movie reviews	As interest *increases*, time spent reading *increases*.
9. Comics and cartoons	As interest *increases*, time spent reading *increases*.
10. TV situation comedies	As liking *increases*, time spent reading *increases*.
11. TV game shows	As liking *increases*, time spent reading *increases*.

Reliance on Sources of Information

One half the respondents were asked which media they relied on for their sources of information concerning job possibilities, local political activities, community events, and making major purchases such as a car or stove. The possible responses were television, radio, newspaper, organizations (e.g., church, social agencies), family and friends, others, and not sure. A total of 837 Anglos and Hispanic adults responded to this series of questions. Results appear in Tables 4.39 through 4.42.

The review of previous research suggested a consistent trend for Hispanic Americans to rely primarily on the electronic media for information. The data for this study do not support such a trend; in fact, Hispanics preferred the newspaper as their primary source of information in all four situations. The newspaper was the preferred medium of 52 percent of the entire sample for information on job possibilities, with 59 percent of the Anglos and 44 percent of the Hispanics naming newspapers as their preferred sources of information on this question. The family was a distant second as the preferred choice of job information for both groups, and the broadcast media were named by relatively few people as a preferred source of information.

TABLE 4.39. Preferred sources of information on job possibilities.

| | Ethnicity | | | |
	Anglo	Hispanic	Total	Significance
1. TV	2%	6%	4%	*
2. Radio	3	8	5	
3. Newspaper	59	44	52	
4. Organizations	8	20	15	
5. Family	22	16	18	
6. Other	3	2	3	
7. Not sure	3	4	3	

*Denotes a significant difference between groups ($p < .05$)

TABLE 4.40. Preferred sources of information on local political activities.

| | Ethnicity | | | |
	Anglo	Hispanic	Total	Significance
1. TV	13%	21%	17%	*
2. Radio	4	10	7	
3. Newspaper	54	39	46	
4. Organizations	9	10	9	
5. Family	10	7	9	
6. Other	4	2	3	
7. Not sure	6	11	9	

*Denotes a significant difference between groups ($p < .05$)

TABLE 4.41. Preferred sources of information on community events.

| | Ethnicity | | | |
	Anglo	Hispanic	Total	Significance
1. TV	4%	10%	7%	*
2. Radio	8	15	11	
3. Newspaper	71	47	58	
4. Organizations	9	15	13	
5. Family	3	7	5	
6. Other	1	1	1	
7. Not sure	4	5	5	

*Denotes a significant difference across groups ($p < .05$)

TABLE 4.42. Preferred Sources of Information on Major Purchases.

	Ethnicity		
	Anglo	Hispanic	Total
1. TV	5	8	7
2. Radio	2	4	3
3. Newspaper	48	47	48
4. Organizations	4	3	4
5. Family	20	20	19
6. Other	17	13	14
7. Not sure	4	5	4

Newspapers were also the preferred sources for information about local political activities by both Anglos and Hispanics, with 54 percent of the Anglos and 39 percent of the Hispanics naming newspapers as their first choice for such information. Although Hispanics were more likely than Anglos to name television as a second choice, this second choice was far behind newspapers as the desired source of information on political activities in the community. There were no significant differences found across study sites.

Anglos and Hispanics both named newspapers as their primary source of information about community events. Organizations and radio were second and third, respectively, but relatively few people in the sample named either of these sources as primary conduits of information about community events. An examination of differences across communities indicated more reliance on television as a second choice only in Salinas. In each city, newspapers were the overwhelming first choice of both Anglos and Hispanics, though Anglos mentioned them more often.

In each city, newspapers were named as the primary source of data for making major purchases; there were no significant differences across study sites. There were also no difference in Anglos and Hispanics on this question, with 48 percent of the Anglos and 47 percent of the Hispanics naming newspapers as their number one choice.

Taken as a whole, it is evident that newspapers are the primary sources of information on the topics asked in this investigation. There is no evidence from these data to suggest that Hispanics rely more on broadcast media, organizations or interpersonal contacts to provide them information on these important topics. It is also clear that the pattern of information seeking is very similar across the diverse markets included in this sample.

SUMMARY

The results section was organized to present data on demographics and language patterns, media use and access, media evaluations and image, functions served by various media, content preferences, and sources of information. This section summarizes differences between Anglos and Hispanics on different questions asked in each part of this survey.

Figure 4.1 summarizes the differences between Anglos and Hispanics on the demographic questions and the questions on language use. Hispanics and Anglos differ on almost every question asked in this section. Hispanics in the sample were younger, less educated, less affluent, and more likely to be first- or second-generation residents of the U.S. Hispanics tend to have been in each community longer than Anglos; both groups are equivalent on their reports of likelihood of moving away from their community. Hispanics are more likely to suggest that they are polarized in terms of their views of the quality of life in the community. Many express the belief that the quality of life is worsening, but many others stated that the quality of life is improving. Hispanics are less likely than Anglos to take a middle position on this issue of quality of life.

FIGURE 4.1. Demographics and language patterns.

Anglos and Hispanics are equivalent
    . . . in their likelihood of moving from the community
Hispanics differ from Anglos in that Hispanics
    . . . have less education
    . . . have less income
    . . . are younger
    . . . have lived in the community longer
    . . . are more likely to be first-generation residents of the U.S.
    . . . are more polarized on the quality of life in the community
    . . . are more likely to be bilingual

Figure 4.2 presents information on several questions about media use and access. As expected by the examination of prior research, Anglos are more likely to read a newspaper, read newspapers more frequently, and subscribe to newspapers more than do Hispanics. Anglos also spend more time reading magazines than do Hispanics, and a greater percentage of the Anglo population read magazines than do Hispanics. All these data indicate that the penetration of all print media in Hispanic households is lower than in the Anglo population. Hispanics are shown to be less frequent, more occasional consumers of print media who tend to purchase such publications in street sales outlets. Given the demographics of the Hispanic population and their claimed purchasing habits, the print media have to deal with the typical young reader problem in order to convert these people to become regular consumers of print journalism.

Hispanics are more likely to spend time watching morning and afternoon television entertainment. They also spend more time with all forms of Spanish-language media and are more likely, as expected, to prefer more Spanish-language programming and print media.

There are a number of items on which Anglos and Hispanics do not differ. Users in both groups spent an equal amount of time with the local daily newspaper and magazines. The same percentage of each group watches local and national news on television. They both spend the same amount of time watching

FIGURE 4.2. Media use and access.

Anglos and Hispanics are equivalent
        . . . on amount of time spent reading newspapers and magazines (among users)
        . . . on percentage who watched local and national news
        . . . on amount of time watching local news and, among users, amount of time watching national news
        . . . on percentage who watch morning and evening entertainment programs
        . . . on amount of time spent watching evening entertainment programs
        . . . on percentage who listened to radio news and entertainment
        . . . on amount of time spent listening to radio news and entertainment
        . . . on number of TVs in household

Hispanics exceed Anglos
        . . . on percentage watching afternoon TV entertainment
        . . . on amount of time watching morning and afternoon entertainment
        . . . on use of all Spanish-language media
        . . . on preference for media in Spanish

Anglos exceed Hispanics
        . . . on percentage who read newspapers and proportion of household who read
        . . . on frequency of newspaper readership
        . . . on percentage who subscribed to newspapers
        . . . on amount of time watching national news (when nonusers are included)
        . . . on number of radios in household
        . . . on percentage who read magazines
        . . . on amount of time spent reading newspapers and magazines (when nonusers are included)

evening prime-time television and the same amount of time listening to radio news and entertainment. All these questions together do not suggest a pattern of extreme broadcast dependence on the part of Hispanics. There are certainly fewer differences than expected between Anglos and Hispanics on many issues concerning media use.

Figure 4.3 presents a summary of some very important data concerning satisfaction with and image of the local media. It has been suggested by many that Hispanics are generally less involved with local media and tend to have very negative evaluations of the media that serve their community. The results of this study suggest that the myth of the alienated and hostile Hispanic is due for revision. Anglos and Hispanics do not differ in their evaluation of several important image items for television and newspapers. Hispanics do not have less trust for nor consider TV and newspapers to be more biased or racist than do Anglos. Moreover, Hispanics indicate more overall satisfaction with local newspapers

FIGURE 4.3. Media evaluations and image.

Anglos and Hispanics are equivalent
>   . . . on overall satisfaction with local radio news
>   . . . on evaluations of local TV coverage of locals and their accomplishments, local cultural activities, and treatment of crime
>   . . . on radio coverage of locals and their accomplishments
>   . . . on evaluations of TV image on trust, personalism, bias, receptivity, racism, community surveillance, accuracy, timeliness, sensationalism, caring, power, community concern, influence, representativeness, and courage
>   . . . on evaluations of *newspaper* image on trust, personalism, bias, receptivity, racism, community surveillance, accuracy, sensationalism, caring, community concern, and representativeness

Hispanics exceed Anglos
>   . . . on overall satisfaction with local newspapers
>   . . . on overall satisfaction with local TV news
>   . . . on satisfaction with local TV coverage of social news in community
>   . . . on satisfaction with local radio coverage of social news in community and local cultural activities
>   . . . in believing TV when news media are in conflict
>   . . . on evaluations of TV image on competence and liveliness
>   . . . on evaluations of *newspaper* image on competence, liveliness, timeliness, power, influence, and courage

Anglos exceed Hispanics
>   . . . on satisfaction with newspaper coverage of locals and their accomplishments, social news of community, local cultural activities, and treatment of crime
>   . . . on satisfaction with local radio coverage of crime
>   . . . in estimate of fairness of coverage of Hispanic community by local media

and local TV news than do Anglos. Across a number of very important issues, Hispanics are generally more positive about all forms of media and their coverage than are Anglos. Community leaders, media decision makers, and many earlier researchers promulgate perspectives about the attitudes of Hispanic Americans that have little, if any, support from the data gathered in this study.

Hispanics do tend to be less satisfied with newspaper coverage of locals and their accomplishments, social news of the community, local coverage of cultural activities, and treatment of crime. They are also more negative about radio coverage of crime and believe in general that the fairness of coverage of the Hispanic community by local media could be improved. However, their concerns about specific coverage of the Hispanic community do not lead to a generalized negative attitude about the local media. These data tend to indicate the recognition of specific problems and the maintenance of relatively upbeat and positive attitudes by Hispanics about how well the media serve the people.

The portrayal of the Hispanic as uninvolved with local print media is certainly disputed by the summary of data presented in Figure 4.4. All local media are considered very important to the Hispanic community as indicated by the fact that Hispanics rate *every* function of newspapers and television the same as or more important than do Anglos. Hispanics again exceed Anglos in their satisfaction with local newspapers' fulfillment of key functions, as well as with the job TV and radio are doing to satisfy functions important to them. Again we see Hispanics as very involved with the media and relatively satisfied with the performance of their local media. Anglos tend to use magazines more and tend to be more satisfied with the functions performed by that print medium.

The conception of the Hispanic as primarily involved with a "use" paper and interested in soft news, features, and advertisements is again unsupported by the data collected in this study. Hispanics are interested in hard news and in fact exceed Anglos in their interest in a variety of news items. Across the board, Hispanics are equal to or exceed the interest of Anglos in almost every content category queried in this research. Hispanics show less interest than Anglos in national politics, local politics and government, business news, and humorous stories and features when such items appear in the media. However, the data on TV news consumption and functions reveal that Hispanics do have a strong interest in local news, if not specifically local politics. Hispanics also report liking to watch a variety of television entertainment programs exceeding that of Anglos. The Hispanic community is very interested in the content offered by the media, involved with its day-to-day presentation, and relatively satisfied with the current product mix offered them by their local media. Figure 4.5 presents a detailed summary of the content preferences of Anglos and Hispanics.

An examination of earlier research and testimony by several sources indicated that Hispanics would be much more likely to rely on broadcast media, organizational support, and interpersonal contacts as sources of information about important issues. This is simply not supported by the data from this investigation. Anglos and Hispanics both rate newspapers as their primary source

FIGURE 4.4. Media functions.

Hispanics rate every function of newspapers and television the same as or more important than do Anglos.

Hispanics exceed Anglos
>   . . . on satisfaction with local newspaper's fulfillment of key functions (among all respondents; among users, ratings are equivalent)
>   . . . on satisfaction with local TV and radio's fulfillment of key functions

Anglos exceed Hispanics
>   . . . on satisfaction with fulfillment of key functions by magazines they read

of information for job opportunities, local political activities, community events, and where to make major purchases. Both groups are relatively equal in their dependence on the broadcast media and other contacts as secondary sources of information on all these issues. Figure 4.6 summarizes the data on sources of information.

In summary, the results from this seven-city survey in the southwestern U.S. offer compelling evidence that many of the previously held assumptions and assertions about Hispanic media use and evaluations are more myth than reality. The current data contrast with the depiction of the Hispanic as distrustful of and uninvolved with English-language media. They further counter the widely held belief that Hispanics are more broadcast-oriented than print-oriented. While it is true that the Hispanics in this survey were less frequent readers of the newspaper and more likely to watch daytime television entertainment, they also reported greater reliance on both media for a number of key functions and expressed favorable evaluations of both in several areas. Additionally, their expressed interest in a wide range of hard news topics as well as soft news and features underscores their generally high level of interest in and dependence on

FIGURE 4.5. Content preferences.

Hispanics and Anglos are equivalent
  . . . in their interest in news of the local economy, agricultural news, real estate and housing, stories on the changing roles of women, consumer information, Good Samaritan stories (people helping people), and things to see and do in the area when such topics appear in newspapers, on TV, and on the radio
  . . . in liking to watch nature and outdoors shows and musical variety shows on TV

Hispanics exceed Anglos
  . . . in their interest in crime news; accidents and disasters; news of Mexico and Latin America; job opportunities; ads and commercials; immigration; stories about discrimination; drug and alcohol problems; bilingual education; problems in the schools; union activities; news about youth gangs; professional sports; local participatory and high school sports; sports from Latin America; churches and religion; food, recipes, and nutritional information; advice on personal problems; health and medical advice; how-to advice; TV and TV personalities; movie reviews; art, dance, theater, and music; stories on retirement and retirement living; and comics, when such topics and features appear in the media
  . . . in liking to watch situation comedies, soap operas, police and detective shows, movies, cartoons, and game shows on TV

Anglos exceed Hispanics
  . . . in their interest in national politics and the president; local politics and government; editorials and letters to the editor; news and features on business; and humorous stories and features, when such topics and features appear in the media

FIGURE 4.6. Sources of information.

Hispanics and Anglos both rate newspapers as their primary source of information for

         . . . job opportunities
         . . . local political activities
         . . . community events
         . . . where to make major purchases

Anglos exceed Hispanics on relying more *exclusively* on newspapers as their primary source of information for

         . . . job opportunities
         . . . local political activities
         . . . community events

Hispanics and Anglos are relatively equal in their dependence on broadcast media as second choices for information.

---

the media for news and information. In these seven cities at least, the typical Hispanic appears not to be alienated and hostile but, rather, receptive and positively disposed toward the media. These findings have important implications for media policy makers and should prompt a rethinking of how the media needs and wishes of Hispanics can best be served.

5

MASS MEDIA USE,
PREFERENCES, AND
ATTITUDES AMONG YOUNG PEOPLE

Bradley S. Greenberg
Carrie Heeter
Michael Burgoon
Judee K. Burgoon
Felipe Korzenny

The comprehensive review of available research evidence on the mass media attitudes and behaviors of Hispanic Americans in chapter 1 yields sparse information about all age groups but a particular scarcity regarding young Hispanics. There was no study of the collective media behaviors, attitudes, and media accessibility for young people from Spanish-speaking families. That gap is corrected in this chapter.

We set out to explore media behaviors and attitudes of Hispanic youth across the widest possible set of media. To provide a direct comparison for the findings, we chose to collect at the same time and from the same place the same information from Anglo youth. Although much mass media data already exist for Anglo youngsters, it seemed unwise to use data from other, likely monocultural environments and from different time periods.

The population growth trend among Hispanics, on their way to becoming the largest U.S. minority, provides a strong incentive for government and industry to understand the information and entertainment resources on which this population group relies.

In addition to a desire for such data because it is not elsewhere available there was a motivation to empirically explore media issues where Hispanic/Anglo differences might be presumed to exist. First, the multicultural orientation of Hispanics suggests a duality of media orientations to both Anglo and Spanish media, alternative content preferences, and differential perceptions of how well the media serve the community (or the subcommunities). Second, to the extent that there are bilingual capabilities, a lesser ability in English, or a desire for bilingual media opportunities, differences could emerge in media postures. Third, proportionately more Hispanics are in lower socioeconomic situations than their Anglo counterparts, and different media choices by socioeconomic status are a demonstrated fact.

Ethnic differences in media behaviors and attitudes have been consistently demonstrated between Black and white American adults and children. None of those studies have included sufficient Hispanic Americans to subdivide the findings and compare Anglos and Hispanics. The Black-white comparisons have repeatedly demonstrated a stronger orientation to broadcast media among the Blacks and more negative attitudes toward print, accompanied by lower usage and lesser expectations of satisfaction.

Although we did not convert those findings into a statement of parallel hypotheses for this study, awareness of those outcomes provided a guide to the present areas of inquiry. It seemed appropriate at this stage of inquiry to be most concerned with investigating normative media behaviors. Subsequently, we could make specific determinations of the impact of the media on Hispanic youth. But first we had to assess what Hispanic-American youths do with the media, why, with what content, for what purpose, and with what intensity.

METHODS

Questionnaires were administered to 738 fifth and tenth graders in five southwestern U.S. cities during May 1980. Contacts in each city's school districts were asked to arrange for 100 fifth graders and 100 tenth graders, half of them Hispanic and half Anglo, evenly divided between males and females. Fifth grade classes were requested to be "standard" (not accelerated or remedial), and tenth grade classes were requested to be from required courses rather than electives.

Approximately one-half the questionnaires were administered by a Hispanic researcher and half by an Anglo researcher. For fifth graders, some to all of the questionnaire was read aloud (depending on time constraints), to insure that respondents understood and followed the response categories and questionnaire format.

Questionnaires were administered in California to 85 youths in San Bernardino, 187 in Salinas, and 144 in Visalia. Other respondents included 157 in Tucson, Arizona, and 162 in Santa Fe, New Mexico.

VARIABLES

The instrument was designed to encompass the major areas of mass media research that have been studied in relation to youth:

- Media access
- Media usage
- Media content preferences
- Media-use gratifications
- Media credibility
- Perceived reality of television
- Parental mediation of media access and content
- Social interaction about media.

Special attention was also given to Spanish-language media.

Thirteen sets of variables were subjected to exploratory factor analysis. The factors and their major contributing variables are presented following the description of each set of variables that was factor-analyzed. Varimax orthogonal rotated classical r-factor analyses were performed, using up to 25 iterations and selecting factors with a minimum eigenvalue of 1.0. The emergent factors were named based on factor loadings, considering the relative strength of each variable that loaded .4 or greater on each factor. The factor score coefficient matrix was used to create indices for each factor; the indices were then treated as new variables and included in the analysis.

Media Access

Television access questions included number of TV sets and number of color TV sets in the household, the percent of respondents having their own sets, and the percent of households receiving cable TV.

Radio access asked for the number of radios in the household, the number of car radios, and the number of radios belonging exclusively to the respondent.

Record/tape access was measured by the number of record/tape players in the household and the number of players belonging to the respondent.

Media Use

Newspaper use questions included an open-ended question: "In the last week, which newspapers did you read?" In this analysis, the results were translated into a variable representing the total number of different newspapers read in the last week. Other newspaper use questions concerned number of days in the last week a newspaper was read, amount of time spent yesterday reading a newspaper, whether a newspaper was delivered to the household, the number of people in the household wo read the paper.

The number of comic books and magazines read in the preceding week was also asked, along with the number of books other than school books read in the last month.

Two types of measures of TV viewing time were used, estimates and logs. Respondents were asked to estimate the number of hours they usually watched TV on a school day before school, after school before supper, and after supper before bed. These estimates were summed for a total school-day estimate. Estimates were also requested for Saturday mornings and afternoons.

Respondents were given a TV program log of the previous day's shows and were asked to circle the shows they actually watched. These circled logs were translated into minutes and grouped into before noon, between noon and 5:30, from 5:30 on, and total TV time. If circled programs overlapped in time, minutes were calculated based on actual time possible to have been watching TV. Prime-time viewing also was calculated (7:00 to 10:00 P.M. in Arizona and New Mexico; 8:00 to 11:00 P.M. in California). San Bernardino data were collected on a Monday, and their log results are reported separately as time watched on Sunday.

Frequency of viewing Saturday cartoons, soap operas, network news, local news, and game shows was also assessed.

Radio use asked for an estimate of the hours usually spent listening on a school day and whether or not the respondent listened to radio news, sports, or music on the preceding day.

Record/tape use asked for an estimate of the hours usually spent playing records/tapes on a school day, and the number of records/tapes purchased in the last month.

Movie use asked the number of movies seen (in theaters, not on TV) in the last month.

Content Preferences

To assess newspaper content preferences, respondents were asked how often they looked at the following items when they read a newspaper:

- Comics and cartoons
- Sports
  Weather
  Headlines

- Advertising
- Front page news
- News inside the paper
- Photos
- TV sections
- Advice columns
- Crime stories
- Stories about Mexico and Latin America
- Stories about young people
- Things to do in town.

Response categories were *Always, Sometimes* and *Never*.

Newspaper content preferences were factor-analyzed and the following factors emerged: (1) *News,* made up primarily of front-page news (loading .75), headlines (.73), news inside the paper (.59), and photos (.43); (2) *Local information,* including stories about young people (.77), things to do in town (.58), crime stories (.41), and advertising (.40); and (3) *Features,* consisting of the television section (.56) and comics and cartoons (.43).

Comic book content preferences were measured in terms of how much the respondent liked to read:

- Love stories
- Horror stories
- Superhero comics
- War stories
- Funny comics.

Response categories were *Very much, Quite a lot, Not much,* and *Never*. The same categories were used for magazines, TV, radio, records, and tapes.

Comic book factors were: (1) *Action,* combining superhero comics (.75), war comics (.72), and horror stories (.61); and (2) *Romance/humor,* comprised of love stories (.67), funny comics (.51), and horror stories (.45).

Magazine types included:

- Sports magazines
- News magazines
- Magazines about cars
- Fashion magazines
- Children's magazines

- Television and movie star magazines
- Music magazines.

Two magazine factors emerged: (1) *Pop culture,* representing television and movie star magazines (.79), fashion magazines (.60), children's magazines (.54), and music magazines (.51); and (2) *Recreation,* combining sports magazines (.84) and magazines about cars (.57).

Television content preferences asked how much respondents liked to watch:

- Soap operas
- Cartoons
- Game shows
- Local news
- Comedies
- Movies
- Police/detective shows
- Shows like "Villa Alegre" and "Sesame Street"
- Shows with singing and dancing
- Network news
- Shows about families
- Baseball
- Shows in Spanish
- News shows like "60 Minutes" and "20/20"
- Sports shows like "Wide World of Sports"
- Soccer

Television content preference factors were: (1) *Sports,* grouping sports shows like "Wide World of Sports" (.73), baseball (.65), soccer (.48), and a dislike of soap operas (−.41); (2) *News,* made up of local news (.78), network news (.77), and shows like "60 Minutes" and "20/20" (.43); (3) *Spanish,* made up of shows in Spanish (.67) and shows like "Sesame Street" and "Villa Alegre" (.65); and (4) *Entertainment,* encompassing shows about families (.55) and comedies (.47).

Radio music content areas tested were:

- Rock
- Top 40
- Classical
- Soul

- Country and western
- "Musica Ranchera"
- Rock in Spanish
- Disco

A *Spanish* factor emerged consisting of "Musica Ranchera" (.83), and rock in Spanish (.80). The *Black music* factor represented soul (.56) and disco (.51), and the *Top 40* factor combined Top 40 (.64) and rock (.42).

Record/tape content preference questions were the same as for radio music, excluding Top 40. *Spanish* and *Black* factors also emerged for records and tapes (the former consisting of rock in Spanish (.89) and "Musica Ranchera" (.80), and the latter of soul (.70) and disco (.45)), and a *Classical/Country and western* factor replaced the radio *Top 40* factor, with classical loading .53 and country and western loading .52.

Movie content preference types included:

- Horror movies
- Comedies
- Love stories
- Westerns
- War movies
- Science fiction
- Movies in Spanish
- Detective movies
- Animal movies

Movie factors were: (1) *Adventure,* made up of war movies (.64), science fiction (.62), western (.59), and detective movies (.49); (2) *Romance* (love stories .62); and (3) *Spanish,* with a strong dislike of comedy (−.52) and a positive preference for movies in Spanish (.48).

Media Use Gratifications

To measure motivations for reading newspapers, respondents were asked how much the following were their reasons for reading the paper:

- Because I want to know what's going on
- Because it's funny
- So I can learn to do new things
- Because it excites me

- Because it relaxes me
- Because it cheers me up
- So I can forget about my problems
- To look at the pictures
- For the local news
- For the national news
- To get advice on problems
- To find out about new places and people
- To get the headlines
- To find out more about things I heard about
- To find out what's happening to people in town
- Because it gives me things to talk about
- I don't read because it's boring

Three factors emerged for newspaper gratifications: (1) *News,* combining reading for the local news (.81), for the national news (.75), to get the headlines (.56), to know what's going on (.52), and to find out more about things I heard about (.45); (2) *Diversion,* including because it cheers me up (.66), to forget my problems (.62), because it excites me (.57), because it's funny (.48), to get advice on problems (.45), because it relaxes me (.44), because it gives me things to talk about (.44), and to look at pictures (.43); and (3) *Social Learning,* made up of to find out about new places and people (.63), to find out what's happening to people in town (.57), to find out more about things I heard about (.53), to know what's going on (.48), and to learn to do new things (.43).

Television gratification questions were very similar; the following completions to "I watch TV . . .":

- Because it excites me
- So I can learn to do new things
- Because it relaxes me
- Because it teaches me things I don't learn in school
- Because it shows me how other people deal with the same problems I have
- Because everyone else does
- Because it helps me know how I'm supposed to act
- When I'm lonely
- So I can forget about my problems
- For the local news
- To get advice on problems
- Because it cheers me up

- To find out more about things I heard about
- Because it gives me things to talk about
- I don't watch because it's boring

Television gratification factors parallel the newspaper factors: (1) *Diversion* grouped because it cheers me up (.67), to forget my problems (.60), when I'm lonely (.54), because it excites me (.53), because it relaxes me (.46), and because it gives me things to talk about (.45); (2) *Social learning* consisted of because it teaches me things I don't learn in school (.69), to learn to do new things (.64), and because it shows me how others deal with the same problems I have (.48); and (3) *News* included to find out more about things I heard about (.75) and for the local news (.48). A fourth factor, *Advice*, also emerged for TV gratifications, comprising because it helps me know how I'm supposed to act (.43) and to get advice on problems (.42).

Media Credibility and Choice

Respondents were asked, "If you had to choose between watching TV and reading the newspaper, which would you do?" They were also asked to choose between TV and radio and between radio and newspapers.
Credibility was measured in two ways:

If the newspaper, radio, and TV all said different things about the same thing, which would you believe?

If you read it in the newspaper (see it on TV, hear it on the radio), it's true [*Yes, Not sure, No*].

Perceived Reality of TV

Perceived reality questions dealt with how true-to-life respondents assessed the following TV images:

People
Places
Young people
Anglos
Mexican Americans
Blacks
Mexican-American families
Anglo families.

Response categories were *Very real, Quite real, A little real, Not real.*

Two factors emerged for perceived reality of TV: (1) *Minorities*, representing Mexican Americans (.79), Mexican-American families (.71), Blacks (.62), young people (.51), and people (.48); and (2) *Anglos,* combining Anglos (.70), Anglo families (.64), people (.40), and young people (.40).

Parental Mediation

Parental mediation of TV measures included the following parental restrictions:

> Are there any shows your parents won't let you watch because they don't think the stories or characters are good for you?
>
> On school days, how late can you stay up to watch TV compared to most kids your age?
>
> Are there more rules about TV, less rules, or about the same as your friends?
>
> Has a parent ever told you that you're watching too much TV?

Frequency of watching TV with a parent, frequency of discussing a show while watching with a parent, and frequency of a parent telling respondents to watch a TV show, read something in the newspaper and read something in a magazine were also asked. Response categories ranged from 7 days a week to less than once a week.

Parental mediation variables loaded onto three factors: (1) *Read,* grouping frequency of a parent telling respondents to read something in a magazine (.76) and to read something in the newspaper (.73); (2) *TV rules,* made up of the number of shows parents wouldn't permit (.66), a negative loading of how late the respondent could stay up to watch TV ($-.58$), and positive loadings for frequency of a parent telling respondents to watch certain TV shows (.42) and for relative number of parental TV rules compared to other kids the same age (.41); and (3) *Co-watching,* made up of how often a parent watched TV with the respondent (.63) and how often parents and respondents talked about a show while watching together (.56).

Social Interactions

Respondents were asked how often they talked with parents and friends about TV and newspapers and how often parents talked with them about TV and newspapers.

Social interaction factors split the variables by media. (1) *NP talk* combined how often respondents talked with a parent (.88), how often they talked with a friend (.65), and how often a parent talked with them about newspapers (.54); (2) *TV talk* combined how often they talked with a parent (.76), how often a parent talked with them (.59), and how often they talked with a friend about TV (.57).

Portrayals of Mexican Americans

For local newspapers, local TV news, and TV shows, respondents were asked how frequently the media portrayed Mexican Americans doing good things and doing bad things. Response categories were *Very often, Quite often, Not very often, Not at all.*

Mexican-American portrayal factors grouped the variables into negative and positive images:

1. *Negative image* included local TV news (.85), local newspapers (.72), and TV shows (.53);

2. *Positive image* consisted of local TV news (.79), local newspapers (.57), and TV shows (.48).

Spanish-Language Media

Spanish-language media questions dealt with *access* to a Spanish-language TV channel, *usage* of Spanish-language TV, radio, records/tapes, movies, magazines, and books; and Spanish-language *content preferences* for TV shows in Spanish, shows like "Villa Alegre" and "Sesame Street," radio rock in Spanish and radio "Musica Ranchera," records/tapes of rock in Spanish and "Musica Ranchera," and movies in Spanish. Daily Spanish-language newspapers were not regularly available in many of the sites. Therefore Spanish-language newspaper questions consisted of, "How often do you look at news about Mexico and Latin America when you read a newspaper?" and, "How much would you like some of the newspaper in Spanish?"

Demographics

Ethnicity and grade were the primary demographic variables in this analysis.

Ethnicity. Respondents were given a list of 12 choices (Chicano, Latino, Mexican, Cuban, Puerto Rican, Spanish American, Mexican American, Asian American, White (Anglo) Black, Native American (American Indian), and Other) and were asked to circle the word that best described their cultural background.

Eighty-seven percent of all respondents chose a single response. A respondent was classified as Anglo if *Anglo* was circled and none of the Hispanic cultural backgrounds were circled, regardless of whether any non-Anglo, non-Hispanic choices were also circled. Ninety-four percent of the 274 Anglos chose a single response; 6 percent selected two responses.

Seventy-nine percent of the 464 Hispanics chose a single response; 10 percent chose 2 responses; 4 percent chose 3 responses; and 7 percent chose between 4 and 9 responses. Of the 368 Hispanics circling a single response, 41 percent chose Mexican American, 20 percent Spanish American, 19 percent Chicano, 18 percent Mexican, 2 percent Latino, 1 percent Puerto Rican, and 0 percent Cuban. Multiple responses were classified as Hispanic if one or more of the seven Hispanic cultural backgrounds were circled, regardless of whether any non-Hispanic cultural background was also circled.

If neither Anglo nor Hispanic cultural backgrounds were circled, the respondent was classified as "other" and excluded from this analysis.

Grade. Questionnaires were administered to 293 fifth graders (198 Hispanic and 95 Anglo) and 442 tenth graders (263 Hispanic, 179 Anglo). The age range for fifth grade was 10 to 13 and 14 to 19 for tenth. In San Bernardino, data were collected from tenth graders only.

Sex. Forty-six percent of Anglos and 49 percent of Hispanics were male; 50 percent of fifth graders and 48 percent of 10th graders were male.

Other Demographics. Additional demographics collected concerned number of people in the household, whether there was a telephone in the home, grades in school, and languages spoken and written (English and Spanish in varying combinations of proficiency).

Hispanic respondents reported larger households (5.8 people, compared to 4.4 for Anglos). Fewer Hispanic youth (94 percent) reported having a telephone in their home than Anglos (97 percent), although that difference was not significant.

Anglos reported getting better grades in school than did Hispanics, and fifth graders exceeded tenth graders. The means for all four subgroups fell between average and good.

Eight percent of the Anglo youth spoke some Spanish and 10 percent read some Spanish. About 80 percent of the Hispanic respondents were bilingual. Nineteen percent spoke only English, 39 percent spoke mostly English and some Spanish, 26 percent spoke English and Spanish about equally, and 16 percent spoke mostly Spanish. That bilingualism drops sharply in terms of language reading ability. Half the Hispanic youth could read only English; 28 percent read some Spanish; 14 percent were equally proficient in both languages; and 9 percent could read mostly Spanish and some English. About 10 percent more tenth graders than fifth graders could read some Spanish.

ANALYSIS

Two-by-two analysis of variance was the principal statistical tool used in this study, comparing means by ethnicity (Hispanic and Anglo) and grade (fifth and tenth) and their interactions for each variable and factor.

Forward stepwise multiple regression analyses were conducted to determine the subsets of media use, demographic, gratification, parental mediation, credibility, and content preference variables that best predicted usage of each mass medium. Two hierarchical steps were defined within the overall stepwise design such that all demographic (and presumably antecedent) variables were given first priority to enter the equation when their significance level met the statistical requirements for entry and removal ($F = 3.84, p < .05$). The demographic variables included age, gender, size of household, grades in school, reading and speaking ability in and dependence on Spanish and English, and ethnicity. Cultural self-referents among Hispanics were contrast-coded to permit the following orthogonal comparisons: Hispanics selecting the self-referent *Mexican* versus all other Hispanics; Hispanics (excluding those who selected *Mexican*) who selected *Chicano* versus *Mexican American, Spanish American,* or other Hispanic self-referents; Hispanics not selecting *Mexican* or *Chicano* who selected *Mexican American* versus *Spanish American* or *Other;* and *Spanish American* versus *Other.* This order of inclusion reflected a continuum of most-traditional, least-assimilated Hispanic self-referents to most assimilated.

All media variables were entered at the second hierarchical level. For each specific medium being predicted, only that medium's access and content preference indices were entered. In addition, the indices for the remaining variable sets were entered, together with other media use variables. There were a total of 40 to 45 variables entered into each regression analysis.

Missing values were replaced by the mean for a respondent if 10 percent or less of the variables entered into the analysis were missing for that person. (If more than 10 percent were missing, the case was dropped from the analysis.) Missing values on the individual variables ranged from 0 to 2.8 percent; for the factor score indices, the range was 1.8 to 7.7 percent. The missing value replacement criteria yielded a minimum of 639 qualified cases for each independent-dependent variable pair.

RESULTS

Results are grouped into eight major variable categories: (1) *Media access,* (2) *Media use,* (3) *Content preferences,* (4) *Media gratifications,* (5) *Media credibility,* (6) *Media attitudes,* (7) *Social interaction about media,* and

(8) *Parental mediation of media use.* For each, we identify similarities and differences between the Hispanic and Anglo youth samples and between fifth and tenth graders as well as the absolute levels of these media behaviors. Interactions between ethnicity and grade are also examined.

Media Access

Access to electronic media is in Table 5.1. Ethnic similarities in media access outnumber differences. Hispanic youths report more access to cable television and fewer personal radios than do Anglo youths. On all other access variables Hispanic and Anglo youths are quite similar. Each group claims to have two television sets in the home, of which one is color; each family has four radios, including two car radios, and almost three record/tape players in the home. Two-thirds of the youngsters indicate that one of the players is their own.

TABLE 5.1. Media access by ethnicity and grade.

	Ethnicity			Grade		
	Hispanic	*Anglo*	*(p)*	*5*	*10*	*(p)*
TV						
a. How many TV sets?	2.08	2.14	ns*	2.06	2.13	ns
b. How many color TVs?	1.24	1.27	ns	1.17	1.31	.02
c. Have own TV?	43%	40%	ns	45%	40%	ns
d. Get cable TV?	43%	31%	.01	33%	43%	.01
Radio						
e. How many radios?	3.91	4.15	ns	3.63	4.24	.01
f. How many yours?	1.21	1.46	.01	1.03	1.48	.01
g. How many car radios?	1.83	1.87	ns	1.77	1.89	ns
Records/tapes						
h. How many record/tape players:	2.76	2.74	ns	2.66	2.81	ns
i. Have own record/tape player?	65%	73%	ns	59%	74%	.01

*ns = not significant

By age, tenth graders report more color television sets in the home, more access to cable television, more radios in the home, more personal radios, and more personal ownership of a record or tape player than do fifth graders.

Media Use

Newspaper Use. Table 5.2 presents the results on newspaper usage. Again, there are more similarities between the Hispanic and Anglo youth than differences. Each reads one newspaper a week and on about three days a week. Each spends from 5 to 15 minutes reading the newspaper and did so on the

TABLE 5.2. Newspaper use by ethnicity and grade.

	Ethnicity			Grade		
	Hispanic	Anglo	(p)	5	10	(p)
a. Number of newspapers read last week?	.85	.97	ns	.64	1.06	.01
b. Days last week read newspaper?	2.86	3.24	ns	1.96	3.70	.01
c. Time spent reading newspaper yesterday?*†	.93	.90	ns	.77	1.02	.01
d. Is newspaper delivered? (percentage yes)	50%	73%	.01	56%	60%	ns
e. How many people in household read newspaper?	3.04	2.99	ns	2.86	3.13	.01

*Significant interaction between ethnicity and grade.

†Response categories and values: 0 = 0; 1 = 5 to 15 minutes; 2 = 16 to 30; 3 = 31 to 45; 4 = More than 45 minutes

preceding day. These findings differ from the adult survey results, where Anglos were more frequent newspaper readers. In each household about three people read the newspaper. The only significant difference by ethnicity among the youth is that the newspaper is substantially more likely to be delivered to Anglo homes (73 percent) than to Hispanic homes (50 percent); this is consistent with the adult survey findings.

As anticipated, tenth graders were far more likely to make use of the newspaper than fifth graders. The tenth graders read more newspapers on more days during the week, spend more time reading them and report that more members of their household read the paper.

A significant interaction between ethnicity and grade for time spent reading the newspaper does not alter the interpretation of the grade difference. The source of the interaction was fifth-grade Anglos, who were substantially lower than any other subgroup in time spent reading the newspaper.

The multiple regression analysis of frequency of reading the newspaper reported in Table 5.3 accounted for 47 percent of the variance. The significant predictors are reported in order of strength of their standardized beta weights. Simple correlations (r) are also reported. A sentence describes the direction of each reported relationship. Finally, we identify at the bottom of each multiple regression table those variables (if any) that appeared as significant predictors in earlier solutions but did not emerge as significant in the final, most comprehensive and parsimonious solution.

The household environment predicting that a child reads the newspaper is one in which others in the household read the newspaper, the number of

TABLE 5.3. Predictors of frequency of reading the newspaper.

	Variable	Description of Relationship	Simple r†	Beta
1.	Newspaper readers in household	As number of newspaper readers in the household *increases*, the newspaper is read *more* often.	.491	.328
2.	Liking of newspaper news	As liking of newspaper news *increases*, the newspaper is read *more* often.	.485	.165
3.	Age	*Older* youth read newspapers *more* often.	.342	.161
4.	Talk about newspaper	As the newspaper is discussed *more frequently* with friends and parents, the newspaper is read *more* often.	.382	.129
5.	Reading the newspaper for news	Those who read the newspaper *for news* read *more* often.	.434	.106
6.	Magazine reading	As *more* magazines are read, the newspaper is read *more* often.	.280	.101
7.	Newspaper subscription	Those who have a newspaper delivered to the home read *more* often.	.268	.096
8.	Household size	As household size *increases*, frequency of reading the newspaper *decreases*.	−.075	−.089
9.	Radio listening	As time spent listening to radio *increases*, the newspaper is read *more* often.	.250	.067
10.	Perceived reality of Anglos	As Anglos on TV are perceived to be *more* true to life, the newspaper is read *more* often.	.080	.060

$R^2 = 47\%$

*Other Significant Variables***

1.	Mexican cultural identity	Hispanics who select the self-referent *Mexican* read the paper *less* often.	.087	——
2.	Grades	Those who receive *better* grade in school read the newspaper *more* often.	.101	——

†All standardized betas and simple correlations are significant ($p \leq .05$).

**Variables identified here meet the multiple regression analyses inclusion criteria in a preliminary solution, but failed to do so in the final solution.

people living in the household is relatively small, the newspaper is discussed with parents and friends, and the newspaper is delivered to the home. Another cluster of strong correlates of newspaper readership reflect a news orientation: liking hard news content and reading the newspaper to seek news. Magazine reading and radio listening are other media-use variables that increase with newspaper reading.

Demographic correlates suggest that older youth and those who receive better grades in school read more frequently, while youngsters from larger household and Hispanics selecting the self-referent *Mexican* read less often. It is important to note that neither the analysis of variance results nor the multiple regression solution identify an overall ethnicity difference in newspaper reading between Hispanics and Anglos. The *Mexican* versus *non-Mexican* difference is within Hispanics only. Overall, Anglo/Hispanic newspaper reading frequency is equivalent for these young people.

The multiple regression analysis reported in Table 5.4 accounted for 31 percent of the variance in amount of time spent reading the newspaper. The three largest predictors (greater number of other newspaper readers in the household, more discussing the newspaper with friends and family, the more liking newspaper news) are also the three largest predictors of frequency of newspaper readership. The remainder of the time-reading correlates are unique to this solution. A local information and advice-seeking orientation to media accompanies greater time spent reading the newspaper; the news-seeking gratification is not significant. Talking about newspapers, talking about TV, and watching TV for advice are all related to newspaper reading time, suggesting that when those media are more relevant to a youngster's life, more time is spent with the newspaper.

The content orientation that accompanies time spent reading the newspaper is specific: Reading is clearly associated with both an overall liking for news in the newspaper and a specific liking for local information. Those who spend more time reading claim to believe the media have fewer positive portrayals of Mexican Americans. Although age was a significant variable in the analysis of variance comparison and initially emerged as a significant regression predictor, the other variables discussed here are more important overall. No ethnicity difference was detected, nor any within Hispanic self-referent distinctions.

Other Print Media Use. Table 5.5 indicates that Hispanic youth read nearly twice as many comic books (.93 in the preceding week) as Anglo youth (.48) but do not differ in frequency of reading magazines or books other than school books.

The grade differences reflect differential orientations of more mature youngsters. Comic book reading is a fifth-grade phenomenon, and general magazines are more often read in tenth grade. Substantially more non-school books are

TABLE 5.4. Predictors of time spent reading the newspaper.

Variable	Description of Relationship	Simple r	Beta
1. Newspaper readers in household	As the number of newspaper readers in the household *increases,* time spent reading the paper *increases.*	.373	.248
2. Liking newspaper news	As liking of newspaper news content *increases,* time spent reading the paper *increases.*	.381	.227
3. Talk about newspaper	As the newspaper is discussed *more frequently* with parents and friends, *more* time is spent reading the paper.	.386	.201
4. Liking local information	As liking of local information in the newspaper *increases,* time spent reading the paper *increases.*	.213	.101
5. Positive Mexican-American media image	As perceptions of positive portrayals of Mexican Americans *decrease,* time spent reading the paper *increases.*	−.029	−.093
6. Comic book reading	As *more* comic books are read, *more* time is spent reading the paper.	.105	.081
7. Talk about TV	As TV is discussed *more frequently* with parents and friends, time spent reading the newspaper *increases.*	.115	.079
8. Sex	*Males* spend *more* time reading the paper.	−.045	−.078
9. Watching TV for advice	Those who watch TV *for advice* spend *more* time reading the newspaper.	.047	.075

$R^2 = 31\%$

Other Significant Variables

1. Age	*Older* youth spend *more* time reading the newspaper	.149	——

read by fifth graders (2.0 in the last month) than by tenth graders (1.4). The source of the significant interaction of nonschool book reading was fifth-grade Anglos, whose reported reading of that material (2.3) was strikingly higher than for any other age-ethnicity subgroup.

Thirty-four percent of the variance in comic book reading is predicted by the multiple regression solution in Table 5.6. Congruent with the

TABLE 5.5. Other print media use by ethnicity and grade.

	Ethnicity			Grade		
	Hispanic	Anglo	(p)	5	10	(p)
How Many						
a. Comic books read in last week?	.93	.48	.01	1.36	.36	.01
b. Magazines read in last week?	1.53	1.70	ns	1.40	1.72	.01
c. Non-school books read in last month?*	1.64	1.62	ns	2.04	1.35	.01

*Significant interaction between ethnicity and grade.

TABLE 5.6. Predictors of number of comic books read.

Variable	Description of Relationship	Simple r	Beta
1. Age	As age *increases,* number of comic books read *decreases.*	−.362	−.255
2. Liking action comics	As liking of action comics *increases,* number of comics read *increases.*	.413	.243
3. Magazine reading	As *more* magazines are read, *more* comics are read.	.224	.187
4. Non-school book reading	As *more* non-school books are read, *more* comics are read.	.302	.122
5. Positive portrayals of Mexican Americans	As *more* positive media portrayals are perceived, *more* comics are read.	.246	.106
6. Newspaper reading time	As *more* time is spent reading the newspaper, *more* comics are read.	.105	.101
7. Speaking Spanish	As Spanish-language ability and dependence *increases,* *more* comics are read.	.187	.095
8. Grades in school	As *worse* grades are received, *more* comics are read.	−.056	−.076
9. Record/tape playing	As *more* time is spend playing records/tapes, *more,* comics are read.	.103	.075

$R^2 = 34\%$

Other Significant Variables

1. Sex	Females read *fewer* comics.	.111	——
2. Mexican cultural identity	Hispanics who select *Mexican* as a cultural self-referent read *more* comics.	.111	——

analysis of variance comparison just reported, age is the strongest predictor of number of comic books read; younger children read more. Further, an overall reading orientation emerges in a cluster of positive relationships, including magazine reading, non-school book reading, and time spent reading the newspaper. Record/tape playing, more frequently done by older children, is nonetheless a significant predictor of comic books read.

Dependence on and ability to speak Spanish is a better predictor of comic book reading than the Hispanic-Anglo distinction, which is not a significant predictor. Selecting *Mexican* as a self-referent among Hispanics was significant early in the analysis, but did not meet the minimum statistical significance level in the final solution.

Those who receive poorer grades in school read more comics, and females read fewer comics, although gender also did not remain in the final set of best predictors.

Twenty-five percent of the variance in number of magazines read is accounted for by the variables in Table 5.7. Multiple reading behaviors are strongly related to magazine reading. Non-school book reading, comic book reading, newspaper reading, and parental encouragement of reading all significantly predict number of magazines read. Older youths, females, and those from smaller households read more magazines overall. Those who prefer sports and car magazines also read more magazines.

TABLE 5.7. Predictors of number of magazines read.

Variable	Description of Relationship	Simple r	Beta
1. Book reading	As *more* non-school books are read, *more* magazines are read.	.311	.251
2. Comic book reading	As *more* comic books are read, *more* magazines are read.	.224	.196
3. Age	*Older* youth read *more* magazines.	.123	.178
4. Liking recreation magazines	As liking of car and sports magazines *increases, more* magazines are read.	.199	.168
5. Newspaper reading frequency	As frequency of reading the newspaper *increases, more* magazines are read.	.280	.156
6. Household size	As household size *increases,* number of magazines read *decreases.*	−.094	−.111
7. Sex	*Females* read *more* magazines.	−.014	.088
8. Parental encouragement of reading	As parents make *more* suggestions of articles to read in newspapers and magazines, *more* magazines are read.	.221	.087

$R^2 = 25\%$

The significant predictors of number of non-school books read could account for only 20 percent of the variance in that media behavior and are reported in Table 5.8. Consistent with the other multiple regression analyses of print media variables, magazine and comic book reading are significant positive correlates of this book reading. Movie-going, another medium that requires active personal and financial participation, is also related. Younger respondents, females, and those reporting better grades at school read more non-school books.

TABLE 5.8. Predictors of number of non-school books read.

Variable	Description of Relationship	Simple r	Beta
1. Magazine reading	As *more* magazines are read, *more* non-school books are read.	.311	.279
2. Comic book reading	As *more* comic books are read, *more* non-school books are read.	.302	.182
3. Age	*Younger* youth read *more* non-school books.	−.207	−.173
4. Sex	*Females* read *more* non-school books.	.069	.089
5. Movie-going	As movie-going *increases,* number of non-school books read *increases.*	.139	.088
6. Grades	As *better* grades are received at school, *more* non-school books are read.	.083	.076

$R^2 = 20\%$

Television Viewing. Table 5.9 presents the two measures of television viewing time. The upper half of the table reflects results from the youngsters' estimates of how many hours they said they usually watched television in different time periods. The lower half of the table was created from the respondents' circlings of shows they watched "yesterday," as identified in the local newspaper's television log listing. Possible "yesterdays" were Monday through Thursday in the different sites.

The *estimated hours* in the upper half of Table 5.9 reflect consistent differences between Hispanic and Anglo youth, with the Hispanic youngsters persistently reporting that they watch more television—before school, after school before supper, and after supper before bed. Hispanics estimated watching an hour more of television per day than Anglos, with absolute levels at 5 hours per day for Hispanics compared to 4 hours for Anglo youth. That pattern continues on Saturday as well. For both Saturday morning and Saturday afternoon, Hispanics estimate more viewing, with an additional Saturday hour.

Even larger than this ethnic difference is the grade difference. The

TABLE 5.9. Television viewing time by ethnicity and grade.

		Ethnicity			Grade		
		Hispanic	*Anglo*	*(p)*	*5*	*10*	*(p)*
Estimates							
Hours usually watching							
a.	Before school	.57	.30	.01	.74	.28	.01
b.	After school, before supper	2.06	1.65	.01	2.37	1.59	.01
c.	After supper, before bed	2.42	2.14	.01	2.69	2.07	.01
	Total†	5,03	4.09	.01	5.80	3.94	.01
Hours usually watching Saturday							
d.	Saturday morning	2.07	1.52	.01	2.53	1.42	.01
e.	Saturday afternoon	1.76	1.30	.01	1.69	1.53	ns
Logs							
Minutes watched "yesterday"**							
f.	Before noon	39.73	23.24	.03	48.40	14.73	.01
g.	Between noon and 5:30	79.44	68.29	ns	96.08	49.75	.01
h.	From 5:30 on	152.33	138.67	ns	188.25	112.82	.01
i.	*Total:*	280.29	237.29	ns	330.22	182.18	.01
j.	Prime-time only††	86.53	78.58	ns	98.77	70.83	.01

†Totals are based only on those respondents who answered all measures being summed, and thus may differ slightly from the sum of the internal means.

**Respondents were given logs of the previous day's (weekdays only) television schedule and were asked to circle the programs they actually watched. Data collection complications led to some respondents receiving partial or no logs, resulting in lower Ns for this variable set. Ns were as follows: f = 444, g = 444, h = 569, i = 443, j = 569.

††Prime time is 8 to 11 P.M. in the California sites and 7 to 10 P.M. in Tucson and Santa Fe.

fifth graders watch more during every weekday time period studied. The fifth graders estimated nearly 6 hours of weekday television viewing as their usual pattern, compared to 4 hours for tenth graders. Fifth graders also report an added hour of Saturday cartoon watching.

In the bottom half of Table 5.9, where logs were used, most of the viewing differences between Hispanic and Anglo youth were reduced. The only significant ethnicity difference using the log method is for weekday morning watching. Average weekday viewing for Hispanic youth is 40 minutes greater than for Anglo youngsters. Comparing the total daily viewing time obtained by these two methods, the Hispanic youngsters' totals were somewhat more discrepant than the Anglos'. Estimating their usual watching resulted in a 5-hour daily average; using logs to identify yesterday's viewing resulted in 4.7 hours of viewing. By both methods, the Anglo youngsters average 4 hours of viewing.

The possibility of cultural differences in giving time estimates should be explored in future studies.

The differences between fifth and tenth graders persists using the program log identification procedure. The fifth graders watched significantly more during every time block comparison made. The fifth graders estimated and logged 6 hours of viewing on the average; tenth graders estimated 4 hours of normal viewing but log an average of 3 hours' television viewing "yesterday."

In general, the log procedure yielded somewhat lower viewing times than did sheer estimation questions. Had we asked only for estimated viewing, the unambiguous conclusion would be that the Hispanics watch far more television on weekdays and weekends than Anglos. Such a conclusion is more ambiguous in light of the log procedure results.

For estimated time spent watching TV on a school day, 39 percent of the variance is predicted by the multiple regression results in Table 5.10. Younger respondents, Hispanics, and especially self-identified *Mexicans* estimate that they watch the most television. Six of the remaining eight predictors are TV variables: having one's own TV, having fewer parental rules (both of which yield greater opportunity to watch), talking about TV with family and friends, watching for diversion, watching for social learning, and liking family and comedy TV shows. Watching TV for news and watching TV for advice do not predict total time spent watching. News-seeking from newspapers is negatively related, suggesting a lesser overall news orientation among heavy viewers.

It is important to note that television is largely independent of other media use behaviors. Record/tape playing is the only media use variable positively related to television watching, and TV time itself does not significantly predict time spent with any other mass medium.

The multiple regression solution in Table 5.11 accounts for 43 percent of the variance in frequency of viewing Spanish TV shows. Hispanics watched more often than Anglos. Linguistic ability is highly related: Those who have greater dependence on and ability to speak and read Spanish watch more frequently. Among Hispanics, those selecting the self-referent *Mexican* watch more often, as do those wanting more newspaper stories about Mexico and Latin America.

Liking Spanish-language TV shows is not a significant predictor of Spanish-TV viewing. However, co-viewing TV with parents is significant, suggesting that watching Spanish television because others are doing so occurs more often than watching as a preferred content choice. Watching TV to seek diversion, social learning, and advice all predict Spanish-TV viewing; news-seeking from TV does not. Those watching more Spanish TV shows perceive more positive media portrayals of Mexican Americans. In larger households, there is more watching of Spanish shows, but this variable did not remain in the final analytic solution.

TABLE 5.10. Predictors of time spent watching television.

Variable	Description of Relationship	Simple r	Beta
1. Age	*Younger* youth spend *more* time watching TV.	−.386	−.259
2. Liking family and comedy shows	As liking of family and comedy shows *increases,* time spent watching TV *increases.*	.400	.204
3. Watching TV for diversion	Those who watch TV for *diversion* watch *more* TV.	.392	.159
4. Talk about TV	Those who talk *more* about TV with friends and parents spend *more* time watching TV.	.377	.146
5. Parental TV rules	Those with *fewer* parental TV rules spend *more* time watching TV.	.092	−.127
6. Ethnicity	*Hispanics* spend *more* time watching TV.	−.196	−.125
7. Watching TV for social learning	Those who watch TV for *social learning* spend *more* time watching TV.	.293	.102
8. Having own TV	Those having their *own TV* watch *more.*	.216	.100
9. Reading the newspaper for news	Those who read the newspaper for *news* watch *less* TV.	−.127	−.085
10. Mexican cultural identity	Hispanics selecting the self-referent *Mexican* watch *more* TV.	.074	.077
11. Record/tape playing	As *more* time is spent playing records/tapes, *more* time is spent watching TV.	.108	.064

$R^2 = 39\%$

Other Significant Variables

1. Grades	As *worse* grades are received in school, *more* TV is watched.	−.044	——

Table 5.12 reflects our assessment of television usage in asking the youngsters how often they watched five types of programs. Hispanic youngsters report significantly more viewing of each program type. Specifically they watch Saturday cartoons, soap operas, network news, local news, and game shows more frequently. Most-viewed program types for both ethnic subgroups are Saturday cartoons and local news programs.

Fifth graders are more likely to watch Saturday cartoons, soap

TABLE 5.11. Predictors of viewing Spanish television shows.

Variable	Description of Relationship	Simple r	Beta
1. Desire for newspaper stories about Mexico and Latin America	As desire for newspaper stories about mexico and Latin America *increases,* Spanish TV shows are watched *more* frequently.	.462	.207
2. Spanish-reading ability and dependence	As Spanish-language reading ability and dependence *increases, more* Spanish TV shows are watched.	.497	.170
3. Mexican cultural identity	Hispanics selecting *Mexican* as a self-referent watch *more* Spanish TV shows.	.344	.170
4. Spanish-speaking ability and dependence	As Spanish-language speaking ability and dependence *increase, more* Spanish shows are seen.	.522	.162
5. Ethnicity	*Hispanics* watch *more* Spanish TV shows than Anglos.	.390	.108
6. Positive image of Mexican Americans	As *more* positive portrayals of Mexican Americans are perceived, *more* Spanish shows are watched.	.301	.101
7. Watching TV social learning	Those who watch TV for *social learning* watch *fewer* Spanish shows.	.010	−.080
8. Watching TV for diversion	Those who watch TV for *diversion* watch *more* Spanish shows.	.135	.078
9. Watching TV for advice	Those who watch TV for *advice* watch *more* Spanish shows.	.208	.075
10. Co-viewing TV with parents	Those who watch *more* TV with parents watch *more* Spanish shows.	.066	.065

$R^2 = 43\%$

Other Significant Variables

1. Household size	As household size *increases, more* Spanish shows are watched.	.300	——

operas, network news, and game shows. Only local news does not differ between the age groups. The significant interaction for Saturday cartoons stem from conspicuously low viewing by tenth-grade Anglos. Fifth-grade Hispanics and Anglos view Saturday cartoons equivalently.

TABLE 5.12. Frequency of viewing types of television shows by ethnicity and grade.

		Ethnicity			Grade		
		Hispanic	Anglo	(p)	5	10	!p)
a.	Saturday cartoons?*†	2.89	2.44	.01	3.50	2.20	.01
b.	Soap operas?**	1.74	1.56	.03	1.80	1.60	.02
c.	Network news?	1.89	1.70	.02	1.93	1.74	.02
d.	Local news?	2.61	2.42	.01	2.49	2.57	ns
e.	Game shows?	2.38	2.12	.01	2.79	1.95	.01

*Significant interaction between ethnicity and grade.

†Response categories and values: 4 = Every Saturday, 3 = 2 to 3 Saturdays/month, 2 = About 1 Saturday/month, 1 = Less or never.

**Response categories and values for items b through e: 4 = 5 days/week, 3 = 3 to 4 days, 2 = 1 to 2 days, 1 = Less or never.

Radio, Record and Movie Use. Table 5.13 identifies exposure to radio, records/tapes, and movies. For radio, the Hispanic and Anglo youth are the same. They both listen somewhat more than 2 hours a day to radio; they listened to news, music and sports with equal regularity.

TABLE 5.13. Radio, record, and movie use by ethnicity and grade.

		Ethnicity			Grade		
		Hispanic	Anglo	(p)	5	10	(p)
Radio							
a.	How many hours listen on an average school day?	2.20	2.33	ns	1.51	2.75	.01
b.	Listen to news yesterday? (percent yes)	40%	45%	ns	27%	52%	.01
c.	Listen to music yesterday?	90%	87%	ns	80%	95%	.01
d.	Listen to sports yesterday?	10%	14%	ns	11%	12%	ns
Records/tapes							
e.	How many hours play records/tapes on an average school day?	1.42	1.17	.01	1.21	1.44	.03
f.	How many records/ tapes bought in last month?*	2.03	1.42	.01	2.21	1.54	.01
Movies							
g.	How many seen (in theatres only) in last month?	1.43	1.39	ns	1.39	1.44	ns

*Significant interaction between ethnicity and grade.

Tenth graders are far more likely to be oriented to radio than fifth graders. They listen nearly 3 hours a day and are more often consumers of news and music.

The significant predictors of time spent listening to radio reported in Table 5.14 account for 34 percent of the variance in that media behavior. A youngster's access to his or her own radio is an important predictor of time spent listening. Playing records and tapes strongly correlated with the amount of time spent with radio. A content preference for soul and disco music (particularly high among Hispanics) also positively related to time spent with radio. Those who read the paper more frequently spend more time listening to radio and read less often to seek diversion.

Older children and females tend to listen more. Hispanics selecting *Mexican* as a self-referent listen less.

Hispanic youngsters play records more regularly (1.4 hours per day compared to 1.2) and buy them more frequently (2 per month versus 1.4). Tenth graders play records more regularly but Hispanic fifth graders buy substantially more records (2.6 per month) than any other subgroup, accounting for the significant interaction and the grade difference.

TABLE 5.14. Predictors of time spent listening to radio.

Variable	Description of Relationship	Simple r	Beta
1. Record/tape playing	As more time is spent playing records/tapes, *more* time is spent listening to radio.	.440	.355
2. Age	*Older* youth spend *more* time listening to radio.	.341	.224
3. Having own radio	Those having their *own radio* spend *more* time listening to radio.	.304	.134
4. Liking soul and disco music	As liking for soul and disco music *increases,* time spent listening to radio *increases.*	.135	.104
5. Newspaper reading frequency	As the newspaper is read *more* often, *more* time is spent listening to radio.	.250	.100
6. Sex	*Females* spend *more* time listening to radio.	.124	.094
7. Reading the newspaper for diversion	Those who read the newspaper for *diversion* spend *less* time listening to the radio.	−.162	−.085

$R^2 = 34\%$

Other Significant Variables

1. Mexican cultural identity	Hispanics choosing the ethnic self-referent *Mexican* spend *less* time listening to radio.	−.110	——

The multiple regression equation presented in Table 5.15 accounts for 36 percent of the variance in record/tape playing. Radio listening and record/tape playing are strongly related behaviors. As with radio listening, there is a distinct access dimension. Both ownership of more record/tape players and buying more records/tapes by youngsters are firmly associated with more time spent playing them. As with radio, preference for soul and disco music predicts more time spent with the medium. Magazine reading is also positively related to this media behavior. Among Hispanics, those selecting the self-referent *Chicano* play more record/tapes than those who select *Mexican American* or *Spanish American*. Unlike radio listening, ethnicity (Hispanic versus Anglo) emerged as a significant predictor early in the regression process, although it was dropped. Poorer school grades are also associated with more record/tape playing time.

TABLE 5.15. Predictors of time spent playing records/tapes.

Variable	Description of Relationship	Simple r	Beta
1. Radio listening	As *more* time is spent listening to radio, *more* time is spent playing records/tapes.	.440	.352
2. Record buying	As *more* records/tapes are purchased, *more* time is spent playing records/tapes.	.403	.302
3. Record/tape player ownership	As *more* record/tape players are owned, *more* time is spent playing records/tapes.	.281	.111
4. Chicano cultural identity	Hispanics who select *Chicano* as their cultural self-referent spend *more* time playing records/tapes than those who choose *Spanish American* or *Mexican American*.	.153	.092
5. Like soul and disco records	As liking of soul and disco records *increases, more* time is spent playing records/tapes.	.202	.088
6. Grades	As *worse* grades are received in school, *more* time is spent playing records/tapes.	−.138	−.073
7. Magazine reading	As *more* magazines are read, *more* time is spent listening to records/tapes.		.072

$R^2 = 36\%$

Other Significant Variables

1. Ethnicity	*Hispanics* spend *more* time playing records/tapes.	−.093	——

Movie going is not different by either ethnicity or grade, with an average of 1.4 movies seen per month. Only 10 percent of the variance in movie going was accounted for by the multiple regression solution, insufficient to report in detail.

Content Preferences

Newspaper Preferences. Table 5.16 reports newspaper content preferences. That table serves as a prototype for the other media content preference tables. The youngsters were asked how often they look at 14 different newspaper content categories and were given the response categories of *Never,*

TABLE 5.16. Newspaper content preferences by ethnicity and grade.

	Ethnicity			Grade		
	Hispanic	*Anglo*	*(p)*	*5*	*10*	*(p)*
How Often Look in						
Newspaper at†						
a. Comics and cartoons?*	1.42	1.42	ns	1.49	1.37	.02
b. Sports?	1.07	1.11	ns	.86	1.24	.01
c. Weather?	.87	.79	ns	.69	.93	.01
d. Headlines?	1.12	1.31	.01	.88	1.39	.01
e. Advertising?	.87	.75	.01	.64	.94	.01
f. Front page news?	1.25	1.32	ns	.96	1.48	.01
g. News inside paper?	1.02	1.06	ns	.84	1.16	.01
h. Photos?	1.29	1.31	ns	1.19	1.37	.01
i. TV section?	1.27	1.00	.01	1.26	1.10	.02
j. Advice columns?	.74	.77	ns	.69	.80	ns
k. Crime stories?	1.11	.88	.01	1.04	1.02	ns
l. Stories about Mexico and Latin America?	.67	.16	.01	.48	.48	ns
m. Stories about young people?	1.00	.93	ns	.81	1.08	.01
n. Things to do in town?	1.01	.92	.03	.82	1.09	.01
*Factors***						
I. *News* (f, d, g, h)	1.17	1.25	.02	.97	1.37	.01
II. *Local information* (m, n, k, e,)	.90	.84	.01	.73	.98	.01
III. *Features* (i, a)	1.35	1.21	.01	1.34	1.24	.01

*Significant interaction between ethnicity and grade.

†Response categories and values: 0 = *Never,* 1 = *Sometimes,* 2 = *Always.*

**Letters in parentheses indicate which of the variables in the table loaded .4 or higher on the factor and are ordered by strength of the factor loading scores. A negative sign (−) preceding any variable in a factor subset indicates a negative loading for that variable; this notation will be so used for all relevant tables presenting factors. Factor score ethnicity differences are computed using factor score coefficient indices. The significant levels reflect those computations. However, the mean scores reported in these tables are recalculated using raw scores to facilitate interpretations in reference to the same response categories as the other items in each set.

Sometimes, Always. The top half of Table 5.16 reports their responses to the individual newspaper content items. The lower half of the table presents newspaper content preference factors that emerged from the factor analysis of the individual items, identifying which items clustered together. Each factor has been given a label that reflects the common elements of the items grouped on that factor. For example, the *News* factor in Table 5.16 is dominated by the individual content items of front-page news, headlines, news inside the paper, and news photographs. This news emphasis was interpreted to be the common factor of these individual items, suggesting the factor label.

In order to provide some parsimony in this results section, we will report primarily the factor results, permitting the reader to inspect the individual content preference category listings for additional information. The results indicate that the Anglo youth are significantly more likely to look at that subset of *News* content items than are Hispanic youngsters. In contrast, frequency of reading what we have called *local information* items, including stories about young people and things to do in town, reflect a significantly stronger preference among Hispanic youngsters. In parallel fashion, Hispanic youngsters are more likely to read material categorized under *Features,* including the television section of the newspaper and the comics and cartoons.

Best-read sections of the newspaper, regardless of ethnicity or age are comics and cartoons, the TV section, front-page news, and headlines.

The significant interaction for comics and cartoons results from Hispanic fifth graders strongly preferring that newspaper content and Hispanic tenth graders disliking it, whereas Anglos of both grades were between the two Hispanic extremes. The grade difference occurs only among Hispanics.

These factors reflect different proportions of the set of newspaper content preference items measured. The *News* factor is the dominant content preference factor. It alone accounted for 31 percent of these youngsters' newspaper content likes and dislikes, whereas the local information and features factors each summarize about 10 percent of the measured preferences.

Comic Book and Magazine Content Preferences. Table 5.17 provides content preference information for two other print media, comic books and magazines. For each of these we have provided again the individual content categories and the factors that identify groups of specific content preferences. Two basic comic book factors emerged from this analysis. One is *Action,* focusing on war and superhero comics. Hispanics more strongly preferred this type of comic book. The second comic book factor was labeled *Romance/humor,* reflecting its basic ingredients. Again, there is a stronger preference for this among Hispanics than Anglos. Basically, every comic book type was more preferred by the Hispanic youngsters. By age, fifth graders like every type of comic book more than do tenth graders, with the exception of love stories. Among both ethnicities and grades, funny comics were most preferred, followed by horror comics.

TABLE 5.17. Comic book and magazine content preferences by ethnicity and grade.

	Ethnicity			Grade		
	Hispanic	*Anglo*	*(p)*	*5*	*10*	*(p)*
How Much Like to Read†						
Comic book types						
a. Love story comics?	1.17	.79	.01	1.06	1.01	ns
b. Horror stories?	1.73	1.26	.01	2.14	1.16	.01
c. Superhero comics?	1.46	1.11	.01	1.99	.89	.01
d. War comics?	1.17	.82	.01	1.48	.74	.01
e. Funny comics?	2.28	1.84	.01	2.55	1.82	.01
Comic Book Factors:						
I. *Action* (c, d, b)	1.66	1.25	.01	1.99	1.21	.01
II. *Romance/Humor*						
(a, e, b)	1.73	1.29	.01	1.85	1.34	.01
How Much Like to Read†						
Magazine types						
a. News magazines?	.96	.81	.01	.73	1.02	.01
b. Sports magazines?	1.54	1.40	ns	1.50	1.47	ns
c. Magazines about cars?	1.71	1.27	.01	1.69	1.45	.02
d. Fashion magazines?	1.41	1.34	ns	1.31	1.43	ns
e. Children's magazines?	1.09	.64	.01	1.62	.46	.01
f. TV and movie star						
magazines?	1.97	1.59	.01	2.22	1.57	.01
g. Music magazines?	1.62	1.49	ns	1.47	1.64	.04
Magazine Factors						
I. *Pop culture*						
(f, d, e, g,)	1.52	1.26	.01	1.59	1.21	.01
II. *Recreation* (b, c)	1.62	1.34	.01	1.62	1.48	ns

†Response categories and values: 0 = *Not at all*, 1 = *Not very much*, 2 = *Quite a bit*, 3 = *Very much*.

The *Action comics* factor accounted for 51 percent of the comic book preference variance and the *Romance/humor* factor accounted for 21 percent.

Looking at magazine content preferences, the lower half of Table 5.17 isolates two basic content preference factors. One of these, *Pop culture*, reflects a preference for television and movie star content, fashion magazines, and music. The second reflects sports and car interests; we have called that *Recreation*. Both are more strongly preferred by Hispanic youngsters than by Anglo youngsters. The pop culture preference was also manifested more among fifth graders than tenth graders, with no age difference for the second factor. Each factor accounted for 25 to 30 percent of the variance. News magazines are among the least preferred magazine types and did not fit on either of the factors. The data show that Hispanic youngsters have a stronger preference for news magazines than do Anglo youngsters, as do tenth graders in contrast to fifth graders.

Television Content Preferences. Sixteen categories of television content were assessed in the questionnaire and are itemized in Table 5.18. For 10 of these, there are significant ethnicity differences and for nine of them, that difference is in the direction of stronger content preferences among Hispanics. Hispanics more strongly prefer soap operas, cartoons, game shows, local news, movies, police and detective shows, shows like "Sesame Street" and "Villa Alegre," shows with singing and dancing, and shows in Spanish. The single stronger preference among Anglo youth was for comedies. Preferred above all other show types on an absolute basis by both Anglo and Hispanic youngsters are TV movies and comedies. The significant interaction for movies on television locates the strongest difference between Hispanic and Anglo fifth graders, with Hispanics more strongly preferring TV movies. Hispanic preference for movies decreases slightly in tenth grade, and Anglo tenth-grader preference increased substantially from fifth-grade levels.

These individual content preference differences did not manifest themselves in the factor results noted at the bottom of Table 5.18. The only factor that yielded ethnicity differences is a greater preference for shows containing Spanish-language content among Hispanic youngsters. In essence, then, English-language television content factors consistently differentiating preferences between Anglo and Hispanic youth were not found; the individual rather than the collective content types yield those distinctions.

In contrast to the ethnicity results, the age groups show differences on all four of the identified factors. The younger children express greater preference for content types reflected on the *Sports* factor, the *Entertainment* factor, and the *Spanish-language content* factor. The tenth graders have a larger preference for news programming. *Sports* and *Entertainment* factors accounted for 15 to 20 percent of the variance; and *Spanish* and *News* factors accounted for 8 to 10 percent.

Radio Music Content Preferences. The youngsters were asked how much they liked to listen to eight different kinds of music. These factored into the three basic types, identified in Table 5.19. The emergent factors include *Spanish-language music,* soul and disco or *Black music,* and the *Top 40* sound. The Anglo youngsters express a significantly greater preference for Top 40. Hispanic youngsters report relatively stronger preferences for the other two music factor types. The *Spanish music* factor accounted for 27 percent of the variance, with the other two factors accounting for 15 to 17 percent. The significant interaction between ethnicity and grade for Black music reflects minimal liking for both soul and disco music by the tenth grade Anglo youngsters in this study; disco is the primary choice among Hispanics. The significant grade-ethnicity interaction for *Rock in Spanish* was due to the large drop in preference among Hispanics from fifth to tenth grade. Anglo preference was minimal in both grades. For *Rock,* a strong ethnic difference emerged between Hispanic and

TABLE 5.18. Television content preferences by ethnicity and grade.

	Ethnicity			Grade		
	Hispanic	Anglo	(p)	5	10	(p)
How Much Like to Watch†						
a. Soap operas?	1.20	.97	.01	1.04	1.16	ns
b. Cartoons?	2.05	1.68	.01	2.47	1.54	.01
c. Game shows?	1.58	1.38	.03	1.77	1.32	.01
d. Local news?	1.45	1.28	.01	1.20	1.51	.01
e. Comedies?	2.31	2.43	.03	2.40	2.32	ns
f. Movies?*	2.51	2.33	.01	2.44	2.45	ns
g. Police/detective shows?	2.06	1.71	.01	2.06	1.84	.01
h. Shows like "Sesame Street"?	.71	.27	.01	.86	.34	.01
i. Shows with singing, dancing?	1.56	1.28	.01	1.62	1.35	.01
j. Network news?	1.20	1.11	ns	1.05	1.24	.01
k. Shows in Spanish?	1.12	.11	.01	.89	.65	.04
l. Shows about families?	1.81	1.72	ns	1.90	1.70	.01
m. Baseball&	1.39	1.21	ns	1.56	1.16	.01
n. Shows like "60 Minutes"?	1.43	1.46	ns	1.31	1.53	.01
o. Sports?	1.83	1.83	ns	1.86	1.81	ns
p. Soccer?	.85	.71	ns	1.01	.66	.01
Factors						
I. *Sports* (o, m, p, a)	1.35	1.25	ns	1.50	1.26	.01
II. *News* (d, j, n)	1.36	1.30	ns	1.22	1.48	.01
III. *Spanish* (k, h)	.91	.19	.01	.79	.46	.01
IV *Entertainment* (l, 3)	2.06	2.08	ns	2.13	2.03	.01

*Significant interaction between ethnicity and grade.

†Response categories and values: o = *Not at all,* 1 = *Not very much,* 2 = *Quite a bit,* 3 = *Very much.*

Anglo tenth graders, with Hispanics lower than the relatively homogeneous fifth graders and Anglos higher in preference level.

Greater preference for listening to Spanish music exists among fifth graders than among tenth, with no difference for the other two music factors.

Record/Tape Music Preferences. The music categories used for this more personal medium are identical to those asked about for radio except that Top 40 was excluded. Table 5.20 parallels the radio music results. First, note that the two primary factors, *Spanish music* and *Black music* are the same as for radio preferences. Further, ethnicity differences are the same; the Hispanic youth show an orientation toward both Spanish and Black music whereas the Anglo youngsters express greater rejection of both. The same interaction was found with regard to Black music on records, with the tenth-grade Anglos showing a very

TABLE 5.19. Radio music content references by ethnicity and grade.

	Ethnicity			Grade		
	Hispanic	Anglo	(p)	5	10	(p)
How Much Like to Listen to†						
a. Rock?*	1.75	2.29	.01	1.94	1.97	ns
b. Top 40?	1.83	1.95	ns	1.91	1.85	ns
c. Classical?	.62	.52	ns	.66	.53	ns
d. Soul?*	1.34	.77	.01	1.02	1.20	.01
e. Country and Western?	.84	1.29	.01	1.15	.92	.01
f. Rock in Spanish?*	.90	.06	.01	.77	.47	.01
g. "Musica Ranchera"?	.84	.09	.01	.67	.50	ns
h. Disco?*	2.18	1.26	.01	2.29	1.54	.01
Factors						
I. *Spanish* (g, f)	.87	.07	.01	.65	.43	.01
II. *Black* (d, h)*	1.76	1.02	.01	1.66	1.38	ns
III. *Top 40* (b, a)	1.79	2.12	.01	1.95	1.89	ns

*Significant interaction between ethnicity and grade.

†Response categories and values: 0 = *Not at all*, 1 = *Not very much*, 2 = *Quite a bit*, 3 = *Very much*.

substantial rejection of that music. The Anglo preference for rock is significantly larger than among Hispanics. There is also a significantly greater preference for country and western music among the Anglos. For all other music types, there is greater preference among the Hispanic youth.

Table 5.20 shows four significant interactions between ethnicity and grade. Each is a function of more extreme responses from the tenth grade

TABLE 5.20. Records/tapes content preferences by ethnicity and grade.

	Ethnicity			Grade		
	Hispanic	Anglo	(p)	5	10	(p)
How Much Like to Play†						
a. Rock?*	1.80	2.33	.01	2.00	2.00	ns
b. Disco?*	2.30	1.42	.01	2.50	1.63	.01
c. Classical?*	.67	.48	.01	.72	.52	.01
d. Soul?*	1.38	.64	.01	1.09	1.12	ns
e. Country and western?	.84	1.17	.01	1.10	.87	.01
f. Rock in Spanish?	.86	.10	.01	.73	.48	.01
g. "Musica Ranchera"?	.85	.08	.01	.66	.50	ns
Factors						
I. *Spanish* (f, g)	.85	.09	.01	.61	.43	.02
II. *Black* (d, b)*	1.84	1.02	.01	1.77	1.37	ns
III. *Classical/Country, and western* (c, e)	.75	.83	ns	.91	.72	.01

*Significant interaction between ethnicity and grade.

†Response categories and values: 0 = *Not at all*, 1 = *Not very much*, 2 = *Quite a bit*, 3 = *Very much*.

Anglos. They showed stronger preferences for rock and much weaker preferences for disco, classical music, and soul than the other subgroups, which generally are more comparable to each other. The primary Anglo preference is for rock; it is disco for Hispanics.

Differences in music preference between fifth and tenth graders are also a function of higher preferences by fifth graders for Spanish-language music, classical, and country and western music. Tenth graders have no preferences stronger than their younger counterparts. The *Spanish-language music* factor accounts for 32 percent of the variance; the other two factors range from 15 to 18 percent.

Movie Content Preferences. Table 5.21 shows that both ethnic groups have similar preferences for *Adventure* type movies, including war movies, science-fiction movies, westerns, and detectives. There is a stronger orientation among Hispanic youngsters for movies about romance and of course for movies in Spanish. Anglos report a stronger absolute preference for comedy movies, although comedies were ranked the most preferred movie type by both groups. Liking Spanish-language movies correlated negatively with liking comedies.

The tenth graders are the romantics in movie content preferences, whereas the younger respondents show more orientation toward both adventure and Spanish-language films. Preference for comedies is stronger among tenth

TABLE 5.21. Movie content preferences by ethnicity and grade.

	Ethnicity			Grade		
	Hispanic	*Anglo*	*(p)*	*5*	*10*	*(p)*
How Much Like to Watch†						
a. Horror movies?	2.32	2.16	.05	2.41	2.16	.01
b. Comedy movies?*	2.41	2.56	.01	2.38	2.52	.02
c. Love stories?	1.72	1.64	ns	1.42	1.87	.01
d. Westerns?	1.45	1.50	ns	1.53	1.43	ns
e. War movies?	1.56	1.42	ns	1.70	1.38	.01
f. Movies in Spanish?	1.03	.06	.01	.80	.59	ns
g. Science-fiction movies?*	1.75	1.75	ns	2.01	1.57	.01
h. Detective movies?	1.80	1.65	ns	1.92	1.63	.01
i. Animal movies?	1.59	1.59	ns	1.94	1.36	.01
Factors						
I. *Adventure* (e, g, d, h)	1.64	1.58	ns	1.78	1.54	.01
II. *Romance* (c)	1.72	1.64	.01	1.42	1.88	.01
III. *Spanish* (−b,f)	1.03	.06	.01	.72	.53	.01

*Significant interaction between ethnicity and grade.

†Response categories and values: 0 = *Not at all*, 1 = *Not very much*, 2 = *Quite a bit*, 3 = *Very much*.

graders; the significant interaction results from tenth-grade Anglos exhibiting the strongest preference. The science-fiction interaction finds Anglos having a more extreme positive preference in fifth grade and a more extreme dislike for science-fiction movies in tenth grade compared to Hispanics.

Media-Use Gratifications

Newspaper Reading Gratifications. Table 5.22 identifies why these youngsters read the newspaper in terms of their acceptance or rejection of 17 possible motivations derived from prior research. These newspaper reading gratifications were factor-analyzed and three primary factors emerged. The *News* factor is the strongest, accounting for 31 percent of the variability in these judgments. The *Diversion* factor accounted for 14 percent and the *Social Learning* factor for 6 percent of the variance. It is of primary importance to note that reading the newspaper to seek news is not different between Anglo and Hispanic youngsters either on the overall factor or on any of the major individual items comprising that factor. Hispanic and Anglo youth approach the newspaper with equivalent news-seeking motivations. Hispanics significantly exceed Anglos in their use of the newspaper for both diversion and social learning. Hispanic youngsters are more likely to say that the newspaper cheers them up, helps them forget their problems, offers some excitement, and provides some relaxation. They are also more likely than Anglo youngsters to say they use the newspaper to find out what's going on in a variety of ways. The major orientation difference in terms of newspaper gratifications is not in terms of news reliance but in terms of secondary functions of the newspaper, i.e., as a source of diversion and social learning. For both ethnic groups, the top-most gratifications sought are to know what's going on, to see what's happening in town, and to check on things heard about.

Age group differences manifest themselves heavily in the news orientation. The younger respondents tend to reject the news function and to be heavily reliant on the diversion function. Tenth graders are far more likely to use the newspaper for local news, for national news, for headlines, to know what's going on, and to find out more information. Fifth grade gratification-seeking from the newspaper is far more affective: for fun and excitement. For the significant interaction in the individual gratification "Because it's funny," the ethnic difference exists entirely among fifth graders; fifth-grade Hispanics are highest; fifth-grade Anglos are second highest; both groups exceed the tenth graders. The significant interaction "To find out more about people in town" reflects a substantially lower motivation among fifth-grade Anglos.

Television Gratifications. Table 5.23 presents results for 15 possible television watching gratifications. Factors emerging from this analysis reflect all the factors found for newspaper reading gratifications plus an *Advice* factor. *News* as a television gratification is not differentiated by ethnicity, nor is *Diver-*

TABLE 5.22. Newspaper reading gratifications by ethnicity and grade.

	Ethnicity			Grade		
	Hispanic	Anglo	(p)	5	10	(p)
I Read the Newspaper†						
a. To know what's going on	1.31	1.22	.03	1.11	1.39	.01
b. Because it's funny*	.74	.57	.02	.97	.48	.01
c. To learn to do new things	.98	.74	.01	.97	.83	.04
d. Because it excites me	.72	.54	.01	.87	.52	.01
e. Because it relaxes me	.78	.57	.01	.71	.70	ns
f. Because it cheers me up	.56	.36	.01	.62	.39	.01
g. To forget my problems	.55	.36	.01	.74	.31	.01
h. To look at pictures	.88	.76	ns	1.03	.71	.01
i. For the local news	.87	.93	ns	.60	1.09	.01
j. For the national news	.68	.78	ns	.55	.83	.01
k. To get advice on problems	.58	.47	ns	.64	.48	.01
l. To find out about new places and people	1.01	.78	.01	.92	.92	ns
m. To get the headlines	.92	.97	ns	.76	1.06	.01
n. To find out more about things I heard about	1.25	1.32	ns	1.13	1.37	.01
o. To find out what's happening to people in town*	1.24	1.04	.01	1.02	1.26	.01
p. Because it gives me things to talk about	.87	.59	.01	.92	.67	.01
q. I don't read because it's boring	.59	.46	ns	.71	.42	.01
Factors						
I. *News* (i, j, m, a, n)	1.00	1.05	ns	.84	1.16	.01
II. *Diversion* (f, g, d, b, k, e, p, h)	.67	.51	.01	.76	.51	.01
III *Social learning* (l, o, n, a, c)	1.15	1.03	.01	1.02	1.17	ns

*Significant interaction between ethnicity and grade.

†Response categories and values ("How much is this like you?"): 0 = *Not like me*, 1 = *A little like me*, 2 = *A lot like me*.

sion. As with newspaper reading, Hispanic youth watch television more for anticipated social learning reasons than do Anglos. They are more likely to watch television because it teaches things they don't learn in school, to learn to do new things, and because it shows them how others solve problems similar to their own. This *Social learning* factor is supplemented by Hispanic youngsters' de-

TABLE 5.23. Television watching gratifications by ethnicity and grade.

	Ethnicity			Grade		
	Hispanic	*Anglo*	*(p)*	*5*	*10*	*(p)*
I Watch TV†						
a. Because it excites me	1.25	1.07	.01	1.54	.94	.01
b. To learn to do new things	.98	.68	.01	1.12	.70	.01
c. Because it relaxes me	1.38	1.32	ns	1.40	1.33	ns
d. Because it teaches things I don't learn in school	.96	.71	.01	1.05	.74	.01
e. Because it shows me how others deal with my problems	.99	.86	.05	1.00	.90	ns
f. Because everyone else does	.40	.28	.04	.44	.29	.01
g. Because it helps me know how I'm supposed to act	.51	.25	.01	.64	.26	.01
h. When I'm lonely	1.11	1.03	ns	1.32	.92	.01
i. To forget my problems	.78	.66	ns	.93	.60	.01
j. For the local news	.82	.82	ns	.67	.92	.01
k. To get advice on problems	.53	.38	.02	.66	.35	.01
l. Because it cheers me up	1.02	1.03	ns	1.26	.87	.01
m. To find out more about things I heard about	1.16	1.06	ns	1.25	1.03	.01
n. Because it gives me things to talk about	1.08	.84	.01	1.21	.84	.01
o. I don't watch because its boring	.35	.30	ns	.33	.33	ns
Factors						
I. *Diversion* (l, i, h, a, c, n)	1.10	.99	ns	1.25	.94	.01
II. *Social learning* (d, b, e)	.97	.75	.01	1.04	.80	.01
III *News* (m, j)	.99	.94	ns	.96	1.00	ns
IV. *Advice* (g, k)	.52	.32	.01	.62	.32	.01

†Response categories and values ("How much is this like you?"): 0 = *Not like me*, 1 = *A little like me*, 2 = *A lot like me*.

pending more on television for advice on problems and for learning how they are supposed to act. No television watching gratification is reported at a higher level for Anglos than for Hispanics. For both groups, television serves primarily as a relaxer and an exciter (an interesting paradox), and as a companion—all components of the *Diversion* factor.

Age differences are also reflected in the factor structure. Surprisingly, the fifth and tenth graders do not differ in terms of their news orientation to television. The fifth graders, however, report using television more for social learning purposes, for diversion, and advice. Looking through the set of individual items, all significant differences reflect greater watching gratification levels among fifth graders than tenth graders, except for watching television for local news. For that single purpose, tenth graders exceed fifth graders.

Only the *Diversion* factor is substantial, accounting for 32 percent of the variance. The other three factors range from 7 to 9 percent in their accounted-for variance.

Media Credibility

Three items in our questionnaire tapped what are summarized as the relative credibility of the different media. Results are in Table 5.24. The relative credibility of the media for Anglo and Hispanic youngsters is quite similar. There is equal belief that what is seen, heard, or read on television, radio, or in the newspaper is true. If forced to select one medium, both ethnic groups claimed

TABLE 5.24. Media credibility by ethnicity and grade.

	Ethnicity			*Grade*		
	Hispanic	*Anglo*	*(p)*	*5*	*10*	*(p)*
Forced Choice Between Media†						
a. Percentage choose TV over newspaper	89%	85%	ns	92%	85%	.01
b. Percentage choose radio over TV	59%	54%	ns	45%	66%	.01
c. Percentage choose newspaper over radio	12%	12%	ns	14%	11%	ns
*Believing One Medium over Others***						
d. Percentage believe newspaper	27%	38%	——	34%	29%	——
e. Percentage believe radio	25%	21%	——	20%	26%	——
f. Percentage believe TV	48%	41%	——	46%	45%	——
Media Credibility††						
g. Newspaper is true	1.35	1.33	ns	1.39	1.32	ns
h. TV is true	1.28	1.20	ns	1.28	1.23	ns
i. Radio is true	1.25	1.25	ns	1.32	1.21	.01

*If you had to choose between [medium] and [medium], which would you choose?"

**"If the newspaper, radio, and television all said different things about the same thing, which would you believe?"

††Response categories and values ("If you see/hear/read it in the newspaper/on TV/on radio, it's true."): 0 = *No,* 1 = *Not sure,* 2 = *Yes.*

they would choose television over the newspaper by a 9-to-1 margin. A bare majority of each claim they would choose radio over television, and radio also wins out over newspapers by a 9-to-1 margin. Hispanic and Anglo children do not differ from each other in these media judgments.

All respondents were asked, "If the newspaper, radio and television all said different things about the same thing, which would you believe?" Table 5.24 indicates that proportionately more Hispanic children claim they would believe television (48 percent versus 41 percent) and proportionately more Anglo children claim they would believe the newspaper (38 percent versus 27 percent). In other words, there is a significant relationship between ethnicity and believing one medium over another. That is the only aspect of this credibility dimension that generated a significant difference.

There are some age-group differences as well. The fifth graders are more likely to choose television over the newspaper, if they have to choose between the two, and the tenth graders are more likely to choose radio over television. Both age groups chose television and radio over newspapers by a 9-to-1 margin. When asked which medium would be most believable in a conflicting information situation, the differences were not significant.

Media Portrayal Perceptions

Perceived Reality. The respondents were asked for their assessment of how real-to-life several dimensions of television content were. The results are in Table 5.25. Eight different television content areas were assessed; for five of

TABLE 5.25. Perceived reality of television by ethnicity and grade.

	Ethnicity			Grade		
	Hispanic	*Anglo*	*(p)*	*5*	*10*	*(p)*
How Real to Life are TV†						
a. People?	1.73	1.53	.04	2.04	1.40	.01
b. Places?	1.95	1.88	ns	2.03	1.85	.01
c. Young people?	1.93	1.65	.01	2.24	1.56	.01
d. Anglos?	1.57	1.47	ns	1.59	1.49	ns
e. Mexican Americans?	1.78	1.43	.01	1.98	1.44	.01
f. Blacks?	1.85	1.61	.01	2.02	1.59	.01
g. Mexican-American families?	1.70	1.24	.01	1.78	1.38	.01
h. Anglo families?	1.56	1.44	ns	1.58	1.48	ns
Factors						
I. *Minorities* (e, g, f, c, a)*	1.80	1.50	.01	1.99	1.49	.01
II. *Anglos* (d, h, a, c)	1.74	1.55	ns	1.94	1.49	ns

*Significant interaction between ethnicity and grade.

†Response categories and values; 0 = *Not real*, 1 = *A little real*, 2 = *Quite real*, 3 = *Very real*.

those the Hispanic youth made higher perceived-reality assessments than the Anglos. These five items loaded together as a *Minority* factor. The Hispanic youths assess the portrayal of Mexican Americans, Mexican-American families, and Blacks on television as substantially more real than do the Anglo youngsters. The level of perceived reality placed the mean for Hispanic youngsters as judging that the Mexican-American portrayals were "quite real" and for Anglos as "a little real."

For the *Minority* factor portrayals, fifth graders differ significantly from tenth graders by perceiving more realism. The significant interaction reflects a substantially higher perceived reality among fifth-grade Hispanics than any other subgroup. That factor accounted for 48 percent of the variance among these items.

The groups do not differ in terms of their judgments of the second factor, *Anglo* portrayals, as individuals or in family portrayals. However, considering the relative ranking within each ethnicity, Anglos perceived portrayals of Anglo families and Anglo individuals to be more realistic than portrayals of Mexican Americans, whereas Hispanics perceived Mexican Americans and Mexican American families as more realistic. The *Anglo* factor accounted for 13 percent of the variance. Places, young people, and Blacks are perceived as most real among both Hispanics and Anglos on an absolute basis.

Perceptions of Mexican Americans. Another series of questions asked the youngsters about Mexican-American portrayals in the local newspapers, on local television news programs, and on TV shows in general. Specifically, it asked the extent to which those media portrayed Mexican Americans in positive and negative behavioral situations, that is, doing good things or bad things. The results in Table 5.26 are the same for each of the three media. The Hispanic youngsters report their belief that the local newspapers, the local television news, and television shows in general portray Mexican Americans doing more good things than are reported by the Anglo respondents. Further, there is no difference whatsoever between Hispanic and Anglo youth reports of these media portraying Mexican Americans doing bad things. The comparative perceptions of doing good and bad things is distinctly on the negative side. All mean scores for perception of portrayals of bad things exceed the mean perception of the frequency of portrayals of good things for each ethnic group.

By age group, there are equally interesting results. The fifth graders consistently perceive more positive portrayals than do the tenth graders, and the tenth graders consistently perceive more negative portrayals than do the fifth graders. The age group difference appears to be critical in that the interim years make for a very different outcome in judgments of what the media do with Mexican Americans.

The significant interaction is important in understanding the results. The locus of the positive perception of media portrayals is located almost entirely among fifth-grade Hispanic youngsters. Their positive perception of what these

TABLE 5.26. Perceived media portrayals of Mexican Americans by ethnicity and grade.

	Ethnicity			Grade		
	Hispanic	*Anglo*	*(p)*	*5*	*10*	*(p)*
How Often Do†						
Local newspapers portray						
Mexican Americans						
a. Doing good things?	1.20	1.03	.01	1.24	1.08	.01
b. Doing bad things?	1.75	1.69	ns	1.56	1.84	.01
Local TV news programs						
portray Mexican Americans						
c. Doing good things?*	1.29	1.06	.01	1.34	1.11	.01
d. Doing bad things?	1.64	1.66	ns	1.51	1.74	.01
TV shows portray						
Mexican Americans						
e. Doing good things?*	1.39	1.13	.01	1.52	1.15	.01
f. Doing bad things?	1.52	1.53	ns	1.44	1.58	.04
Factors						
I. *Negative Image* (d, b,f)	1.64	1.63	ns	1.53	1.71	.01
II. *Positive image* (c, a,e)*	1.30	1.07	.01	1.35	1.11	.01

*Significant interaction between ethnicity and grade.

†Response categories and values: 0 = *Not at all*, 1 = *Not very often*, 2 = *Quite often*, 3 = *Very often*.

media do with Mexican Americans are exceptions. The tenth-grade Hispanic perceptions are really no different from both Anglo groups.

The *Negative image* factor accounted for 33 percent of the variance and the *Positive image* factor accounted for 29 percent.

Social Interactions About Media

Table 5.27 identifies the extent to which these youngsters talk with friends and parents about television and about the newspaper. Both with individual items and with the emerging factors for both newspapers and television, there are no ethnicity differences of any consequence. By age group, fifth graders do more talking about television with both friends and parents, whereas tenth graders are more oriented to peers for newspaper discussions. Two factors emerged, *Newspaper talk* and *Television talk*. The former accounted for 50 percent of the variance and the latter accounted for only 18 percent. This does not mean that there is more talking about the newspapers. An inspection of the means in Table 5.27 indicates that television talking occurred more frequently than newspaper talking when the talking originates with the respondents. The differential strength of the factors indicates that the newspaper talk behaviors more consistently cluster together.

TABLE 5.27. Social interactions about media by ethnicity and grade.

	Ethnicity			Grade		
	Hispanic	*Anglo*	*(p)*	*5*	*10*	*(p)*
How Often Do You Talk With†						
a. Friends about TV?	2.36	2.31	ns	2.61	2.16	.01
b. A parent about TV?	2.22	2.06	ns	2.39	2.00	.01
c. Friends about newspaper?	1.80	1.73	ns	1.69	1.83	.01
d. A parent about newspaper?	1.98	1.86	.05	1.88	1.97	ns
How Often Does a Parent Talk With You						
e. About TV?	2.10	1.98	ns	2.29	1.89	.01
f. About newspaper?	2.15	2.05	ns	2.14	2.09	ns
Factors						
I. *Newspaper talk* (d, c, f)	1.96	1.86	ns	1.89	1.97	.01
II. *TV talk* (b, e, a)	2.23	2.12	ns	2.42	2.04	.01

†Response categories and values: 4 = *6 to 7 days/week*, 3 = *3 to 5 days*, 2 = *1 to 2 days*, 1 = *Less*.

Parental Mediation

Table 5.28 examines a variety of mediation strategies and policies available to parents. The individual item results indicate that Hispanic youngsters' parents guide them to watch certain shows more often and guide them to read items in the newspaper more often. There are no other mediational differences between Hispanic and Anglo youngsters.

Younger children are guided to TV shows by their parents more regularly, whereas older children are guided to newspaper and magazine items more often. There also are more television restraints on fifth graders, including the prohibition of specific shows, the overall number of rules, and the deadline for going to bed. These are reflected in the two factors *Reading* and *Television rules;* the *Co-watching* factor yield neither ethnicity or grade differences. The significant ethnicity-grade interactions for the *Television rules* factor and its strongest two items (number of shows parents won't let respondents watch and how late respondents can stay up to watch TV) reflect a crossover pattern. Hispanic fifth graders claim somewhat fewer restrictions than Anglo fifth graders. Among tenth graders the situation is reversed and the ethnicity difference is stronger, with Hipsanics experiencing more restrictions than Anglos. The *Read* factor accounts for 28 percent of the variance; *Television rules* and *Co-watching* accounted for 13 to 15 percent.

TABLE 5.28. Parental mediation of media by ethnicity and grade.

	Ethnicity			Grade		
	Hispanic	Anglo	(p)	5	10	(p)
How Often Do(es)†						
a. A parent watch TV with you?	1.75	1.74	ns	1.77	1.73	ns
b. You talk with a parent about a show while watching together?	1.51	1.49	ns	1.56	1.46	ns
c. A parent tell you there are certain shows you should watch?	1.16	.92	.01	1.36	.87	.01
d. A parent tell you to read something in the newspaper?	1.00	.84	.01	.78	1.05	.01
e. A parent tell you to read something in a magazine?	.75	.69	ns	.61	.81	.01
f. Has a parent ever told you you watch too much TV? (percentage yes)	48%	46%	ns	52%	44%	.05
g. Are there many shows parents won't let you watch?* **	1.09	.89	ns	1.57	.64	.01
h. How late can you stay up to watch TV?*††	5.49	5.58	ns	4.48	6.23	.01
i. Do you have more TV rules than other kids your age?***	1.71	1.73	ns	1.82	1.65	.01
Factors						
I. *Read* (e, d)	.87	.76	.03	.73	.92	.01
II. *TV rules* (g, −h, c, i,)*	1.32	1.18	ns	1.58	1.05	.01
III. *Co-watching* (a, b,)	1.63	1.61	ns	1.66	1.60	ns

    *Significant interaction between ethnicity and grade.

    †Response categories and values: 0 = *Not at all*, 1 = *Not much*, 2 = *Often*, 3 = *Very often*.

    **Response categories and values: 0 = *No*, 1 = *One or two*, 2 = *A few*, 3 = *Several*, 4 = *A lot*.

    ††Response categories and values: 1 = *8 P.M.*, 2 = *8:30 P.M.*, 3 = *9 P.M.*, 4 = *9:30 P.M.*, 5 = *10 P.M.*, 6 = *10:30 P.M.*, 7 = *11 P.M.*, 8 = *later*.

    ***Response categories and values: 1 = *Fewer rules*, 2 = *About the same*, 3 = *More rules*.

SUMMARY

Here we will draw together the findings of the youth study across media, identifying similarities and differences first by ethnicity and then by age group.

Figure 5-1 summarizes the results for media use and access by ethnicity. Most media are equally accessible to the Hispanic and Anglo youth. As was determined in the adult study, Anglo households are more likely to have the newspaper delivered than are Hispanic households. Unlike the adult findings, however, Hispanic and Anglo youth are equivalent newspaper readers in terms of frequency, recency, and amount, regardless of whether the newspaper is delivered to the home. The Hispanic youths are more frequent consumers of television across all program types and across all parts of the day than the Anglo youngsters. The Hispanic homes also have more television fare available through their greater subscription to cable TV. For all other majority mass media there are no important use or access differences between these groups.

Figure 5.2 summarizes content preferences of the youth. The Anglo youngsters have a more cosmopolitan news orientation than the Hispanics; in contrast, the Hispanics have a stronger local news orientation in their newspaper content preferences. Preference for news on TV is equivalent.

Overall, the Hispanic youth give stronger ratings to television content choices than the Anglo youth, but the relative order of television program preferences is more similar than different.

Substantial differences also occur in terms of music preferences. Disco is the most-preferred type of music among Hispanics, followed by rock

FIGURE 5.1. Media use and access by ethnicity.

Hispanic and Anglo youth are equivalent
      . . . in ownership of TV sets, radios, and record/tape players
      . . . in frequency, recency, and amount of newspaper reading
      . . . in magazine and non-school book reading
      . . . in logged TV viewing "yesterday" afternoon and evening
      . . . in listening to radio
      . . . in listening to radio news, music, and sports
      . . . in going out to the movies

Hispanics exceed Anglos
      . . . in access to cable TV
      . . . in comic book reading
      . . . in estimated hours of TV viewing before school, after school, and after supper
      . . . in estimated hours of TV viewing on Saturday morning and afternoon
      . . . in logged TV viewing "yesterday" before noon
      . . . in frequency of watching cartoons, soap operas, news, and game shows on TV
      . . . in listening to records/tapes and in the number of records bought

Anglos exceed Hispanics
      . . . in home delivery of the newspaper
      . . . in personal radio ownership

FIGURE 5.2. Content preferences by ethnicity.

Hispanic and Anglo youth are equivalent
         . . . for sports, fashion, and music magazines
         . . . for *adventure* films (westerns, war, science-fiction, detective movies)
         . . . for *sports* on TV (shows like "Wide World of Sports," baseball, soccer)
         . . . for *news* on TV (local news, network news, shows like "60 Minutes")

Hispanics exceed Anglos
         . . . for *local information* in the newspaper (things to do in town, advertising, stories about young people, crime stories)
         . . . for newspaper features (TV section, comics)
         . . . for all types of comic books
         . . . for romantic films, for films in Spanish, and for horror films
         . . . for Spanish, disco, and soul music on radio and on records/tapes
         . . . for shows in Spanish on TV
         . . . for soap operas, cartoons, game shows, crime shows, movies, and shows with singing and dancing on TV

Anglos exceed Hispanics
         . . . in preference for *general news* in the newspaper (front-page news, headlines, news inside the paper, photos)
         . . . for comedy films and comedies on TV
         . . . for rock, country and western, and top-40 radio music
         . . . for rock and country and western music on records/tapes

and soul. Among Anglos, rock is more preferred, with disco somewhat less and country and western preference outweighing soul. Although Hispanics indicate more desire for media content in Spanish than Anglos, the absolute level of Hispanic preference for Spanish-language content is very weak compared to the other content preferences measured. This differs from the adult findings, where Hispanic adult preferences for Spanish-language media were strong.

In Figure 5.3 the functions or gratifications of the mass media are summarized. The youth are equivalent in their use of both newspapers and television for news-seeking purposes.

In contrast, both media are used more for social learning gratifications by the Hispanic youngsters than by the Anglos. The Hispanics tend to read the newspaper and to watch television to find information and models that would help them adjust or acclimate to the majority culture environment. In addition, the Hispanic youngster makes more use of the newspaper for affective purposes; both groups make equivalent use of television for those same diversionary purposes.

No media functions are more strongly sought by Anglos than by Hispanics.

Figure 5.4 characterizes the groups' evaluations of the media. The

FIGURE 5.3. Media functions by ethnicity.

Hispanic and Anglo youth are equivalent
. . . in reading the newspaper for *news-seeking* purposes (for local news, national news, headlines, to know what's going on, to find out more about things heard about)
. . . in watching TV for *news-seeking* purposes (for local news, to find out more about things heard about)
. . . in watching TV for *diversion* purposes (to forget problems, to get cheered up, when lonely, for excitement, to relax)

Hispanics exceed Anglos
. . . in reading the newspaper for *diversion* purposes (to get cheered up, to forget problems, for excitement, because it's funny, to relax, to look at pictures, for things to talk about)
. . . in reading the newspaper for *social learning* purposes (to find out more about new places and people, to know what's going on, to learn to do new things, to find out what's happening to people in town)
. . . in watching TV for *social learning* purposes (to learn to do new things, because it teaches things not learned in school, because it shows how others deal with my problems)
. . . in watching TV for *advice* (to get advice on problems, because it helps me know how I'm supposed to act)

FIGURE 5.4. Media evaluation by ethnicity.

Hispanic and Anglo youth are equivalent
. . . in whether what they see on TV, hear on the radio and read in the newspaper is true
. . . in the extent to which TV and radio are chosen over newspapers if only one medium were available
. . . in judgment of how real-to-life Anglos and Anglo familes are portrayed on TV
. . . in perceptions of the frequency of portrayals of Mexican Americans doing bad things in the newspaper and on TV news and entertainment

Hispanics exceed Anglos
. . . in choosing TV over other media as the most believable when conflicting reports appear
. . . in judgment of how real-to-life Mexican Americans, Mexican-American families, and Blacks are portrayed on TV
. . . in perceptions of the frequency of portrayals of Mexican Americans doing good things in the newspaper and on TV news and entertainment

Anglos exceed Hispanics
. . . in choosing the newspaper over other media as the most believable when conflicting reports appear

greater Hispanic orientation to television accompanies their greater choice of television as the most believable medium. Radio and TV are preferred overwhelmingly to the newspaper by both groups of youngsters. The Hispanic youth believe that the minorities they see on television are relatively realistic more so than Anglo youngsters. They also perceive both newspapers and television as including more positive portrayals of Mexican Americans in media news and entertainment components than Anglos perceive—although both groups agreed that negative portrayals outnumbered positive portrayals.

Figure 5.5 presents the pattern of interpersonal interaction with parents and friends about media. By and large, the equivalencies exceed the differences, and in none of these situations did the Anglo youngsters indicate more activity than the Hispanic youngsters. The children reported more positive parental media recommendations by Hispanic parents of things to watch on TV and read in newspapers and magazines. For all other social interactions and parental media input, the two groups did not differ.

Now we will provide a summary of the key differences identified between the fifth and tenth graders. Figure 5.6 does this for media use and access. The older youngsters target their interest more to print media and to media that provide music. This manifests itself in larger amounts of newspaper and magazine reading and more intensive use of radio, record players, and tape units. In contrast, the younger children attend more to the fantasy world in comic books and on television. Their reported television viewing time is larger for all specified times of day on both weekdays and weekends.

Homes with older children more frequently subscribe to cable television; newspaper subscription is equivalent for both grades. The major access difference by grade parallels the use difference: tenth graders have more radios and record/tape players.

The content preferences summarized in Figure 5.7 confirm the notion suggested by the use data that the younger children have a softer, more fantasy-

FIGURE 5.5. Media interactions with friends/parents by ethnicity.

Hispanic and Anglo youth are equivalent
      . . . in frequency of talking with friends and parents about TV
      . . . in frequency of talking with friends and parents about the newspaper
      . . . in co-viewing TV with a parent
      . . . in discussing TV shows with a parent while watching
      . . . in parental banning of TV shows and in the amount of parental TV rules, including how late TV can be watched
      . . . in parental recommendations of articles in a magazine to read

Hispanics exceed Anglos
      . . . in frequency of talking with a parent about the newspaper
      . . . in parental recommendations of TV shows to watch
      . . . in parental recommendations of newspaper articles to read

FIGURE 5.6. Media use and access by grade.

Fifth and tenth graders are equivalent
    . . . in overall ownership of TV sets and record/tape players and in having their own TV
    . . . in home delivery of the newspaper
    . . . in listening to sports on the radio
    . . . in going out to the movies
    . . . in watching local news on TV
    . . . in estimates of TV viewing on Saturday afternoon

Fifth graders exceed tenth graders
    . . . in comic book and non-school book reading
    . . . in watching cartoons, soap operas, and game shows on TV
    . . . in estimated hours of watching TV during all parts of weekdays
    . . . in estimated hours of watching TV on Saturday morning
    . . . in logged TV viewing yesterday for all parts of the day
    . . . in number of records/tapes brought

Tenth graders exceed fifth graders
    . . . in ownership of color TV sets, household and personal radios, and personal record/tape players
    . . . in receiving cable TV
    . . . in frequency, recency, and amount of newspaper reading
    . . . in magazine reading
    . . . in overall radio listening and listening to radio news and music
    . . . in playing records/tapes

oriented set of preferences. They turn more to comics in the newspaper than the older children and have parallel preferences with a focus on fantasy in comic books, movies, and television.

The tenth graders have much stronger preferences for general news and for local information in the newspaper, and they prefer news magazines and news shows on television more than do the fifth graders. Sometime between fifth and tenth grades, the age groups represented in this study, a persistent shift to reality-seeking in media content preferences occurs for both Hispanics and Anglos.

Some preferences do not change within that age range. Most notably, there is equivalence in some major music preferences and in desire for sports content.

Also noteworthy is the absence of any difference between the age groups in terms of their desire for newspaper, movies, and "Musica Ranchera" in Spanish. Fifth graders more strongly prefer TV shows and rock music in Spanish, and in no content area do tenth graders express stronger preference for the Spanish language.

In Figure 5.8 it can be noted that tenth graders use the newspaper more for news-seeking purposes but that both age groups sought television news equivalently. This again seems to reflect the greater print orientation of the older

FIGURE 5.7. Content preferences by grade.

Fifth and tenth graders are equivalent
       . . . for advice columns, crime stories, and stories about Mexico and Latin America
       . . . for love story comic books
       . . . for sports and fashion magazines
       . . . for rock music, "Musica Ranchera," and top-40 music on radio
       . . . for rock music, "Musica Ranchera," and soul on records/tapes
       . . . for movies in Spanish
       . . . for soap operas, comedies, sports shows like "Wide World of Sports," and movies on TV

Fifth graders exceed tenth graders
       . . . for *newspaper features* (TV section, comics)
       . . . for children's magazines, TV and movie star magazines, and magazines about cars
       . . . for horror, superhero, war, and funny comic books
       . . . for *adventure* films (westerns, war, science-fiction, detective films) as well as horror and animal films
       . . . for disco, country and western music, and rock in Spanish on radio and records/tapes
       . . . for TV shows in Spanish, baseball and soccer, family shows, cartoons, game shows, crime, and children's shows

Tenth graders exceed fifth graders
       . . . in preference for *general news* in the newspaper (front-page news, headlines, news inside the paper, photos)
       . . . for *local information* in the newspaper (things to do in town, advertising, stories about young people)
       . . . for sports and weather in the newspaper
       . . . for news and music magazines
       . . . for romantic movies and comedy movies
       . . . for soul music on radio
       . . . for news shows on TV (local news, network news, shows like "60 Minutes")

children (probably due in part to stronger reading ability). The equivalency in TV news-seeking contradicts the trend for tenth graders to be more news-oriented across other media.

The fifth graders turn to both newspaper and television more for affective reasons, for excitement, for relaxation, and to be amused or cheered up. Both groups use the newspaper to the same extent to find out more about their immediate social environment, but fifth graders are more dependent on television for advice and social learning functions.

Figure 5-9 identifies the media evaluations of those two age groups. The radio orientation of the teenagers is reflected in their greater choice of radio over television if only one of those two media were available to them. The fifth graders judge more of the people and things they see on television as realistic; this is in accord with substantial evidence from earlier prior research

FIGURE 5.8. Media functions by grade.

Fifth and tenth graders are equivalent
> . . . in reading the newspaper for *social learning* purposes (to find out more about new places and people, to know what's going on, to learn to do new things, to find out what's happening to people in town)
> . . . in watching TV for *news-seeking* purposes (for local news, to find out more about things heard about)

Fifth graders exceed tenth graders
> . . . in reading the newspaper for *diversion* purposes (to get cheered up, to forget problems, for excitement, because it's funny, to relax, to look at pictures, for things to talk about)
> . . . in watching TV for *diversion* purposes (to forget problems, to get cheered up, when lonely, for excitement, to relax)
> . . . in watching TV for *social learning* purposes (to learn to do new things, because it teaches things not learned in school, because it shows how others deal with my problems)
> . . . in watching TV for *advice* (to get advice on problems, because it helps me know how I'm supposed to act)

Tenth graders exceed fifth graders
> . . . in reading the newspaper for *news-seeking* purposes (for local news, national news, headlines, to know what's going on, to find out more about things heard about)

FIGURE 5.9. Media evaluations by grade.

Fifth and tenth graders are equivalent
> . . . in believing what they see on TV and read in the newspaper is true
> . . . in choosing TV over other media as most believable when conflicting reports appear
> . . . in judgments of how real-to-life Anglos and Anglo families are portrayed on TV

Fifth graders exceed tenth graders
> . . . in believing what they hear on the radio is true
> . . . in the extent to which TV would be chosen over the newspaper if only one medium were available
> . . . in judgments of how real-to-life people, places, young people, Mexican Americans, Mexican-American families, Blacks, people, and young people are portrayed on TV
> . . . in perceptions of the frequency of portrayals of Mexican Americans doing good things in the newspaper and on TV news and entertainment

Tenth graders exceed fifth graders
> . . . in the extent to which radio would be chosen over TV if only one medium were available
> . . . in perceptions of the frequency of portrayals of Mexican Americans doing bad things in the newspaper and on TV news and entertainment

FIGURE 5.10. Media interactions with friends/parents by grade.

Fifth and tenth graders are equivalent
         . . . in frequency of talking to/with a parent about the newspaper
         . . . in co-viewing TV with a parent
         . . . in discussing TV shows with parents while watchnig

Fifth graders exceed genth graders
         . . . in frequency of talking to/with a parent about TV
         . . . in frequency of talking to/with friends about TV
         . . . in parental recommendations of TV shows to watch
         . . . in being told they watch too much TV
         . . . in parental banning of shows

Tenth graders exceed fifth graders
         . . . in frequency of talking with friends about the newspaper
         . . . in parental recommendations of something to read in the newwspaper and in magazines

indicating that perceptions of the reality of television content are inversely related to the age of the viewer. Fifth graders also perceive more positive and fewer negative media portrayals of Mexican Americans than do tenth graders.

Perhaps most important in the set of evaluation results is the fact that at both age levels television is claimed the most believable medium overall.

Finally, Figure 5.10 identifies social interactions about the mass media with the parents and friends of these youngsters. On all items where fifth graders exceeded tenth graders, the subject is television. The younger respondents talk more with everybody about television, are more likely to have shows recommended to them by their parents, are more likely to be criticized for the amount they watch, and are more likely to have some shows banned. In contrast, tenth graders' media interactions deal with print media more often than do fifth graders'.

CONCLUSIONS

Initial conclusions derive from the findings that ran counter to our expectations, to the extent that we had expectations. First there is a stronger orientation to the print media—newspapers, magazines, and books—among Hispanic youngsters than lore has suggested. In fact, the prevalent assumption that Hispanics are not print-oriented is contradicted by these youngsters' responses, although the assumption may be more true for their parents. The young people are equivalent on newspaper usage criteria, and this holds for magazine and non-school book reading as well. The equivalent access and time spent with those media is an important finding. Access to all the media studied was quite uniform, and time spent with all the media may be characterized as more similar than would have been anticipated. Clearly that is the case with the print media.

The television viewing time estimates are more of an anomaly. Certainly the pervasive content preferences—liking more of almost everything—by the Hispanics justify the results from the time estimations that Hispanics watch more television most of the time. That matches expectations developed from earlier studies of the television dependence of ethnic minority groups. The log estimates suggest that we must re-examine the dependency proposition. Although Hispanics claimed to like more and to watch more, it may be the case that actual viewing behavior is more similar than different and more similar than anticipated. The collected logs will eventually enable us to compare specific program choices within given time frames to determine if the expressed content preference differences manifest themselves in specific choice discriminations.

Hispanic youngsters from families long-established in the U.S. and others from more recent immigrant families have shown consistently greater preference than Anglos for Spanish-language content in all media studied. However, that desire is not strong by any of the measures invoked; it is there, but it is weak, consistently demonstrating a quite low-ranking request within each set of content choices. Nevertheless, the cultural duality does persist for these youngsters, a wish to maintain some specific language tie with their ethnic roots. The majority mass media may wish to consider means of accommodating this preference, rather than merely deferring to more specialized media.

Within each medium, there are reliable distinctions in content preferences. The 10- and 15-year-old Hispanics express either stronger content preferences or different ones. Save for music preferences, however, the discriminations made are in terms of strength of choice, not choice of content. It is important not to confuse significant differences in magnitude of newspaper and television content preference with what subject matter is preferred. As one looks at the relative ordering of content preferences for these major media, both groups of young people show essentially the same ordering; the priorities are the same— how much a content area is desired is the locus of difference. Only for music choices are there strong content choice differences as well as strength of choice differences. Acculturation may account for a large share of the differences, but one can only speculate as to how these differences become established at such an early age and whether they will persist or will merge. They do suggest different marketing strategies and thematic emphases. For example, promoting the newspaper features and its local pages should work better in the Hispanic community than hard news promotion; soul and disco and Spanish music should do better with Hispanics than with Anglos.

A further unexpected finding is the generally more positive responses from the Hispanic youngsters regarding portrayal of their own ethnic group in both television and newspapers. Clearly, their perceptions seemed not to match those of community leaders from the same cities. The Hispanic and Anglo youngsters agree that overall there are more negative than positive portrayals of Mexican Americans. However, the Hispanics judge that there are more positive images available than do the Anglos. Their experiences with Spanish-language media might have influenced Hispanics' responses; the instrument did not ask for the source of their impressions.

A related set of findings indicates that Hispanics find the fictional portrayals of Mexican Americans more realistic. Perhaps they are happy just to see *any* Mexican faces in a population of television characters largely devoid of such faces. Perhaps seeing some is judged better than seeing few or none. But those are interpretations unsupported by the present findings. It remains to be determined just what Hispanics react to as realistic or positive or negative. Chapter 6, analyzing news content in newspapers in these communities, provides some baseline information on this issue but does not probe sufficiently into the origins of these judgments by the Hispanic youths. We will subsequently analyze TV and radio news content.

The activity of Hispanic parents is also noteworthy. They invoke similar levels of restrictions and co-watching with their children. They are reported as more active in positive suggestions regarding watching and reading activities. Perhaps this ties to the Hispanic youth's use of television and newspapers for advice-seeking and social learning.

Here are some key issues for continuing research analysis:

1. These results are geography-bound in the southwestern portion of the U.S.; parallel data from other regions and from other Hispanic subgroups (*e.g.*, Puerto Ricans and Cubans) remain to be developed.

2. Comparative analyses of Hispanic boys' and girls' media habits and attitudes should be examined.

3. The factor analytic results reported combine the Anglo and Hispanic data; separate factoring procedures may yield alternative cognitive mappings that could add to our understanding of ethnic similarities and differences.

4. Two methodological issues remain central: One is the variability in Hispanic use of time estimates and time logging procedures; the second is the possible general tendency of Hispanic youth to use more extreme response categories on scaled items and the possibility that some differences reflect scale usage rather than substantive differences.

5. One anticipates a greater orientation to Spanish-language media among those more capable in that language; a subsequent analysis will compare respondents' estimates of their bilingual capabilities with media use and content preferences.

6. The young Hispanic respondents are offered seven different options for identifying their cultural origins; four were chosen most frequently: Mexican

American, Mexican, Spanish American, and Chicano. Why one over another? What implications does cultural identity have for media behaviors and attitudes? What meanings are conveyed by the different labels?

Chapter 5 has presented a baseline for probing these kinds of issues.

6

A CONTENT ANALYSIS OF NEWSPAPER COVERAGE OF MEXICAN AMERICANS

Bradley S. Greenberg
Carrie Heeter
Judee K. Burgoon
Michael Burgoon
Felipe Korzenny

This chapter systematically examines the coverage of Hispanic Americans in six U.S. daily newspapers, all serving communities with substantial Hispanic-American populations.

Sanchez (1970) conducted the first major empirical study by selectively analyzing newspaper coverage of Mexican Americans on 19 dates between January and June 1970. Dates were chosen on which Mexican Americans could have received some form of national newspaper coverage, as indicated by reports in *Facts on File*. From 10 newspapers, 337 articles were examined. Sanchez found a preponderance of stories dealing with conflict, in contrast to cooperation or conflict resolution. A majority of the stories were classified as local, but the newspapers included the country's major news centers, e.g., New York, Washington, Chicago, and Los Angeles. Conflict stories were not different in length from nonconflict stories, Mexican-American sources were used in 30 percent of the stories, and equivalent space allocation was found in newspapers close to and distant from the centers of Mexican-American activity.

In a much more limited study of two English-language dailies in New York City, Fishman and Casiano (1969) found that three-fourths of a total of 64 stories dealing with Puerto Ricans centered on intergroup relations and that 85 percent of these were problem-oriented stories. They concluded, "Puerto Ricans are discussed and reported in the English press primarily in the context of the problems or difficulties that they pose for Anglo society, whereas their cultural activity and creativity is by and large overlooked.''

In a more recent review of news coverage of Hispanics, Gutierrez (1980a, b) claims that (1) news coverage has been small, but is increasing; (2) coverage is concentrated in times when Hispanics are judged to be a threat; (3) the news media often have used negatively perceived symbols, e.g., *wetback, alien, Chicano,* to designate Mexican-American groups; (4) reporters rely on sources outside the Mexican-American community for information about Mexican Americans; and (5) coverage has focused on negative or unfavorable community issues.

The major shortcoming of the earlier studies is their concentration on specific events or kinds of coverage, e.g., immigration stories. No systematic analysis of normal or typical coverage of Hispanic Americans in their local communities has been identified. One purpose here is to provide such evidence as a baseline for examining subsequent changes in coverage of the Hispanic community. What is coverage like, with respect to news stories, announcements, photos, etc., in a normal time period, without a crisis as the focal point? That is the purpose of this chapter.

Interviews with Hispanic community leaders and the newspapers' key executives in the field study sites had yielded their perceptions of newspaper coverage before this content analysis was undertaken. Community leaders believed there was an overplay of the negative and underplay of the positive in news content; these leaders believed their constituencies resented the magnitude of coverage of Hispanic crime-related events without a sufficient counterbalance of positive events. The leaders also reported that coverage was weak in terms of frequency and poor where the frequencies were higher. They complained about the location of Hispanic items within the paper, the emphasis on ethnicity, the length of the pieces, and so on. Publishers indicated that coverage was increasing but probably still insufficient; uniformly, they said that the most central complaint from the Hispanic community dealt with crime coverage.

These perceptions of both groups warrant verification through such procedures as this content analysis. Although this study avoids making judgments about the positive or negative attributes of any content item, it does examine considerations of emphasis and prominence. The methods used to conduct this study are described in the next section.

METHODS

Daily newspapers were collected by private mail-order subscription from six southwest cities for the first three weeks of September 1980. A composite, two-week sample of Monday-through-Saturday editions was selected randomly from that time period. Newspapers analyzed included the *Salinas Californian,* the *Stockton Record,* the San Bernardino *Sun,* and the *Visalia Times-Delta* in California; the *Tucson Citizen* in Arizona; and the Santa Fe *New Mexican* in New Mexico. Issue dates sampled were September 3, 4, 6, 8, 9, 12, 15, 16, 17, 18, 19, and 20.

Southwest locations were selected because the large concentration of Hispanics in that region was likely to yield sufficient local news coverage of Hispanics for quantitative analysis. Interviews with Hispanic community leaders in each of the sites identified the local newspaper as a key source of local information for the community. Only two of the cities (Tucson and Salinas) had a local television-network affiliate that broadcast local news. Thus, in four of the cities the newspaper was the primary source of local information, competing with or supplemented by brief local radio newscasts. The communities in this study reflected a variety of Hispanic and Anglo populations, diverse in proportion of Hispanics to Anglos, socioeconomic status, overall community size, integration, length of residence in the U.S., and population stability. Population size varied from 27,268 in Visalia to 262,933 in Tucson according to the 1970 Census. Estimates from the 1970 Census and by Hispanic community leaders and local newspaper publishers placed Hispanic-Anglo proportions in the range of 55 to 65 percent Hispanic in Santa Fe and 20 to 30 percent in the other five sites.

The primary daily newspapers analyzed here also reflected a variety of newspaper attributes, including morning and afternoon publication, circulation size, extent and frequency of community penetration, and size of total local and nonlocal *newshole*. (Within each newspaper, the total space in square inches devoted to local news, sports, editorials, bulletins, and photographs was measured by measuring each item and summing them. These composite measurements are referred to as the local newshole.)

Content Definitions

This analysis focused exclusively on local items. A local item was defined as follows: (1) non-wire service, non-syndicated; (2) having either a local dateline or no dateline (nearby suburbs did not qualify as local); (3) not specified and not national or syndicated; (4) attributed as written by a staff member of the local paper. Classified ads, comics, paid legal announcements, and advertising were excluded.

Coders identified each item in each of the 72 sampled issues as local or non-local. Local items were classified as one of five types for further analysis: bulletin, photo, editorial, sports story, or news story. Bulletins were defined as sets of brief announcements that shared essentially the same format and content. Bulletins included sets of birth, death, wedding, engagement, and divorce announcements; crime briefs; drunk driving arrests; calendar formats reporting on upcoming events and things to do in town; and occasional sports briefs. A minimum of two announcements was required for an item to qualify as a bulletin.

Local photos included artists' renderings and cartoons but excluded comics. Wire service photos were excluded when so identified. Editorials included letters to the editor (regardless of the city of the author), local editorials, and local columns. Editorials were required to appear on the editorial page(s). Sports stories included all articles (other than bulletin-format repetitive announcements) that centered on sports content, regardless of their location in the paper.

Local news stories were broadly defined as all local items that did not qualify as bulletins, editorials, photos, or sports. All local items were read by coders and identified as Hispanic or non-Hispanic. An item was considered Hispanic if it contained one or more Spanish surnames, referred to a Spanish-speaking country, culture, or custom, or otherwise mentioned Hispanics or Hispanic issues.

The 1980 Census List of Spanish Surnames was used to identify Spanish surnames. Passel and Word (1980) describe the process by which that list was derived, based on the principle that "for a particular surname to be considered Spanish, the geographic distribution of persons with that surname must be 'similar' to the distribution of the Hispanic population [p. 2]." Beginning with a formula that operationalized the name distribution function, a large initial list was derived that was refined and underwent corrections for known inclusions and exclusions, leading eventually to the 1980 list containing 12,497 names. The list was checked against 1980 Census returns, which included surnames and self-identification as Hispanic, to calculate an error estimate. Two types of identification error were expected: errors of commission, where a person qualifies as having a Spanish surname but does not identify himself or herself as Hispanic (whether by choice or because he or she has a different ethnic origin); and errors of omission, where a person identifies himself or herself as Hispanic, but does not have a surname appearing on the list. Passel and Word report the error rate in identifying Hispanic males in the Southwest as being 6.3 percent commission errors and 11.5 percent omission errors. They also point out that a person's self-identification as Hispanic has been found to change over time. The error rates are higher for females than for males and less high than in the 1970 List of Spanish Surnames.

When more information than surname was available in an item, allowing the coder to verify the accuracy of labeling an individual Hispanic or non-Hispanic based on surname, this was done. For example, one news story centered on a famous concert pianist with a surname appearing in the Census list, who was identified in the article as Yugoslavian. Despite the Spanish surname, that item was not considered Hispanic. Similarly, a photograph of a woman with a non-Hispanic surname identified in the accompanying article as from Mexico was considered Hispanic, despite the non-Hispanic surname.

Newshole Computation

The local Hispanic newshole for each of the five types of items measured and summed to yield the local newshole—local news, sports, editorials, bulletins, and photographs was calculated by summing only those items that qualified as Hispanic. By definition, bulletins contain large numbers of small items, some Hispanic-related and some not. The local Hispanic bulletin newshole was defined as the space devoted to bulletins (sets of announcements) that contained at least one Hispanic announcement, and not the measurement and summation of the individual items within a given bulletin. The local non-Hispanic bulletin newshole was the total space per paper of bulletins containing no reference to Hispanics.

Comparisons Across Item Type

There were 810 local Hispanic items identified in the 2-week, 72-issue sample, including 200 Hispanic bulletins, 132 Hispanic photos, 300 Hispanic news stories, 129 Hispanic sports stories, and 49 Hispanic editorial page items. That set of items was content-analyzed in more depth, concentrating on four basic characteristics: *prominence, reasons the item qualified as Hispanic, representation of Hispanics compared to non-Hispanics,* and *content*.

The newshole computations permit direct comparison of overall local Hispanic coverage to local non-Hispanic coverage. However, no comparable data set exists for the in-depth content analysis, i.e., we did not do in-depth analysis of non-Hispanic content. Lacking that, the analyses will concentrate on comparing different subsets of Hispanic coverage within and across item types.

Prominence

For each item, the page number it appeared on relative to the section it appeared in, the page number relative to the total number of pages in that issue, the section number, and the total number of pages in the issue were recorded. Location within the newspaper page was recorded as another measure of prominence for photos, editorials, news, and sports items. An item was coded as appearing above the fold if (1) it appeared exclusively above the center fold; (2) it began at the top of the page, regardless of how far below the fold it continued; or (3) most of the item was located above the fold. An item was coded as below the fold if all or most of it fell below the fold and coded as across the fold if it was close to evenly divided.

Page number and section number prominence measures were coded for bulletins, primarily to use for comparisons of content and representation differences across bulletin sets. Item prominence within a bulletin set was not analyzed.

In addition to the newshole computations, the size in square inches to the nearest one-tenth of an inch for individual photo, news, and editorial items was calculated.

Reasons Items Qualified as Hispanic

There were five possible criteria by which items qualified as Hispanic. At least one and up to five of the criteria could have occurred for each item. Inclusion of *Spanish surnames* was the most common reason an item was identified as Hispanic. Mention of *Hispanic culture* was another option, encompassing references to customs, language, habits, arts, heritage, or other traditions from an Hispanic country or hybrid U.S.-Hispanic group. Coders were asked to list the basis of this and the other non-surname qualifying reasons when they occurred. Mention of *Hispanic ethnicity* was defined as reference to issues, problems, and information relating to Hispanics as a minority in the U.S., including identifying an individual as Hispanic. Mention of a *Hispanic country* was the fourth way a story could qualify. The intent was to identify the extent of representation by country of origin, if it were reported. The final category was a residual one, to encompass that which was clearly Hispanic for some unanticipated reason.

Representation

For photos, the total number of surnames and the total number of Spanish surnames in available cutlines were counted, recorded separately, and compared as a measure of the proportion of Hispanics to Non-Hispanics appearing in photos qualifying as Hispanic. The same comparison was made for surnames appearing in news and sports items. When a person was otherwise identified as Hispanic but had a non-Hispanic surname, the surname was counted as Hispanic, and vice versa. Editorials were assumed not to contain any personal references; so a name comparison assessment was not made, beyond identifying whether the editorial qualified because of Spanish surnames.

Representation in bulletin sets was measured by counting the number of Hispanic announcements within the bulletin and comparing that to the total number of announcements.

Content Topics

During the coding process, 40 separate content topic categories were assessed as being central to the story or photo, as mentioned but peripheral, or as not mentioned. This set was used for photos, news and sports stories, and editorials. The categories included a number of minority issues and content areas expected to be of interest, based on interviews with community leaders and the limited literature on news coverage of Hispanics. The frequency of occurrence of central topics in the 610 items coded using those categories led to collapsing the 40 topics into eight broader categories. A general *Crime* category subsumed white-collar crime, civil offense, violent crime, crime against Hispanics, and crime by Hispanics. *Minority issues* combined discrimination, youth gangs, busing, migrant workers, poverty and unemployment, ethnic conflicts, bilingualism, unions and strikes, immigration, and the reporting of Hispanic inequalities with the majority population, e.g., less education, lower income. *Cultural features* included stories/photos about culture and the arts, religion, foods and recipes, and features on Spanish countries. *Noncultural features* included personality profiles, humorous stories, Good Samaritan stories, and other feature-angle reports, e.g., education and the elderly. *Hard news* (excluding crime) included political elections and functions, accidents and disasters, stories on business and the economy, and agricultural news. *Advice* grouped advice on personal problems, how-to advice, things to do in town, health and medical advice, and consumer education. *Sports* continued as its own category. An *Other* category included items that did not qualify as central in any of the other categories. Items could qualify in more than a single category. Among photos, 94 percent were coded in only one category, 6 percent in two. Within news items, 74 percent were coded in a single content category, 23 percent in two categories, and 3 percent in three categories. Sports items occurred exclusively in the *Sports* category due to the nature of the stories, not to any particular coding requirement. Editorials generated the most multiple content areas, with 55 percent coded in a single category, 41 percent in two categories, and 4 percent in three.

For bulletins, nine mutually exclusive categories were used: births, deaths, weddings, divorces, crimes and arrests, other legal, sports, calendar announcements, and other.

Item-Specific Content Coding

Photos. Photo captions were coded, in place of headlines, when they occurred. The type of photo was assessed as either a *news photo,* defined as a photo whose content (or whose accompanying story's content) could not logically be carried in its current form a week later or a week earlier and have the same impact; a *feature photo,* which was a non-news photo; or an *artist's rendering,* which referred to a drawing.

Total number of people in a photo were counted. Only those individuals who were clearly identifiable were counted. Blurred images and parts of bodies (e.g., in football pictures) were not counted. Beyond total number of people in a photo and the general content categorization, the visual content of photos was ignored. Representation measures (Hispanic–non-Hispanic proportions) were based exclusively on surnames in the cutline.

News and Sports. Stories were coded as having a byline or not, and if so, whether the byline name was on the Spanish surname list. Sources of information who were directly quoted in the articles were also coded as having a Spanish surname or not, and a judgment was made about whether each source was directly or incidentally involved with the story. Most sources were directly involved (i.e., having an ongoing relationship with the content), whereas incidental sources were more man-on-the-street-interview types of quotes or witnesses to a crime, disaster, etc. The coding system allowed for zero to three sources. In only one story of the 429 did the number of sources exceed three.

As with photos, news stories were classified as current breaking news or features.

The focus of news, sports, and editorials was coded as local, state, national, international, or other. For news, sports, and editorial items, a judgment was made as to whether the story focused primarily on a Hispanic individual and/or Hispanic-related topics and issues or was a secondary Hispanic story. A story was coded as primary Hispanic if one or more of the reasons the story qualified (individual with a Spanish surname, ethnicity, culture, or country) was central to the story. A news story that centered on an individual with a Spanish surname was coded as primary Hispanic even if no mention of the person's ethnicity occurred. A story that quoted a single Hispanic individual among a number of other quotes was a secondary Hispanic story.

Editorials. Editorials were classified by type, as a local column (usually with byline and published regularly), local editorial (without byline), letter to the editor from a Hispanic, or letter to the editor from a non-Hispanic.

Reliability

Intercoder reliability on the 32 categorical variables was 88 percent or higher. Coding of number of surnames yielded 95 percent agreement between two coders, with per-story differences not exceeding one surname. Identification of surnames as Hispanic or non-Hispanic yielded 83 percent agreement, again with plus or minus one surname accounting for the differences. Coding story size in square inches was significantly correlated among three coders at .93 using Kendall's W, with differences accounted for by plus or minus 2 square inches.

RESULTS

Local News

This section reports on the analysis of local news stories.

Space. In all, 300 local news stories qualified as Hispanic news items in the 72 issues of the sample, or four per day per newspaper. The average story size was 36 square inches. Hispanic news stories were identified in 26 percent of the total local newshole.

Prominence. One-third of local Hispanic news stories were in the first section of the newspaper, one-third in the second section, and the remainder in subsequent sections. Three-fifths of these news stories were above the fold and 29 percent were below the fold. Twenty percent of the stories were front-page items.

Byline. Sixteen percent of these stories carried a byline with a Hispanic surname, 36 percent carried a non-Hispanic surname, and the remainder had no byline. Stories with no byline were smaller; more frequently qualified as Hispanic only because of Spanish surnames; more frequently dealt with crime content; less frequently dealt with minority issues; included fewer Spanish surnames, fewer total surnames, and contained proportionately more Spanish-total surnames. Non-byline stories were not significantly different in whether they were primary or secondary Hispanic stories, or in page location.

Approximately one-half the Hispanic byline articles, compared to 37 percent of non-Hispanic bylines, qualified for reasons other than or in addition to inclusion of Spanish surnames. Hispanic byline articles were less likely than non-Hispanic byline articles to center on hard news content but were equivalently likely to deal with minority issues and crime.

Hispanic byline articles contained significantly more Spanish surnames (an average of 4.4 per story) than did non-Hispanic bylines (2.7) and contained more total surnames.

Reasons for Inclusion. The vast majority of the news stories qualified because they contained a Hispanic surname—65 percent qualified solely for this reason and an additional 26 percent qualified for this reason plus some other. The other bases for inclusion—ethnicity (minority issues or labeling an individual as Hispanic), cultural content, and Hispanic countries—each accounted for about 10 percent of the reasons for inclusion.

Stories that qualified exclusively because of Spanish surnames were larger (48.6 versus 28.7 square inches) and contained more Spanish surnames than stories that qualified for multiple or other reasons (3.49 compared to 1.94 per story).

One-third of the stories that qualified exclusively because of surnames were primary Hispanic stories, compared to 74 percent of the multiple or other qualifying stories. When the story focused on a Hispanic individual, culture or ethnicity was more frequently mentioned than when the Hispanic individual was secondary to the story.

Seventy-eight percent of the crime stories qualified by surname only, with no ethnicity attribution; 37 percent of cultural features, 50 percent of minority issue topics, 68 percent of hard news, and 70 percent of noncultural features qualified in the same way. The first or only source quoted had a Spanish surname in one-half the multiple or other qualifying stories and 36 percent of the surname-only stories.

Content. News story content is indexed in the following table:

	Single Topic	Multiple Topic
Hard news (e.g., politics, accidents)	25%	14%
Crime	4%	17%
Cultural features	13%	7%
Minority issues	9%	7%
Advice	4%	9%
Noncultural features	4%	6%
Other	14%	0

Hard news stories predominated as the focus of Hispanic news coverage. Crime, cultural features, and minority issues news stories also occurred regularly.

Emphasis and Sources. Nearly one-half the local Hispanic news stories were judged to be primarily Hispanic items focusing on Hispanic individuals or activities. Hard news and feature content were significantly less likely to have a primary Hispanic emphasis, i.e., they were general news stories, not Hispanic. Crime news, in contrast, was significantly more likely to have a primary Hispanic emphasis.

In primary Hispanic stories, 51 percent of the named individuals had Hispanic surnames, with more Hispanics and fewer total names mentioned than in secondary Hispanic stories, where 22 percent of individuals mentioned had Spanish surnames. Primary and secondary Hispanic stories did not differ in their prominence, size, or byline.

The sources used in the stories were also identified as having Hispanic surnames or not. Seventy-nine percent of the stories quoted at least one source, and 39 percent of all sources quoted were Hispanic. If the first or only source was Hispanic, the story was more likely to have a primary Hispanic emphasis.

Newspaper Differences. The Santa Fe and Tucson newspapers carried an average of 6 items each day; it was 5 in Salinas, 3.5 in Stockton, and 2.5 in Visalia and San Bernardino. The following table compares average local newshole proportions per day with the Hispanic proportion of the population in those cities.

	Local Newshole, All Hispanic Items	Local Newshole, Primary Hispanic Items	Hispanic Population
Santa Fe	61%	23%	55–65%
Salinas	32%	20%	20–30%
Tucson	24%	12%	20–30%
San Bernardino	23%	12%	20–30%
Stockton	17%	5%	20–30%
Visalia	12%	7%	20–30%

The first four cities listed in the table allocated local newshole space to Hispanic items in proportions equal to or greater than the Hispanic population segment. Only Stockton and Visalia allocated substantially less space than their population proportion of Hispanics. The ratios of *primary* Hispanic stories within the local newshole were considerably lower than Hispanic population proportions except in Salinas.

Comparisons by city of news story size showed considerable variability. In Tucson, the average local news story that qualified as a Hispanic story was 66 square inches; the San Bernardino stories averaged 42; Salinas, 38; Stockton, 23; Visalia, 17; and Santa Fe, 18. These differences were statistically significant.

Hispanic sources for news stories were significantly more likely to be used in Santa Fe and San Bernardino than in the other cities.

Content emphases also differed by community. In Santa Fe, with the largest proportion of Hispanics, only 1 in 13 Hispanic stories had crime content. In Tucson and San Bernardino, it was 1 in 4, and in the other three sites, it was 1 in 2.5. Hard news regarding Hispanics was maximally likely in Tucson. Santa Fe, Visalia, and Stockton reported least often on minority issues in the community.

Editorials

The analysis of editorial page content included an examination of local columns relating to Hispanics, letters to the editor from Hispanics and non-Hispanics, and locally written editorials containing some reference to Hispanics.

Space. A total of 49 items relating to Hispanics was found in the 72 newspaper issues, or about two items every 3 days. Of the total local editorial newshole (measured in square inches), 15 percent contained editorial page material that qualified as Hispanic. One-half this material was located above the fold, one-fourth cut across the fold, and one-fourth was below the fold. The matter above the fold was significantly more likely to contain Hispanic surnames.

Content. One-half the material coded as Hispanic editorial page items consisted of letters to the editor written by persons with Spanish surnames; 37 percent was general newspaper editorials; 8 percent was letters in the editor from non-Hispanics; and 4 percent was local columns. Fifty-nine percent of the items dealt with local issues, 27 percent with state issues, 10 percent international, and 2 percent with national and other items.

The distribution of Hispanic editorial page items by content topic was as follows:

	Single Topic	Multiple Topics
Minority issues (e.g., bilingualism, discrimination)	12%	41%
Hard news (e.g., politics, accidents, disasters)	12%	18%
Crime	4%	25%
Cultural features	6%	4%
Sports	4%	0
Noncultural features (e.g., personality profiles, humor)	4%	6%
Other	12%	0

The designation as a single topic means that only that content area was present in the editorial page item; for multiple topics, that content area was among others coded for that item.

Editorial page material inclusive of Hispanics centered on minority group problems, crime, and other areas of hard news. Letters from Hispanics focused on minority issues significantly more than other content types.

Reasons for Inclusion. The bases for identifying editorial page content as Hispanic were as follows:

	Single Qualifying Reason	Multiple Reasons	Total
Spanish surname	33%	35%	68%
Hispanic ethnicity	14%	43%	57%
Hispanic culture	——	14%	14%
Hispanic country	——	33%	33%
Other	2%	6%	8%

As stated earlier, one-half the Hispanic editorial page items were letters to the editor from a person with a Spanish surname. One-third of those letters qualified only because the author was Hispanic. In contrast to news stories, where 65 percent qualified exclusively because of surnames and 91 percent included some Spanish surnames, 33 percent of the editorial items qualified exclusively by the criterion and 68 percent included surnames. Excluding letters to the editor from Hispanics, Spanish surnames accounted for only 8 percent of the reasons the other editorial page content qualified. Editorials were much more likely than news items to deal with Hispanic ethnicity and minority issues.

Newspaper Differences. One-half the editorial page items relating to Hispanics appeared in the Tucson newspaper, nine others were found in the 12 issues examined from Santa Fe, and each of the other four sites yielded either three or four items across the 2-week time period. The following table shows the proportion of editorial newshole in each site containing Hispanic items and the Hispanic proportion of the population:

	Editorial Newshole, Hispanic Items	Proportion Hispanic Population
Santa Fe	30%	55–65%
Tucson	24%	20–30%
San Bernardino	22%	20–30%
Stockton	11%	20-30%
Visalia	5%	20-30%
Salinas	3%	20-30%

Two newspapers carried editorial page content about Hispanics in proportion to the population of Hispanics in their community. The others are particularly discrepant with that criterion. In sum, Tucson ran two items a day; Santa Fe ran three items every 2 days; Stockton, San Bernardino, and Salinas ran one item every 3 days; and Visalia ran one item every 4 days.

Local Sports News

Because sports news was anticipated to be a major carrier of Hispanic items, it was analyzed separately from general news.

Space. Of 429 local news stories that included some Hispanic referent, 129, or 31 percent, were local sports stories. This was 1.8 local sports stories per day per newspaper with some Hispanic-related information. The average story size was 33 square inches, virtually identical to that of non-sports local news stories with Hispanic information. These sports stories constituted 48 percent of the total local sports newshole across the six cities.

Prominence. One-fourth of the local Hispanic sports stories were on the front page of the sports section, one-fourth were on the second page, and the remainder were in later pages. Two-thirds of the stories were above the fold in the sports section.

Byline. Six percent of the stories carried a byline with a Hispanic surname, 46 percent had a non-Hispanic byline, and the remainder had no byline. Byline stories by Hispanics were significantly shorter than non-Hispanic byline stories; stories by the former did not feature Hispanic participants to any greater extent.

Reasons for Inclusion. There was a single basis for categorizing these stories as Hispanic: 98 percent had one or more Spanish surnames within the body of the story. The ethnicity of Hispanic participants was mentioned in 2 percent or less of the stories.

Emphasis and Sources. Typically, these were general sports stories that did not emphasize Hispanic participants; 93 percent fit that description, while 7 percent (about 10 stories) centered on Hispanic participants or activities. The primary Hispanic sports stories were no more likely to be written by a Hispanic reporter but contained proportionately more Hispanic individuals.

An average of 4.62 Spanish surnames and 19.17 total surnames appeared in each sports story; 24 percent of the surnames were Hispanic.

Compared to news stories, sports had 2.14 more Spanish surnames and 11.50 more total surnames per story. Hispanic surnames comprised 32 percent of news story surnames and 24 percent of sports surnames.

The sources cited in the stories also were examined for ethnic surnames. Single sources and first sources quoted were less likely to be Hispanic (20 percent) by comparison with second (26 percent) and third sources (36 percent). Thus, if more than one source was cited, the subsequent ones were more likely to be Hispanic; but even a substantial proportion of the first sources were Hispanic.

Newspaper Differences. The Tucson and Visalia papers carried an average of 2.5 local sports stories with Hispanic information each day; Stockton, Salinas, and Santa Fe ran 1.7 items per day, and San Bernardino carried less than one such story per day. The following table compares the sports newshole proportion per day with the Hispanic proportion of the population in those cities:

	Sports Newshole, Hispanic Items	Hispanic Population
Santa Fe	80%	55–65%
Visalia	65%	20–30%
Salinas	58%	20–30%
Tucson	35%	20–30%
Stockton	36%	20–30%
San Bernardino	24%	20–30%

All newspapers were larger in allocation of sports newshole to items inclusive of Hispanics than their Hispanic population proportions. All were substantially larger, save San Bernardino. It is also important to compare these newshole proportions with those found in the general local news analysis. The Hispanic sports newshole proportions were much larger than their local newshole counterparts, e.g., 32 percent general news and 58 percent sports newshole in Salinas; 17 percent and 36 percent, respectively, in Stockton; and the largest discrepancy, 12 percent for local news and 65 percent for sports news in Visalia.

A comparison of story size by city showed no significant differences. There were also no differences among papers in terms of relative inclusion of Hispanic participants in these stories.

Photos

Photographs were a further source of content in which the display of Hispanics could be examined.

Space. A total of 132 photographs containing Hispanics or Hispanic events were found in the 72 issues of the six newspapers, or just under two photos per issue. These photos filled 22 percent of the total local photo hole in those issues, or about one in five photos can be estimated to have pictured a Hispanic.

Prominence. Ten percent of the Hispanic pictures appeared on the front page. Seventy percent were located above the fold, 15 percent across the fold, and 15 percent below it. Above-fold pictures were more likely found later in the paper. The largest Hispanic photos were in the front section of the paper.

Reason for Inclusion. Eighty-six percent of the photos qualified as Hispanic because the cutline included a Hispanic surname; 21 percent included a reference to a Hispanic cultural activity; no other specific basis for inclusion was found. The fact that so many of the photos qualified solely because of the names cited (71 percent) means that the photos were not connected with uniquely Hispanic activities. Had they been, then culture or ethnicity would have been coded as well. Thus, the inclusion of Hispanics in photos occurred largely in non-ethnic contexts. Photos that qualified only because of Hispanic surnames were more likely in later sections of the paper.

Content. Three-fourths of the pictures were news photos, and the remainder were feature photos. Hispanic surnames constituted 74 percent of all surnames in the photos. The number of people in the Hispanic photos varied: 3 percent had no people, 39 percent were of a single person, 22 percent were of two people, 12 percent were of three people, and 24 percent contained four or more people.

The following table displays the featured content basis for the photographs:

	Total Referents*
Sports	26%
Culture	24%
Hard news	17%
Advice (e.g., gardening tips)	8%
Features	5%
Crime	2%
Minority issues	2%
Other	23%

*Multiple content areas were not reflected in any more than 3 percent of any single content category: exclusive and multiple topics have been combined.

Sports and cultural event photos were dominant; crime and minority issue photos were insignificant with respect to incidence of Hispanics.

When there was a cutline, it included an average of 1.78 Spanish surnames and 2.39 total surnames. Fourteen percent had no cutline. Photos with more people had lower proportions of Hispanic surnames to total surnames. Hard-news photos contained fewer Spanish surnames. Forty-two percent of surnames appearing in hard-news stories were Hispanic, compared to 77 percent in feature photos.

Newspaper Differences. Santa Fe carried 3.4 Hispanic photos per issue, Tucson ran 2.7, Visalia published 1.7, and the remaining cities averaged 1. Thus, the overall average of just under 2 per day has much variance across the study sites.

Again, a useful means of examining the relative use of photos with Hispanics involves a comparison with the community's representation of Hispanics. This is in the following table:

	Local Hispanic Photo Hole /Total local Photo Hole	Hispanic Population Proportion
Santa Fe	52%	55–65%
Tucson	24%	20–30%
Visalia	21%	20–30%
Salinas	17%	20–30%
Stockton	13%	20–30%
San Bernardino	11%	20–30%

The display of Hispanics in photo coverage in Santa Fe, Tucson, Visalia, and Salinas corresponds quite closely with the Hispanic population in those communities. Stockton and San Bernardino fare less well using that criterion.

Bulletins

The analysis of bulletins included examining listings of births, deaths, crimes, weddings, community events, etc.

Space. This process identified exactly 200 bulletins in the 72 issues that contained one or more Hispanic-related items, or three bulletins a day across six different newspapers. The newshole for bulletins containing Hispanic item(s) was 50 percent of the total newshole for bulletins. Essentially one of every two bulletins in these papers contained some Hispanic announcement.

The remainder of the analysis centers only on those bulletins that did contain one or more Hispanic announcements. From this analysis, we find:

1. The average length of Hispanic announcements (4.1 column inches) filled one-third of the average bulletin space in which they were included.
2. The average number of Hispanic items (4.5) in these bulletins was one-third of the total items in these listings.

Given this comparability in length and frequency and the fact that one-half the total bulletin newshole contained any Hispanic listings, it may be inferred that one-sixth to one-seventh of the newspapers' bulletin items referred to Hispanics.

Content. The distribution of bulletins containing Hispanic items was as follows:

Deaths	19%
Weddings	16%
Crime	13%
Community events	10%
Legal	9%
Sports	8%
Births	8%
Divorce	3%
Other	16%

Deaths, weddings, and crime announcements were most likely to include Hispanic entries, but these differed in terms of Hispanic representation. Across the four papers that carried bulletins of this type, among bulletins containing Hispanic announcements 25 percent of the wedding announcements and 34 percent of the death announcements were Hispanic. However, 40 percent of the crime announcements were Hispanic.

Reasons for Inclusion. In this content category, 96 percent of the items qualified because they contained a Hispanic surname.

Prominence. One-half the bulletins containing Hispanic items were located in the first five pages of the newspaper section in which they appeared; 4 percent were found on the first page of that section. The second section of the paper was predominant in containing these bulletins (44 percent).

Newspaper Differences. Above, we reported an average of 3 Hispanic bulletins a day across the six newspapers studied. This varies from just under 2 bulletins per day in Santa Fe and Visalia to 4.5 per day in Tucson; the other three cities averaged 3 bulletins per day. This variability can be examined better by a comparative analysis of bulletins with and without Hispanic items, in relation to the Hispanic population in the several communities, as in the following table:

	(1) Local Newshole w/Hispanic Bulletins	(2) Local Hispanic Items in Hispanic Bulletins*	(3) Local Hispanic Items/ Total Items†	(4) Hispanic Population
Santa Fe	76%	23%	17%	55–65%
Tucson	52%	27%	14%	20–30%
Stockton	54%	16%	9%	20–30%
Salinas	45%	38%	17%	20–30%
San Bernardino	36%	29%	10%	20–30%
Visalia	25%	26%	7%	20–30%

*This is computed only among bulletins with one or more Hispanic announcements.

†This is computed by multiplying columns 2 and 1. It makes the assumption that the newshole space without Hispanic items has a proportionate number of total items.

Column 1 indicates the proportions of newshole space that contain one or more Hispanic items. Three-fourths of the total space encompassed by bulletins in Santa Fe, for example, contains some space with Hispanic announcements, whereas in Visalia the parallel proportion is 25 percent.

Within the newshole space, column 2 identifies the Hispanic proportions. They range from 16 percent in Stockton to 38 percent in Salinas. This is a measure of density of Hispanic items within bulletins containing any Hispanic items.

Column 3 contains the critical findings. Salinas comes the closest to announcing Hispanic events in proportion to the Hispanic population in that community, followed by Tucson. Stockton, San Bernardino, and Visalia are considerably more discrepant with that criterion. The Santa Fe data are the most extreme in terms of the size of the disparity between their use of Hispanic bulletin items and the proportion of Hispanics residing in that city.

The distribution of Hispanic announcements by content was also quite variable by city. We looked at the proportion of Hispanic weddings, deaths, and crimes reported in four cities (the two smallest did not print crime bulletins).

	Weddings	Deaths	Crime
Salinas	42%	53%	53%
San Bernardino	26%	27%	45%
Tucson	20%	12%	27%
Stockton	27%	31%	38%

Crime bulletins contained the largest proportions of Hispanic items.

SUMMARY AND DISCUSSION

In addition to summarizing the key findings for the several kinds of news material examined, here we have an opportunity to comment on certain implications for subsequent news coverage of the Hispanic community. Because a common goal is the possible improvement in coverage of Hispanic people and activities, we can speculate in a fashion designed to further that goal. We will examine each major news content area separately.

Local News

One-fourth of the total local newshole in the newspapers studied contained items that mentioned Hispanic individuals or reported on Hispanic activities; the number of stories averaged four each day of the study period. These were spread equally through the first, second, and subsequent sections of the papers. Further, one story in six carried a byline of a Hispanic reporter and two in six of a non-Hispanic reporter. Crime content was no more regular than cultural features on the Hispanic community; both were less prominent than hard-news stories and sports stories. Finally, there was systematic inclusion of Hispanic sources in these stories; Hispanic sources were used in 40 percent of these stories. Taken together, this should serve to dampen criticism of news coverage of Hispanics in local cities, at least for these characteristics. There are Hispanic stories regularly presented; there are Hispanic reporter bylines; and Hispanics themselves are regularly interviewed in the collection of information.

If there is a down side in straight news coverage of Hispanics, it may be in terms of the variability identified across the different newspapers. Story size varied, the number of stories per day varied, and the emphasis on crime differed extensively. It may be more appropriate to look at what specific papers are or are not doing, rather than broadly praising or condemning newspapers in general. Local management varies, and in comparative terms at least, some local newspapers are doing more than an adequate job in reflecting Hispanic news events. That comparative base offers a perspective on judging local coverage that living in but one community cannot provide. Such studies as these can demonstrate what cross-city findings look like; within a community, the task remains with the local newspaper to convince the community that its coverage is comprehensive and balanced.

Editorials

The quantity of editorial page material relating to Hispanics seems deficient. In four sites, there were only three or four codable items in the 2-week period; one site accounted for one-half of all the editorial page items, including editorials, local columns, and letters to the editor. Further, one-half of all the material that qualified consisted of letters to the editor from Hispanic writers. The editorial newshole proportion referring to Hispanic people and issues (15 percent) was the smallest of all the newspaper content areas examined in this study. Crime was more prominent a content topic for editorial page material than for general news or in the paper's photo coverage. Editorials were more likely than other other types of items to deal with minority issues and to have qualified for reasons other than Spanish surnames.

Because local non-Hispanic editorial items were not coded, it is not known how much total local editorial space is devoted to letters to the editor, how much to local columns, and so on. However, it seems that Hispanics are more ignored on the editorial page than in other sections of the newspaper examined.

Sports

Local sports participants obviously include many Hispanic Americans. That is most likely the basis for their extensive inclusion in local sports stories. Sports is the largest single content area containing references to local Hispanics. Nearly 1 of every 2 local sports stories identifies a Hispanic, but total local sports coverage averaged only 4.5 stories each issue. Further, there appears to be more dependence on Hispanic sources in these stories than earlier reports suggested.

Distinctively Hispanic sports stories were rare in the 2-week sample time period, about one per newspaper. This may reflect the organization of local sports activities wtihin the communities, but that possibility should be verified.

Two local sports stories a day identifying Hispanic participants may be adequate coverage; it would be difficult to assess that level of coverage without further information as to the local sports events in each community.

One specific deficiency is in staffing, if we can project from byline usage is that 6 percent of the byline stories were by Hispanic reporters, and that is substantially less than the Hispanic bylines found in the general news section of the papers. Recruitment of more Hispanic sports reporters and/or the kinds of assignments that yield bylines are worth considering.

Photos

These newspapers printed two photographs per issue that contained one or more Hispanics. These photos were prominently displayed, often on the front page of the newspaper, and were about one-fifth of all the local pictures used.

The photos were most often news photos not associated with particular Hispanic community events but were used because of their general news content. However, one-fourth of them were related to Hispanic cultural activities, with sports photos and hard-news photos being the other central content categories. Crime and minority issues, including problem situations, were largely omitted from photo coverage. Thus, the bulk of the photographs that included Hispanics were for non-Hispanic reasons, while a substantial subset did focus on Hispanic events.

Bulletins

It seems reasonable that Hispanics are born, wed, die, and commit crimes at least somewhat proportionately to their presence in a community. Yet, the bulletin listings of these newspapers overall underrepresent Hispanics. At most, one-sixth of all such listings included an individual with a Hispanic surname in communities where the nontransient Hispanic population comprised at least 20 percent of the citizens (and more than 50 percent in one of them). We recognize that the Hispanic population is a younger group, and somewhat fewer people will be reflected in some of these kinds of listings, but the overall pattern of inclusion needs to be considered. Perhaps Hispanics are less likely to report such activities, but birth and death information typically originates with hospitals and weddings with churches, where all newspapers maintain contacts. One-half the bulletin listings carried no Hispanic announcements, among those that did, crime entries occurred more prominently than weddings or deaths. There was considerable variation among the newspapers in terms of their inclusion of Hispanics in these listings, but none appear to reflect the Hispanic community proportions adequately. This seems a simple enough area of reporting to upgrade, if these conclusions are reasonable.

If one were to make a summary evaluation of the extent to which the newspapers studied are servicing the Hispanic community in their locales, and do so solely on the basis of the story types and story attributes studied here, then the report card would look like this:

1. Sports news and photo coverage get high marks for their inclusion of local Hispanics.
2. Local news coverage exclusive of sports gets a passing grade—good, not excellent, but better than it is currently receiving credit for.
3. Editorial coverage and bulletin listings of Hispanic people and activities are below average and in need of considerable attention.

Perhaps more important than this summary is the point that on each one of these content dimensions some newspapers studied are doing very well and others are doing very poorly. From an analytical viewpoint, it is possible to talk about newspapers in general; from a community view, it is the hometown newspaper alone that matters.

7

A STYLISTIC ANALYSIS OF NEWSPAPER COVERAGE OF MEXICAN AMERICANS

Donald G. Ellis
Michael Burgoon
Terry Slater
Rodney Reynolds
Judee K. Burgoon
Bradley S. Greenberg
Felipe Korzenny

The purpose of this investigation was to provide information about some stylistic characteristics of newspapers in communities with large Hispanic populations. Of specific interest was readability, or general comprehensibility of the selected newspapers. Readability is especially important for three reasons. First, compositional factors contribute most to a reader's ability to understand a story. Since a reader's satisfaction and likelihood of purchasing a newspaper are directly related to comprehension, it is in the interest of management to pay special attention to the quality of written material (Burgoon, et al., 1981). Second, the stylistic features of a newspaper can be controlled. A newspaper may have little influence over reader abilities or interests but can manipulate style variables to increase the probability of a reader's comprehending a story. Finally, the readability of community newspapers serves important sociological functions. A satisfying and readable newspaper is central to the well-being of the local culture.

Readability is a category of general stylistic analyses. Stylistic analyses have a long history that encompasses a broad range of interests. Early work was primarily concerned with describing literature and identifying literary styles, authors, and dates. But more contemporary work has turned toward analyses of interaction between a reader and a written document. That is, research questions focus on how stylistic variables act as stimuli to evoke reader responses. This perspective is responsible for generating a large volume of research on how the stylistic qualities of newspapers elicit judgments in readers. The general research strategy has been to identify clusters of stylistic variables that correlate with reader judgments. Lynch (1970) and Burgoon et al. (1981) summarize this research. They report that stylistic research has been concerned with either the actual linguistic make-up of stories or the criteria that readers use to judge stories. Typical stylistic variables are productivity, sentence length, consistency, lexical diversity, syntactic dispersion, abstraction, complexity, redundancy, pausality, personalism, emotiveness, and readability. And reader judgments are usually made with respect to comprehension, human interest, sensationalism, and creativity. The most common research strategy is to correlate a stylistic variable with a judgment category and show how one predicts the other.

The measurement of readability has received the brunt of research attention. Readability is a technique for estimating a reader's probable success in understanding a piece of writing (Klare, 1963). Readability analyses originated in the 1920's and gained popularity thereafter. The formula has been applied to textbooks (Tankard and Tankard, 1977), government regulations (Pyrczak, 1976), and insurance policies. The readability of newspapers has been especially popular. Readability experts have worked with the wire services to make wire stories more comprehensible, and most sections of newspapers have been analyzed for readability. Researchers have studied the readability of various story types (Razik, 1969), news stories versus editorials (Moznette and Rarick, 1968), children's sections (Bittner and Shamo, 1976), and others.

The technique for measuring readability has varied with changing assumptions about what contributes to comprehension. Early theorists maintained that vocabulary was most responsible for determining the reading ease or difficulty of a written passage. Researchers, therefore, measured readability by comparing the words of a passage to lists of common words. A passage was difficult if it contained rare words or a large number of different words. This beginning work was significantly advanced by two researchers who interviewed librarians, teachers, publishers, and other interested parties about what contributed to readability (Gray and Leary, 1935); these interviews produced a large variable list. A research program was set into motion, and in time this list was reduced to five variables that accurately and parsimoniously predicted readability. The variables were (1) number of different words, (2) number of first, second, and third person pronouns, (3) average sentence length, (4) percentage of different words, and (5) number of prepositional phrases. The early work, although useful, often contained two problems. First, lists of difficult or easy words are too subject to historical changes and individual discriminations. Moreover, word lists make difficulty dependent on frequency of usage. The second problem was the absence of a standard scale for interpretation. It was only possible to compare two samples to see which was more or less difficult. An individual score could not be interpreted according to a standard measure.

Flesch worked to improve the readability formula by eliminating the list of uncommon words. Although he thought that abstract words would promote difficult reading, he found that a list of abstract words was no better at predicting readability than counting the number of prefixes and suffixes contained in a written passage. Moreover, Flesch found that "appeal" or human interest was equally as important to readability so he counted the number of personal references in a sample and added this to his formula. After some variations on the original formula Flesch settled on two formulas, one for readability and one for human interest. The Flesch readability formula was used in this research; the formula is reproduced below (Klare, 1963):

$$R = 206.835 - .846X_1 - 1.015X_2$$
$$R = \text{readability}$$
$$X_1 = \text{number of syllables per 100 words}$$
$$X_2 = \text{average number of words per sentence}$$

The creation of a standard scale by means of which Flesch readability scores can be compared to educational level is an especially attractive feature of Flesch's procedure.

Measuring readability in this study was a matter of applying the Flesch formula to selected sections of the newspapers in the target communities. We conducted analyses on the newspapers with the following four variables in mind:

1. *Story type.* We checked for differences among wire stories, local front page, non-Hispanic stories, local Hispanic stories, and editorials.

2. *Market.* There were six markets: Salinas, San Bernadino, Santa Fe, Stockton, Tucson, and Visalia. We then combined story type with market to examine possible interactions.

3. *Day of the week.* Stories were sampled from each day of the week except Sunday to see if readability varied throughout the week. We then made this comparison on Hispanic stories only.

4. *Page.* Here front-page stories were compared to stories not on the front page. This variable was then combined with market to search for a possible interaction between story placement and market.

PROCEDURES

Gannett newspapers from six southwestern U.S. communities were used in this study. Twelve issues per market were used to collect stories for stylistic analysis. The markets included: the *Californian,* Salinas; *The Sun,* San

Bernardino; *The New Mexican,* Santa Fe; the *Stockton Record,* Stockton; the *Tucson Citizen,* Tucson; and the *Times-Delta,* Visalia. Papers were collected during January and February 1980, and a composite 2-week sample, including two issues of each day of the week except Sunday, was randomly selected. January issues included the following: 18 (Friday), 19 (Saturday), 24 (Thursday), 28 (Monday), and 30 (Wednesday). The February issues were 4 (Monday), 5 (Tuesday), 14 (Thursday), 16 (Saturday), 19 (Tuesday), 20 (Wednesday), and 29 (Friday). A total of 72 newspaper issues were studied.

The story types selected for analysis were defined as follows:

1. *Wire:* a front-page UPI or AP story

2. *Local:* a front-page story written by newspaper staff members

3. *Hispanic:* a local story with the primary emphasis on one or more persons with a Spanish surname (surnames had to appear on the 1980 Census List of Spanish surnames), or a story where Hispanic ethnicity or culture was the central theme was selected

4. *Editorial:* a staff-written article located on the editorial or opinion pages voicing the position of the newspaper on a given topic

Data Collection

All stories selected had to be at least 300 words long. Another criterion for selecting stories was that each had to be the leading article of its type. For example, a story qualifying as a leading wire or leading local story had to be on the front page and have the largest headline and occupy the most column inches. The first Hispanic story over 300 words was selected as the leading Hispanic story. The editorial located directly under the headline "Editorial" or "Opinion" was selected as the leading editorial unless it was under 300 words. If the first editorial was less than 300 words, the editorial next to or beneath the disqualified editorial was selected. In most of the newspapers the editorial page was in the first section.

Typically, one example of each story type was selected per issue, but there were some exceptions. Articles under 300 words, regardless of story type, were excluded. When leading wire or local stories were too short, no other article on the front page could qualify as the leading story. Hispanic stories and editorials were excluded for an issue only when no story over 300 words could be located.

Any leading wire story from one newspaper that duplicated a leading wire story from another paper was omitted. When this occurred, no other wire story was selected. If a story was both a leading local story and a leading Hispanic one, it was entered as the leading Hispanic story with no other local story chosen for that issue. When no Hispanic story was printed in an issue, no Hispanic item was submitted; this occurred most frequently in Visalia and

Stockton. Similarly, when no wire or local story appeared on the front page of an issue, no substitute was selected. The same was true for editorials.

Once articles were located, a story of 300 to 350 words with a random start point was selected from each article for analysis. For example, one entry might begin with the first paragraph of an article while another might begin with paragraph seven. In this way we avoided measuring only the beginning 300 to 350 words in every article. Random selection of new items insured the representation of entire stories. A total of 227 stories were analyzed. The number per market was as follows: Salinas, 43; San Bernardino, 43; Santa Fe, 35; Stockton, 33; Tucson, 39; and Visalia, 34. The number per story type was *Wire*, 58; *Local*, 54; *Hispanic*, 51; and *Editorial*, 64.

Analyses

Stories were loaded into the computer for initial analysis. A readability program was accessed to generate the summary variable list. These variables were (1) percent of words of three or more syllables, (2) average number of words per sentence, and (3) average number of syllables per word. The summary variables were then used in calculating the Flesch Index. The Flesch Index is determined by counting the number of syllables per 100 words and the average number of words per sentence and then applying the formula discussed earlier. The result is the Reading Ease score; lower scores represent the most difficult end of the continuum and higher scores represent the easiest. This score is then convertible to a grade-level reading index. The Flesch Index, along with the percent of "hi-calorie" words (three or more syllables) became the dependent variables for this study. The independent variables were story type, market, day of the week, and page.

The statistical analyses were correlations and analysis of variance. First, correlations were run on a set of variables composed of Flesch score, percentage of polysyllabic words, average words per sentence, and average syllables per word to check for theoretically expected relationships. The analyses of variance were used to tap the relationships between the independent and dependent variables. One-way analysis of variance was used to test the effects of story type, market, day of the week, and page. Two-way analysis of variance was used to test the market by page and market by story type relationships. Finally, *post-hoc* tests were conducted using Newman-Keuls procedure.

RESULTS

This section reports the results of the analysis of the data. The chart for converting Flesch score to grade levels appears in Table 7.1.

TABLE 7.1. Grade equivalents for Flesch reading ease scores.

Reading Ease Score	Description of Style	Estimated Reading Grade
90–100	Very easy	5th grade
80–90	Easy	6th grade
70–80	Fairly easy	7th grade
60–70	Standard	8th and 9th grade
50–60	Fairly difficult	10th to 12th grade
30–50	Difficult	13th to 16th grade (college)
0–30	Very difficult	college graduate

Correlations

Since several of the variables might tap the same underlying phenomenon, the first analysis examined the degree to which the measures were correlated with each other (Table 7.2).

TABLE 7.2. Correlation matrix.

	Percent big words	Average syllables per word	Average syllables per word
Average words per sentence	.07		
Average syllables per word	.90	.13	
Flesch score	−.81	−.54	−.87

The average words per sentence and the average syllables per word are both used in the calculation of the Flesch score. Thus, the degree of their correlation with the Flesch score and their lack of correlation with each other are as expected. Given the role of the average words per sentence and the average syllables per word in the Flesch score, we decided that there was no need to include these measures in further analyses.

The percent of big words is determined by a count of the words that have three or more syllables. Thus, the correlation between the count of big words and the average number of syllables per word is obviously high. The conceptual uniqueness of this measure, however, provided the justification for including it in the subsequent analyses.

Differences by Type of Stories

Table 7.3 reports the results of the one-way analysis of variance for the four types of stories. There is a significant difference among types of stories on the percent of words that are big and on the Flesch scores. *Post-hoc* compari-

TABLE 7.3. Dependence variable by story type (all markets combined).

	Wire	Local	Hispanic	Editorial	Grand $\bar{X}$s
Percent					
big words	15	13	14	16	15
Flesch score	52.06	57.61	58.54	51.59	54.70
(n)	(58)	(54)	(51)	(64)	(227)
	Percent big words	$F = 5.306$, $df = 3/223$, $p = .002$, $\omega^2 = .05$			
	Flesch	$F = 8.710$, $df = 3/223$, $p = .001$, $\omega^2 = .09$			

sons of cell differences reveal that both wire stories and editorials differ significantly from local stories and Hispanic stories. The wire stories and the editorials, however, do not significantly differ from each other. Similarly, the local stories and the Hispanic stories do not differ significantly. The *omega*-square statistic indicates that readability and the number of big words account for a moderate to low degree of the variance attributable to differences between the types of stories.

Differences by Market

Table 7.4 provides the results of the one-way analysis of variance for the six markets. There is a significant difference among the markets on the variable for percent of big words and on the Flesch scores. *Post-hoc* comparisons of cell differences reveal that only Salinas (low) and Stockton (high) differ from each other on the number of big words and on the Flesch scores.

TABLE 7.4. Dependent variable by market (all data).

	Salinas	San Bernardino	Santa Fe	Stockton	Tucson	Visalia	Grand $\bar{X}$s
Percent of							
big words	13	16	14	14	15	14	15
Flesch							
score	57.71	52.09	55.73	51.98	54.32	56.24	54.70
(n)	(43)	(43)	(35)	(33)	(39)	(34)	(227)
	Percent of big words	$F = 2.060$, $df = 5/221$, $p = .07$, $\omega^2 = .02$					
	Flesch	$F = 2.298$, $df = 5/221$, $p = .05$, $\omega^2 = .03$					

With differences discovered for both market and story type there appeared to be a potential for an interaction effect in that different newspapers might treat Hispanic-related stories differently. The examination of a possible interaction between market and story type was conducted by the use of a two-way analysis of variance (Table 7.5). The interaction of market and story types was not supported. It should be noted, however, that the interaction did approach significance for Flesch scores. In fact, this trend in the data is due to the fact that in the Santa Fe and Tucson newspapers, Hispanic stories were written at a level about two grades lower than were other local stories. On the other hand, the complexity of writing increased in Stockton and San Bernardino when the content was about the Hispanic community. Part of this interaction is also caused by the extremely complex writing of San Bernardino editorials.

TABLE 7.5. Dependent variable by market by story type (all data).

		Salinas	San Bernardino	Santa Fe	Stockton	Tucson	Visalia	Row $\bar{x}s$
	A.	14	16	17	16	15	15	15
Wire	B.	54.46	51.95	49.95	48.80	51.72	53.38	52.06
	(n)	(12)	(12)	(6)	(8)	(9)	(11)	(58)
	A.	11	15	16	12	15	12	13
Local	B.	63.19	57.27	50.17	56.87	54.70	61.66	57.61
	(n)	(9)	(11)	(6)	(11)	(9)	(8)	(54)
	A.	13	16	13	14	13	13	14
Hispanic	B.	57.59	53.37	64.72	51.20	61.87	56.25	58.54
	(n)	(10)	(10)	(12)	(4)	(9)	(6)	(51)
	A.	15	17	14	16	16	15	16
Editorial	B.	56.96	45.29	52.10	49.45	50.31	54.91	51.59
	(n)	(12)	(10)	(11)	(10)	(12)	(9)	(64)
	A.	13	16	14	14	15	14	15
Column $\bar{x}s$	B.	57.51	52.09	55.73	51.98	54.32	56.24	54.70
	(n)	(43)	(43)	(35)	(33)	(39)	(34)	(227)

By story type
a. = Percent of big words $F = 5.834$, $df = 3/203$, $p = .001$, $\omega^2 = .05$
b. = Flesch $F = 9.691$, $df = 3/203$, $p = .001$, $\omega^2 = .09$
By market
a. = Percent of big words $F = 2.409$, $df = 5/203$, $p = .038$, $\omega^2 = .02$
b. = Flesch $F = 2.824$, $df = 5/203$, $p = .017$, $\omega^2 = .03$
Interactions (market by story)
a. = Percent of big words $F = 1.043$, $df = 15/203$, $p < .05$
b. = Flesch $F = 1.613$, $df = 15/203$, $p = .07$

Differences by Day of the Week

Table 7.6 reports the results of the one-way analysis of variance for the day of the week. There were no significant differences attributable to this

TABLE 7.6. Dependent variable by day of the week (all data).

	Monday	Tuesday	Wednesday	Thursday	Friday	Saturday	Grand $\overline{X}s$
Percent of big words	14	41	14	15	15	15	15
Flesch score	56.42	56.70	54.58	55.11	51.87	53.59	54.70
(n)	(34)	(41)	(38)	(40)	(40)	(34)	(227)
	Percent of big words		$F = .724$, $df = 5/221$, $p > .05$				
	Flesch		$F = 1.359$, $df = 5/221$, $p > .05$				

TABLE 7.7. Dependent variable by day (Hispanic stories only).

	Monday	Tuesday	Wednesday	Thursday	Friday	Saturday	Grand $\bar{X}s$
Percent of big words	13	13	14	14	14	14	14
Flesch score	60.00	63.02	56.32	56.23	60.41	55.61	58.54
(n)	(7)	(9)	(10)	(10)	(8)	(7)	(51)
Percent of big words		$F = .211, df = 5/45, p > .05$					
Flesch		$F = .771, df = 5/45, p > .05$					

variable. Similarly, when Hispanic stories were isolated in the analysis, there were no significant differences found (Table 7.7).

Differences by Page

We suspected that the readability and number of big words might vary as a function of where the article appeared (front page, not front page). Table 7.8 provides the results of the two-way analysis of variance for page and market. There were no main effects for page placement. Further, the potential interactions between page placement and market were also nonsignificant.

TABLE 7.8. Dependent variable by market by page (all data).

		Salinas	San Bernardino	Santa Fe	Stockton	Tucson	Visalia	Row $\bar{x}s$
Front page*	A.	13	15	15	14	14	14	14
	B.	57.84	54.41	53.92	53.26	54.34	55.98	55.10
	(n)	(26)	(26)	(18)	(20)	(20)	(22)	(132)
Not front page	A.	14	17	13	15	15	14	15
	B.	57.52	48.55	57.64	50.02	54.28	56.72	54.16
	(n)	(17)	(17)	(17)	(13)	(19)	(12)	(95)
Column $\bar{x}s$	A.	13	16	14	14	15	14	15
	B.	57.51	52.09	55.73	51.98	54.32	56.24	54.70
	(n)	(43)	(43)	(35)	(33)	(39)	(34)	(227)

By page
a. = Percent of big words $F = 1.740, df = 1/215, p > .05$
b. = Flesch $F = .530, df = 1/215, p > .05$
Interactions (page by market)
a. = Percent of big words $F = 1.182, df = 5/215, p > .05$
b. = Flesch $F = 1.222, df = 5/215, p > .05$

Front-page stories included all wire stories, all local stories, and a subset of the Hispanic stories; *Not front page* stories included in all editorial page material used and the remainder of the Hispanic stories.

Previous research has suggested that newspapers may be biased in their placement of articles about Hispanics. Table 7.9 shows the results of one-way analysis of variance for page placement of Hispanic stories. The analysis of

TABLE 7.9. Dependent variable by page (Hispanic stories only).

	Front Page	Not Front Page	Grand $\bar{X}s$
Percent of big words	14	14	14
Flesch score	57.10	59.46	58.54
(n)	(20)	(31)	(51)
Percent of big words	$F = .082, df = 1/49, p > .05$		
Flesch	$F = .638, df = 1/49, p > .05$		

the data indicate that there are no significant differences in readability of Hispanic stories placed on the front page and those placed elsewhere in the newspapers.

SUMMARY AND DISCUSSION

It is clear from this investigation that the readability of editorials and national reports differs significantly from that of local reports. On the whole, editorials and wire reports are much more difficult to read than any local writing. Stories about Hispanics were no different across all markets combined than were other local stories. The practical implications of such analyses are obvious. If management wishes to raise comprehensibility, careful attention is going to have to be given to editing the wire report, and editorials are going to have to be written at a different level.

There were differences across the markets in overall readability. The writing in Stockton and San Bernardino is the most difficult to read of any in the investigation. Given the demographics of these two communities, the newspapers are possibly more difficult than they should be for large numbers of people in these two communities. The other four markets analyzed in this investigation were not different from each other on overall difficulty of the material analyzed.

There were some important differences of story types across the different markets studied. The first obvious concern is the differences in the wire report. Santa Fe and Stockton have the most-difficult-to-read national stories, and all six markets have national stories that are significantly more difficult than their local report. Any such differences must be due to differential editing practices in the separate newsrooms. The local report for non-Hispanic stories is very difficult in Santa Fe and very easy in Salinas and Visalia. Hispanic stories are written at a much lower grade level in San Bernardino and Tucson than elsewhere. Moreover, in these two cities, stories about Hispanics are written at a much lower level than the rest of the local report. In contrast, stories in Stockton about Hispanics are much more difficult to read. In a similar way, editorials in Stockton and San Bernardino are most difficult to read.

There are probably unintentional factors influencing the writing of specific types of stories in these different communities. The writing style differs depending on the type of story being produced. Moreover, there seems at times to be a mismatch between the complexity of writing in the newspapers studied and the demographics of the community involved. When writing is beyond the comprehension of large numbers of the population in a given city, circulation and user satisfaction can be negatively influenced.

These data suggest that careful attention needs to be paid to the editing of national and local stories. Newsroom managers should carefully consider why stories about Hispanics differ in comprehensibility from the rest of the local report. Moreover, it is clear that differential editing practices affect the comprehensibility of the national report, the editorial page, and the local pages.

There were no differences in readability across days of the week studied. Moreover, stories on the front page were no more readable than stories placed elsewhere in the newspaper. Availability of specific staff members on different days of the week or placement of the story was not an explanation for the differences found in writing style throughout these six newspapers.

These data raise a number of questions about why such differences occur in objective measures of writing style in these different newspapers. Answers to these questions can be the beginning in providing newspapers that serve both Anglos and Hispanics with stories that are comprehensible regardless of whether they originate on the wire or are produced in a local newsroom.

IV

WHAT REMAINS?

8
SUMMARY OF FINDINGS

SUMMARY

The four empirical studies presented for the first time in this volume reflect two major field surveys and two major sets of newspaper analyses. Together they offer a comprehensive examination of Hispanics and the media from the perspectives of both public response and media coverage. We bring together the results of the several studies in a single section to help the researcher and the practitioner sort out relevant and useful findings.

For the field surveys, we have reorganized the results by medium rather than by sets of variables; such a presentation should be especially useful to media-oriented readers.

Adult Survey

In this study, adult Anglos and Hispanics were questioned intensively about three media: newspapers, radio, and television. The summary in this section will focus on these media. In addition, adults' content preferences were assessed without differentiating the originating medium, so we will add a general summary of that critical findings area.

Figure 8.1 presents the newspaper results. Anglos read the newspaper more regularly than do Hispanics, but Hispanics' evaluation of newspapers are as positive or more positive on many key issues. In respect to general measures of satisfaction—overall satisfaction and satisfaction with how well the newspaper is rated in fulfilling those purposes Hispanics deem most important—Hispanics' judgments are more favorable than Anglos'.

One set of 30 items dealt with the possible reasons for reading the newspaper. Respondents rated the importance of each reason as a basis for their own reading. For 21 items, Hispanics' ratings are greater than Anglos'. But eight of the top 10 most important reasons are held in common by both Hispanics and Anglos: immediate knowledge of local, national and international events; comprehensiveness of coverage of local and non-local events; variety of local and non-local news; to keep informed about local events; and for the day's headlines.

Despite these overall positive ratings, however, Anglos exceed Hispanics on each of the measures of newspaper access and use. The positive newspaper judgments do not yet manifest themselves in use of or dependence on the newspaper.

FIGURE 8.1. Newspaper results.

Hispanic and Anglo adults are equivalent
> . . . in amount of time spent reading newspapers and magazines (among readers)
> . . . in positive evaluations of newspaper image on trust, bias, receptivity, racism, community surveillance, accuracy, sensationalism, caring, community concern, and representativeness
> . . . in use of newspapers as the primary source of information for major purchases
> . . . in the relative importance to them of the newspaper's immediacy, comprehensiveness, and variety of coverage of local and non-local news; in keeping them informed about local events; and for the day's headlines

Hispanics exceed Anglos
> . . . in overall satisfaction with local newspapers
> . . . in positive evaluations of newspaper image on competence, liveliness, timeliness, power, influence, and courage
> . . . in rating overall how well their local newspaper satisfies the purposes they cited as important (including nonreaders)

Anglos exceed Hispanics
> . . . in percentage who read newspapers and magazines
> . . . in proportion of household members who read newspapers
> . . . in frequency of newspaper readership
> . . . in percentage who subscribe to newspapers
> . . . in amount of time spent reading newspapers (including nonreaders)
> . . . in satisfaction with newspaper coverage of locals and their accomplishments, local cultural activities, social news, and crime.
> . . . in use of newspaper as the primary source of information for job opportunities, local political activities, and community events

In respect to newspaper image characteristics, more image attributes are rated equivalently by both groups of adults than are rated differently.

The multiple regression analyses within the adult samples yielded six prediction equations in which the variance accounted for exceeded .20, actually ranging from .24 to .35. We will summarize those results here for the composite information they provide.

Among newspaper users, frequency of newspaper readership was largely reflected in certain demographic characteristics—exclusive of ethnicity. Age, income, and schooling (the more of each, the more reading) were strong correlates of frequency of newspaper reading, as was time spent reading.

Satisfaction with the local daily newspaper was best predicted by satisfaction with the other local news media, i.e., local radio news and local TV news. Education was among the best predictors: most educated, least satisfied. Satisfaction with local television news coverage was best predicted by degree of satisfaction with the other local news media. Whereas both groups make similar judgments of the newspaper's accuracy and lack of bias, Hispanics judge the newspaper as more powerful, vibrant, and current than do Anglos.

Anglos tend to be more satisfied with the local newspaper's coverage of local content areas than are Hispanics. This satisfaction is also reflected in Anglos' greater reliance on the newspaper as a primary source of information about local happenings.

Figure 8.2 summarizes the two groups' orientation to television. Virtually everyone has access to television. Hispanics spend more time watching morning and afternoon television, but both groups devote the same amount of time to television entertainment in the evening. On none of the questions about television assessment or use do Anglos exceed Hispanics.

Hispanics are more satisfied in general with television and with television's ability to serve the purposes they cite for watching television.

Eight of the top 10 most important reasons for watching television news were the same for Hispanic and Anglo respondents. Seven were identical to those reported as most important for newspaper reading: immediacy, comprehensiveness and variety of local and non-local news, and to keep informed about local events. In addition, a common important television function was its assistance in selecting the most important news stories for viewers.

Hispanics clearly exceed Anglos in the strength of their preferences for traditional entertainment fare on television. Both groups, however, are quite similar in their satisfaction with local television coverage in either the general community (for Anglos) or the Hispanic community (for Hispanics). That similarity extends to the respondents' ratings of a large set of image characteristics. For 16 of 17 attributes judged, the ratings from Hispanic and Anglo adults were not different from each other.

Generally, the results show similar orientations to television news between these ethnic groups, with a greater orientation or preference for television entertainment among Hispanic adults.

FIGURE 8.2. Television results.

Hispanic and Anglo adults are equivalent

      . . . in use of TV as a secondary source of information for major purchases and local political activities

      . . . in percentage who watch local and national news and, among viewers, in amount of time spent watching local and non-local news

      . . . in percentage who watch morning and evening entertainment shows

      . . . in amount of time spent watching evening entertainment

      . . . in household TV ownership

      . . . in liking to watch nature and outdoor shows and musical varieties on TV

      . . . in the relative importance to them of television news for providing immediacy, comprehensiveness, and variety in local and non-local news coverage; information about local events; and assistance in selecting important news stories

      . . . in satisfaction with local TV coverage of locals and their accomplishments, local cultural activities and crime

      . . . in evaluation of 16 of 17 assessed attributes of TV image

Hispanics exceed Anglos

      . . . in percentage watching afternoon TV entertainment and in amount of time spent watching morning and afternoon entertainment

      . . . in believing TV when news media are in conflict

      . . . in rating overall how well local TV satisfies the purposes they cited as important

      . . . in overall satisfaction with local TV news

      . . . in satisfaction with local TV coverage of social news about the local Hispanic community (compared to Anglo satisfaction with overall coverage of local social news)

      . . . in liking to watch situation comedies, soap operas, crime shows, movies, cartoons, and game shows

---

Radio was studied less intensively than television and newspapers. For the variables in Figure 8.3, the similarities between Hispanics and Anglos with regard to radio are more extensive than the differences, and the differences tend to balance out.

All use measures for radio are equivalent for these adult subgroups, as is dependence on radio as a source of information for community events and job opportunities.

The major difference in satisfaction with local radio coverage of the community occurs in respect to crime coverage. Anglos are more satisfied and Hispanics less satisfied in that coverage area.

Figure 8.4 identifies contrasting content preferences for Hispanic and Anglo adults. The content preference questions were not asked separately by medium; such preferences might possibly have been more or less strong if they

FIGURE 8.3. Radio results.

Hispanic and Anglo adults are equivalent
    . . . in amount of time spent listening to the radio
    . . . in percentage who listen to radio news and entertainment
    . . . in satisfaction with radio coverage of locals and their accomplishments
    . . . in dependence on the radio as a second source of information about the job opportunities and community events

Hispanics exceed Anglos
    . . . in satisfaction with local radio coverage of social news in the Hispanic community and local Hispanic cultural events, compared to Anglo ratings of overall local coverage of cultural events
    . . . in rating how well local radio satisfies the purposes the adults cited as important

Anglos exceed Hispanics
    . . . in household radios owned
    . . . in satisfaction with local radio coverage of crime

---

had been medium-specific. Stronger Anglo preferences exist for political content, both national and local. Anglos also have stronger interests in the opinion sections of the media.

Hispanics express stronger content preferences for a large number of content areas spanning both hard and soft news issues. If anything characterizes the set of content preferences more strongly chosen by Hispanics it is the subset of content issues likely to involve them more directly. For example, their content preferences for stories about discrimination, bilingual education, union activities, local sports and church news, all reflect a greater likelihood for inclusion of participants from the Hispanic community. The remaining cluster of content preferences more strongly preferred by Hispanics tends to reflect the entertainment aspects and the advice columns or features of the media.

Economic content areas appear to be of equivalent interest to the two groups (e.g., news of the local economy, real estate and housing).

The reading of Spanish-language newspapers occurred primarily with magazine reading and of course with the ability to read Spanish. Predominantly English speakers were least likely readers of Spanish-language newspapers.

Watching Spanish television was a concomitant primarily of listening to Spanish radio, watching television entertainment in general, and not reading a newspaper. Also strong was the relationship between positive judgments of quality of community life and watching Spanish TV.

Listening to Spanish radio was part of a media-use complex that included watching Spanish television, reading Spanish-language print media, and listening to radio in general. Of course, it also included Spanish-language ability.

FIGURE 8.4. General results.

Hispanic and Anglo adults are equivalent
   . . . in their interest in news of the local economy, agricultural news, real estate and housing, stories on the changing roles of women, consumer information, Good Samaritan stories (people helping people), and things to do in the area

Hispanics exceed Anglos
   . . . in use of all Spanish language media (newspaper, TV, radio, magazines, records)
   . . . in preference for media content in Spanish
   . . . in their interest in crime news; accidents and disasters; news of Mexico and Latin America; job opportunities; ads and commercials; immigration; stories about discrimination; drug and alcohol problems; bilingual education; problems in the schools; union activities; news about youth gangs; professional sports; sports from Latin America; churches and religion; food, recipes, and nutritional information; advice on personal problems; health and medical advice; how-to advice; TV and TV personalities; movie reviews, art, dance, theater, and music; stories on retirement and retirement living; and comics

Anglos exceed Hispanics
   . . . in estimates of fairness of coverage of the Hispanic community by local media
   . . . in their interest in national politics and the president, local politics and government, editorials and letters to the editor, news and features on business, and humorous stories and features

Youth Survey

What do Anglo and Hispanic youngsters do with each of the mass media examined? This summary focuses on the ethnic comparisons, permitting those more interested in age-group comparisons to examine the data tables in chapter 5.

Figure 8.5 summarizes the results for newspaper habits and attitudes. Access and usage are essentially the same: A single newspaper is read about every other day for perhaps 15 minutes. Hispanic youngsters show a stronger orientation to the features and local information for purposes of diversion and social learning; Anglo youngsters express more orientation to harder news. For both, the newspaper is third in dependency and credibility to radio and television. Both found in newspapers more bad than good things about Mexican Americans, but they find them to the same extent. Hispanic youngsters, however, perceive more good portrayals than do the Anglos. Parental discussion about the newspaper is equivalent, although more Hispanic parental suggestions of articles are reported.

Figure 8.6 presents parallel information for the other print media examined. There are distinct similarities in usage of magazines and non-school

FIGURE 8.5. Newspaper results.

Anglos and Hispanics are equivalent
  . . . in their judgment of the relative credibility of newspapers in comparison with radio or TV
  . . . in talking with peers or parents about the newspaper
  . . . in their estimate of local newspaper portrayal of Mexican Americans doing bad things
  . . . in frequency, recency, and amount of newspaper reading
  . . . in reading the newspaper to satisfy news-seeking motives
Hispanics exceed Anglos
  . . . in parents suggesting they read something in the paper
  . . . in the estimate of local newspaper portrayal of Mexican Americans doing good things
  . . . in content preferences for features and local information
  . . . in reading the newspaper to satisfy diversion needs (for excitement, relaxation, escape)
  . . . in reading the newspaper to satisfy social learning purposes (to find out about things in town and to learn to do new things)
Anglos exceed Hispanics
  . . . in the likelihood that they would believe the newspaper if it conflicted with other media
  . . . in home delivery of the newspaper
  . . . in content preference for news

books for the two ethnic groups, but with a markedly higher usage of comic books for the Hispanics. Their preference for comic books is not content-related—all types are preferred at higher levels. Differences in magazine content preference are either absent or display stronger Hispanic preferences for specific content types.

Figure 8.7 indicates the major results for the television variables. Notably sparse are indicators that Anglos exceed Hispanics on any TV behavior or preference. Generally, the two groups are equivalent, or there is more usage, stronger content preferences, gratifications, and more positive reactions from

FIGURE 8.6. Other print media results.

Anglos and Hispanics are equivalent
  . . . in magazine reading
  . . . in non-school book reading
  . . . in parental urging of magazine item reading
  . . . in preference for sports, music, and fashion magazines
Hispanics exceed Anglos
  . . . in comic book reading
  . . . in preference for all comic book types (horror, superhero, war, funny, and love stories)
  . . . in preference for news, car, children's, and TV/movie magazines

FIGURE 8.7. Television results.

Anglos and Hispanics are equivalent
> . . . in TV sets, in color sets, and in having a personal TV set
> . . . in logged viewing time in the afternoon, evening, and Sunday
> . . . in preference for sports content
> . . . in preference for news and public affairs
> . . . in the relative credibility of TV over other media
> . . . in talking with peers and parents about TV
> . . . in the perceived existence of rules about TV in the home
> . . . in watching with parents
> . . . in their estimate of TV's portrayal of Mexican Americans doing bad things
> . . . in their perception of the portrayal of non-minorities on TV
> . . . in watching TV for news functions

Hispanics exceed Anglos
> . . . in access to cable TV
> . . . in estimated viewing time all day long and on Saturdays
> . . . in logged viewing time in the morning
> . . . in estimated watching of soap operas, news, and game shows
> . . . in preference for Spanish-language content
> . . . in preference for soap operas, cartoons, game shows, movies, crime, and variety shows
> . . . in their estimate of TV's portrayal of Mexican Americans doing good things
> . . . in their perception of the reality of portrayals of minorities on TV
> . . . in watching TV to satisfy social learning needs (to learn how to do things and how to act)
> . . . in watching TV for excitement and for advice

Anglos exceed Hispanics
> . . . in preference for situation comedies

Hispanic youngsters. In particular, access to off-air television is the same, but the Hispanics have more quickly obtained cable reception. Sheer estimates of viewing time showed longer Hispanic viewing in all times of day; specific viewing logs diminished those differences. In addition to a preference for more Spanish-language programs, the Hispanic youngsters indicated greater preference for seven of nine program types, with no difference for news and sports programming. Hispanic youth more often watched television for advice, for excitement, and for social learning purposes. They also were more likely to perceive positive portrayals of Mexican Americans on television than their Anglo counterparts, although both groups made similar estimates of negative portrayals. In addition, the portrayals of Mexican Americans on television were judged as more real-to-life by Hispanic youngsters than by their Anglo counterparts.

Figure 8.8 summarizes the behaviors for radio, record playing, and movie going. Radio listening is not different in quantity for news, music, sports, or general radio listening. A majority of both groups would choose radio over

FIGURE 8.8. Record/movie/radio results.

Anglos and Hispanics are equivalent
> . . . in number of radios in the home and car
> . . . in radio listening in general and in news, music, and sports listening
> . . . in preference for classical music
> . . . in their judgment of the relative credibility of radio in comparison with TV and newspaper
> . . . in home and personal record players
> . . . in movie going

Hispanics exceed Anglos
> . . . in preference for Spanish music and soul and disco on both radio and home record/tape players
> . . . in playing records
> . . . in buying records
> . . . in preference for Spanish and horror movies

Anglos exceed Hispanics
> . . . in number of personal radios
> . . . in preference for the top-40 sound and country and western music on both radio and home record/tape players
> . . . in preference for comedy films

both TV and the newspaper if forced to make such a choice. The homes have four radios, and listening exceeds 2 hours a day, with the preponderance of listening devoted to music. Preferred music types vary widely between the ethnic groups: Hispanics preferred soul and disco and Spanish music, whereas Anglos opt for the top-40 sound (largely rock) and country and western music.

The music type preferences for radio carry over into the more personally controlled playing of records and tapes. But that activity is more often done by Hispanics than by Anglos. Access is equivalent, but Hispanics typically play more records and buy more of them.

Both claim to go to movies once or twice a month. Anglos have stronger preferences for comedies, Hispanics for horror films and Spanish-language movies.

The multiple regression analyses yield more information about these media behaviors and attitudes. Again, we will summarize those results for the several media, given the specificity of detail in chapter 5.

For both frequency of newspaper use and time spent reading the newspaper, the home environment presents the best set of predictors: others in the home reading the paper, discussing news with family and friends, and an affinity for news.

All other print media (comics, magazines, and non-school books) are clustered as concomitant reading behaviors. For comics, younger readers predominated.

Time spent watching television is cast in a nesting of other television variables: having one's own TV, fewer TV restrictions, talking about television, and using it for diversion and social learning. There is also a distinct non-news orientation.

Watching Spanish television occurs among those more able to handle the language and in homes where conjoint viewing with parents more often occurs, as well as a more general interest in what is going on in Spanish-speaking countries.

Radio and record/tape usage co-vary with each other, with access to one's own personal radio and record player, and, interestingly, with an orientation to reading.

Newspaper Style Analysis

The readability or ease of understanding newspaper stories was assessed for six different newspapers. The readability assessment consisted of calculating Flesch scores, which are based on average words per sentence and syllables per word.

The major results of this study may be summarized as follows:

1. Local newspaper stories and local newspaper stories involving Hispanics are significantly easier to understand than wire service stories or local newspaper editorials. Local stories and local Hispanic stories do not differ from each other in terms of readability; wire service stories and editorials are equivalently readable.

2. Newspapers differed significantly from each other in respect to readability of news stories. More importantly, individual newspapers differed greatly in readability of Hispanic and non-Hispanic local stories, but not uniformly. Local Hispanic stories were more readable by two grade levels in two papers. In two others, the Hispanic stories were less readable by two grade levels than other local non-Hispanic stories.

3. Newspaper stories did not differ in readability by whether they appeared on the front page or elsewhere in the paper; this lack of difference also held for front-page and non-front-page local Hispanic news stories.

4. Newspaper stories did not differ in readability on the basis of the day of the week on which they were printed.

Content Analysis of Local Hispanic Coverage

The content of local news stories, local sports stories, editorials, bulletins, and photos in six newspapers was analyzed and compared in terms of their inclusion of Hispanic information.

Local News. The primary findings in this examination of the local news story coverage of Hispanics in communities with populations averaging not less than 20 percent Hispanics include the following:

1. Four local news stories per day were identified as Hispanic.

2. One-fourth of the total space devoted to local news contained articles qualifying as Hispanic news stories.

3. Two-thirds of the qualifying local Hispanic news stories did so solely because they contained one or more Hispanic surnames.

4. Hard news stories (e.g., politics and accidents) were the principal topics of Hispanic news coverage. Crime, cultural features, and news stories dealing with minority issues also were prominent content topics.

5. The newspapers studied differed greatly from each other. Among those with similar population proportions of Hispanics, the range of local news stories per day was from 2.5 to 5. The proportion of local newshole containing Hispanic items ranged from 12 percent to 32 percent across the 2-week sample.

6. Content emphases differed dramatically by newspaper. In the community with the largest population of Hispanics, an average of 1 in 13 Hispanic stories had crime content; in the other communities the range was from 1 in 2.5 stories to 1 in 4 stories.

Editorials. The primary findings in terms of editorial coverage of Hispanic Americans include the following:

1. The several papers averaged less than one editorial page item per day containing Hispanic content from among local columnists, letters to the editor, and locally written editorials.

2. One-half of all the Hispanic editorial page items found appeared in a single community.

3. One-half the material coded as Hispanic editorial page items was letters to the editor written by persons with Hispanic surnames.

4. The content of editorial page items emphasized minority-related issues, hard-news areas, and crime.

5. The several newspapers differed greatly in terms of the inclusion of Hispanic items on the editorial page. The newspaper containing one-half the total items in this category reflected Hispanic items in 24 percent of its total editorial newshole. The remaining newspapers serving similar proportions of Hispanic citizens filled from 3 to 22 percent of their editorial newshole with qualifying Hispanic items.

Local Sports News. The findings in this newspaper content category were:

1. One-third of all local news stories that included some Hispanic reference were local sports stories.

2. Sports stories containing some Hispanic referent comprised one-half the total local sports newshole of the six newspapers during the 2-week sample.

3. Although one-half the local Hispanic sports stories carried a byline, only 6 percent of those stories carried a byline with an Hispanic surname.

4. The single basis for categorizing 98 percent of the local sports stories as Hispanic was the inclusion of one or more Hispanic surnames within the body of that story.

5. Seven percent of all these stories centered primarily on Hispanic participants or activities; the remainder were general sports stories without any particular emphasis on Hispanics.

6. The qualifying sports stories typically had twice as many Spanish surnames per story as the non-sports local Hispanic news stories.

7. Approximately one-fourth of the sources cited in the stories were Hispanic.

8. The proportion of each newspaper's local sports hole containing Hispanic items was larger than the city's Hispanic population proportion; most were substantially larger.

Photos. For photographs including Hispanics, the following was found:

1. About one of every five photos in the papers included Hispanics in some manner.

2. Eighty-six percent of the photos that qualified as Hispanic did so because of the inclusion of an Hispanic surname; 71 percent did so solely for that reason, indicating that the photos were not connected with particularly "Hispanic" activities.

3. Three-fourths of the pictures were news photos; the remainder were feature photos.

4. One-fourth of the photos were sports photos, one-fourth dealt with cultural activities, one-fourth were a miscellaneous collection, and 17 percent were hard-news photos.

5. Only 2 percent of the photos were crime-related.

6. Again, the differences between newspapers were more substantial than the similarities; the range was from 1 Hispanic photo per day to 3.4.

Bulletins. Representation of Hispanics in the local listing of births, deaths, crimes, weddings, and community events produced these major results:

1. One-sixth to one-seventh of the bulletin items in a newspaper referred to Hispanics.

2. Deaths, wedding, and crime announcements were most likely to include Hispanic entries.

3. By our estimation procedure, about 12 percent of the total bulletin item listings were Hispanic entries.

4. Among content categories, the proportion of Hispanic entries in crime listings was larger than their proportion reported in wedding or death announcements.

In summary, then, sports news and photo coverage appear to be most inclusive of local Hispanics. Editorial coverage and bulletin listings of Hispanic people and activities appear to be most deficient. Local news coverage exclusive of sports lies between those two contrasts.

9

A RETROSPECTIVE ANALYSIS
OF PROJECT CASA

Félix Gutiérrez
Jorge Schement

The Communication and Spanish-speaking Americans (CASA) research project at Michigan State University has made a substantial and important contribution to the base of information pertaining to the interaction between Latinos and the mass media in the United States. The results of the primary studies, as reported in the preceding chapters of this book, add greatly to the knowledge regarding Latinos, particularly those in the southwestern United States, as well as their attitudes and behaviors relating to mass communication. As noted elsewhere, this knowledge has been developed on a primarily Chicano population in small and medium-sized cities in the southwest, and it should not be generalized to other Latino populations without additional primary research. Nevertheless, the comprehensiveness and depth of the CASA research make a persuasive case for the use of these data as a baseline against which the findings of other research studies can be compared.

  The substantive findings in the primary research studies are detailed throughout this book. The reviews of prior research regarding Latinos and mass communication assist the reader in placing the content of these new studies in the context of earlier research. In this chapter we will comment on the CASA efforts as they relate to the future development of research on Latinos and the media.

  We begin this assessment by taking a broad look at the context of the study and the way the CASA project was conducted. Since both context and conduct contributed to the ultimate importance of the research findings, it is hoped that such a holistic assessment will be of value to researchers in planning and directing additional research projects on Latinos and the media.

CONTEXT OF THE CASA PROJECT

The first major point regarding the context of the CASA project that strikes these authors is that the study was conducted at a time during which the nation's Latino population was experiencing tremendous growth. Due to this growth, the media and other institutions began reassessing their relationship to the Latino population. In many cases, this reassessment led to the conduct of studies with the Latino population, its characteristics, attitudes, and behaviors.

Gannett was not the only large media corporation to take note of the growing Latino population and to decide to reexamine its own coverage, employment, and marketing strategies as they relate to the Latino community. It was, however, one of the few corporations to go beyond performing a narrow marketing study to improve its penetration of the Latino audience. Instead, Gannett decided to commission a study designed by the communication research arm of a major university. Thus, the CASA project was placed in the context of an academic institution using corporate funds to explore areas of importance both to the corporation and to the university. Placing the study in a university setting facilitated the development of a broad multimethod research project not limited to the gathering of data of use primarily to market researchers.

The CASA project researchers analyzed audience demographics, media preferences, market share, and other topics that marketing directors need. Such marketing information serves a useful purpose for the corporation, since it provides information on the audience and potential audience. Yet that kind of information in itself does little to directly benefit the community from which the data were developed. Nor does it necessarily serve the scholarly needs of the academic community that provided the expertise to design and to conduct the study.

While marketing information on the audience and newspaper product is present in several of the CASA studies, Gannett and the Michigan State University research team also decided to dig deeper into both the Anglo and Latino audience characteristics, the content of the newspapers, and the previous research in the field. Thus, the corporate–university link, in the context of the research, allowed for the development of a comprehensive and ambitious research plan that responded to respective agendas of the corporation and the university. The result was the most comprehensive single study ever performed on Latinos and the mass media in the United States.

The CASA corporate–university partnership also had its limitations. Latinos of the United States, while the target of the research effort, did not participate in the original formulation of the research proposal, except for one Mexican who was an 8-year U.S. resident. The researchers subsequently took an "active audience" approach to determining how and why Latinos use the media.

Once the project and its major components had been funded, Latino leaders in various communities, Latino reporters on Gannett newspapers, and a Latino advisory committee were subsequently involved in the formative stages of the research. Thus, their input was placed in the context of assisting the researchers in the design and implementation of the research plan.

Within this research plan, Latinos were seen as an "active audience" that seeks out and evaluates media. In both the adult and youth surveys, the involvement of the Latino community leaders and the questions were built on the view of Latinos as active participants in the mass communication process. This application of uses and gratifications perspectives in mass communication research has gained wide acceptance, and, as the results of this study indicate, it should also be a part of the context of future studies dealing with Latinos and the media.

The complexity of issues involving Latinos and mass communication was broadly explored in the CASA research through a wide range of research approaches. Some of the findings appear to contradict the results of previous research efforts; others appear to be at odds with the results of other studies within the CASA project itself. These findings, and those that seem to reinforce each other, must be evaluated within the context of both general mass communication research and research on Latinos. Mass communication research is a dynamic field, one in which research findings are rarely conclusive, definitive or final. People change over time, and so do the media that serve them. The same can be said about the Latino population, which continues to grow as a stratified community with at least as much internal diversity as the Anglo population. The complexity of both the research topic and the target population dictate a rejection of quick, simplistic explanations. Research on this topic will need to continue for a long time, will not produce instant definitive answers, and will require a complex array of research tools and perspectives. A major contribution of the CASA project has been in cataloging the research findings and methods of the past and demonstrating, through its own research, the use of multiple methods for research in the present and future.

The findings of the CASA study can stand alone, but they are best understood when viewed in the context of other research. This context should be drawn both from previous studies on Latinos and the media, as well as from studies on specific subject areas. The youth surveys, for example, represent a continuing interest of one of the principal investigators in the interaction between children and media. The analysis of newspaper editorial content should be compared with other studies on newspaper coverage and style. Thus, the chapters in this book should not be isolated as strictly Latino media research, but they should be viewed as additional empirical evidence in a continuing body of knowledge in several areas of mass communication research.

As readers and researchers look for ways in which the CASA findings can impact broadly in mass communication research, they may find themselves pondering a major question posed but not answered by the results of the CASA project. That question revolves around the extent to which it is useful to view Latino ethnic identification as a determinant of media behavior in an audience. While some of the findings in this and other studies indicate a cohesiveness among Latinos in some areas of media behavior and attitudes, other findings do not. It also is not clear whether the cohesiveness is primarily a factor of ethnicity or more a factor of socioeconomic status, education, age, or language dependency. Differences between Anglos and Latinos may also be explained as much by differences in age, education, income, and language as by the difference in ethnicity.

Thus, a major contextual question of this project is the extent to which it demonstrated the importance of conducting research on ethnically distinct groups in the population. Differences between a minority group and other groups may not be so much a factor of ethnicity as a result of other variables. In fact, the greatest similarities may be found in the way media treat different minority groups, not in the way members of minority groups treat the media.

CONDUCT OF THE CASA STUDY

As in the assessment of the context of the CASA study, a single element comes to mind first in reviewing the conduct of the CASA study. This is that the CASA project represents what has become a vanishing type of investigation in mass communication research. The CASA study was a large, well-funded, comprehensive, team research project that took a speedy but thorough look at a particular issue. Such studies are reminiscent of the federally funded research on obscenity, the effects of televised violence on children, and other "super studies" of the 1970's. With the cutbacks in government support for social science and humanities research in the 1980's, it is unlikely that similar projects will be federally funded in the foreseeable future. It is especially significant not only that the study was conducted with funding from the corporate sector, but also that it was allowed to follow the research agenda of the university-based investigators.

The input of the university researchers no doubt facilitated the use of the multimethod approach in gathering the data for the different study parts. The use of multimethods in conducting research on minority group audiences strikes these authors as a particularly useful avenue for future researchers. Standardized sampling plans and instruments typically have been developed on predominantly Anglo, English-speaking populations. Even though the same principles may apply to groups that are culturally distinct, the use of alternative techniques should not be ruled out for verification. Multimethods increase the opportunity for the information gathered to be compared and validated.

Too often investigators have used simplistic designs and methods to investigate minority populations, then generalized their findings broadly to members of the group not necessarily represented in the sample. Certain approaches, such as crosstabulating results by ethnicity on questionnaires administered only in English, mask the complexity of the Latino audience and lead to deceptively simple explanations. The use of multimethods, as demonstrated in the conduct of the CASA project, facilitates the identification of apparent contradictions within the data and ultimately leads to a more sophisticated and valid assessment.

In this regard, the conduct of the interviews with the community leaders in the various cities is of particular importance. While some points raised by the leaders appear to differ from the responses of Latino residents in the same communities, both were critical of media performance as it relates to the Latino community. This use of both qualitative and quantitative research techniques is in the best tradition of research, since it allows for comparisons and contrasts between the findings of different techniques on different strata of the same population. Individual and small group interviews, discussions with media professionals, and other qualitative analyses of mass communication content are important research tools, ones that have often been overlooked in efforts to reduce all possible meaning to numbers. The CASA project makes a contribution to the continued development of qualitative techniques as a companion to quantitative methods in mass communication research.

The conduct of the CASA field research in southwestern cities in which Gannett owns daily newspapers enhanced both the focus of the research and the cooperativeness of the newspaper personnel. It also, no doubt, encouraged community leaders to participate in a project that could potentially improve the performance of the local newspaper. This model should be extended to other corporately funded research projects. Media corporations and media consumers can both benefit from research that views the audience as an active participant in the communication process. Since media corporations traditionally have not extended themselves to the Latino community, both the findings of the CASA project and the research model that produced those findings should be applied in future research on Latinos and the media.

Some important areas were not investigated in this study. Most of these would be classified as institutional studies examining the media and their operations. Studies in these areas would look at: (1) Latino employment patterns on the newspapers, (2) upward mobility of Latinos in the newsroom and management, (3) network analyses of newspaper personnel and their affiliations, and (4) interviews with reporters and editors regarding their perception of Latino coverage. These and other important institutional topics should be included in future studies.

Finally, a research project focusing on a minority community must include members of the community as part of an integrated research team. The CASA project included one Latino as a principal investigator, convened a national Latino advisory panel, and consulted with Latinos in the communities surveyed. The involvement of Latino librarians, sociologists, audience researchers, and/or demographers could have enhanced the conduct of the study and brought to the project staff expertise that could have eased what were otherwise difficult decisions. Latinos should not merely be targets, advisors, and foot soldiers in research. Through the example of the CASA project, future project directors can learn the limitations of such approaches and the benefits to be derived from integrating Latino scholarly talent at all levels of the research process.

CONTENT OF THE CASA PROJECT

The individual chapters describe the results of the CASA research in detail. These chapters present what is undoubtedly the greatest single collection of new primary evidence on the topic of Latinos and mass communication ever assembled in one research project. Certainly no comparable project has had the scope, time frame, and financial support to deal with the topic of Latinos and the media.

Over the coming years, as the findings are compared to those of future studies, their contribution, both individually and collectively, will be measured in many ways. The findings will be applied in the newsroom and referred to by Latino researchers and organizations. The purpose of this portion of the chapter is to look briefly at key portions of those findings and suggest the role they may play in the continuation of research on Latinos and the media. Such an evaluation is made cautiously, since predicting the future in such a dynamic and changing field is a hazardous occupation at best. Moreover, the field is in conflict as accepted notions are increasingly challenged. Our assessments are made in the hope that research interest in this topic will continue to grow, rather than diminish over the next decades.

In reviewing the place of the substance of the CASA findings in the literature, we will review each of the studies separately, commenting both on the contributions of the individual sections and on possible research agendas for the future. These will be reviewed in the order presented in this book.

Mass Communication and Mexican Americans

Chapter 1 presents the most comprehensive review of the research and analytical literature on Latinos and the media to be published to date. The categorization of studies and articles from a variety of sources provides a useful framework for the future study of Latinos and the media, and it helps to put succeeding chapters in their proper historical context. Future researchers will no doubt refer to the previous studies described in this chapter when developing their own studies and when putting the findings of their research in the perspective of prior literature.

The chapter, which is presented as "the first effort to review comprehensively the research literature on the mass communication behaviors of Hispanic Americans," focuses primarily on studies published in established academic disciplines or communication-related publications. While this approach may provide a comprehensive catalog of research in those sources, it does not exhaustively review publications in several other important areas: most notably citations in Latino publications or research centers and studies generated by media marketing firms surveying the Latino audience. While personal inquiries were extended to Latino research centers, a more aggressive search of these potential sources of information is needed before a truly comprehensive review of the literature on Latinos and the media can be presented. Because we are only now identifying and building the literature, a systematic search beyond the academic literature is especially important.

Examples of topics that appropriately belong in such a literature review include historical studies on: (1) Latino media and the past portrayal of Latinos in Anglo media, (2) interaction between Latino media in the United States and media in Latin America, and (3) comparisons of media and media use by Latinos and other groups in the United States. This chapter is, perhaps, a keystone in reviewing the literature on Latinos and mass communication. It is also, however, a keystone whose place must be viewed in relation to other sources of information in order to truly comprehend the field.

Interpersonal Communication and Mexican Americans

Like the literature review on mass communications, chapter 2 attempts a comprehensive review of the findings on interpersonal communication and Latinos.

The organization of the literature into logical subgroupings, the reviews of the findings in each of these groupings, and the accompanying bibliography provide future researchers with a valuable compendium and summary of the work in the field. Again, it is hoped that researchers will use this work as a base for their own library searches and reviews of the literature, rather than merely citing the efforts of the CASA project. Since many of the studies cited, such as those on Latino self-image and Latino values cross over from disciplines other than interpersonal communication, their methodologies and findings must be evaluated before being applied. Differences across time, social class, and geographic location must also be assessed before making sweeping statements that may inaccurately portray Latino realities. Perhaps even more than in the mass communication area, the readers and future users must apply the previous research findings and summaries in the field of interpersonal communication with great care and caution. If, as the research cited indicates, many of the anticipated differences between Latinos and Anglos do not exist, future researchers should have a full agenda investigating why the stereotypes of such differences continue among Latinos and Anglos alike.

Community Leader and Newspaper Executive And Reporter Perspectives on Mexican Americans and the Mass Media

The individual and group interviews with 88 Latino community leaders in six southwestern cities present a valuable insight into the perceptions of media among the Latino leadership sector. The methodology, similar to the focus group interview used by media marketing researchers, usefully probed the attitudes of the respondents on a variety of media-related issues. This use of small group discussion gave the Latino leaders an opportunity to expose their feelings and to pursue points of particular concern to them. Both the depth and the range of the attitudes expressed demonstrate the value of this qualitative research technique. While quantitative research methods often force respondents to react to a set of questions within a fixed range of response categories, the qualitative methods applied in this portion of the project allowed for a wide range of responses and a more complete expression of feelings. This approach is especially useful in situations such as this one, in which the researchers may not be able to fully anticipate either the questions that will trigger responses in the respondents or the range of those responses.

In addition to the methodological contributions the findings in this chapter illustrate the intensity of feelings about the media among Latino leaders. These attitudes can be usefully compared with the feelings of newspaper personnel, adults, and youths to form a more complete picture of the attitudes in a given community. Since leaders are vocal and assertive by definition, it should not be surprising that their feelings are often expressed with greater intensity than those of the general public. The findings in this chapter should be compared to leadership interviews in other communities, and, as in the case of the CASA project, such methods should be utilized to frame questions for public surveys.

The interviews with newspaper personnel present both methodological and substantive contributions to the field. What we find unique is the candor and openness with which the newspaper executives and reporters discussed their feelings on Latino issues. This self-analysis was no doubt a useful exercise for the newspaper personnel, one which also generated a wealth of information on the attitudes of media professionals toward Latinos and Latino issues. It is doubtful that such candor and openness could have been gained if the study had not been sponsored by the corporate home office of the newspapers involved.

Mass Media Use, Preferences, and Attitudes Among Adults

The results of the adult survey in chapter 4 contribute a great deal to dispelling the myth of Latinos as a community unconcerned about media or uninvolved with it. The findings show not only the extent to which Latinos depend on local media, but also the degree to which they are able to comment on its coverage of Latino affairs. The high regard in which Latinos hold media, combined with their specific criticisms of Latino coverage and their lower-than-average readership, should give editors clear direction on the kinds of things that need to be done to improve coverage and readership. At the same time, the comparison of results between Anglos and Latinos should give editors clear guidance as to what kinds of progress can be made without alienating either audience.

The hard-news orientation of the Latinos, coupled with the use of the newspaper for a wider variety of uses than Anglos, indicates that newspapers are, or can be, of primary importance to Latinos when they do their jobs well. However, given the low evaluation of newspaper coverage of Latino activities, along with the overall lower socioeconomic and age status of the Latino respondents, newspapers clearly have to make more than a few cosmetic changes in their product to consistently attract more Latino readers. The CASA survey provides an excellent starting point for editors as they search for ways in which to improve their coverage, employment, and readership among Latinos.

Mass Media Use, Preferences, and Attitudes Among Young People

The questionnaire interviews were conducted among more than 700 fifth and tenth graders in five of the cities. The report in chapter 5 provides provocative comparative data on media use and the feelings of Anglos and Latinos at different grade levels. The similarities between the Anglo and Latino youths in media usage contradict the stereotype of Latinos as not being print-oriented, while the differences in media content preferences indicate that the groups are not identical. Other differences in the evaluation of Latino coverage and portrayals in the media, as well as the influence of parents in recommending television programs, provide a solid foundation for future research to explore these differences between Anglo and Latino youths further.

The findings of this survey can be most productively evaluated when compared with surveys of other youths at comparable grades, socioeconomic levels, and communities. These results are as useful for what they tell readers about the media attitudes and behaviors of United States schoolchildren as they are for the information they reveal about Latino youths. Given the comparatively large proportion of school age Latinos, these data and methods also provide an important model for the inclusion of Latino subsamples in wider surveys of American youths. A logical extension of the methodology in this chapter would be to conduct focus group interviews among the school children, as was done with the adult leaders and newspaper personnel, to allow the students to express their feelings more completely.

Content Analysis of Newspaper Coverage
of Mexican Americans

Like the adult survey, the content analysis in chapter 6 of Latino coverage in the newspapers surveyed runs counter to some expectations developed from previous research. Here the media performed more adequately than expected in local news, sports, and photo coverage of Latinos, but they did not do as well in editorial page items or local community announcements. The heavy representation in sports items and sports photographs suggests that Latino athletes are well covered, particularly when compared with the low representation in community announcements. Similarly, the fact that only one-third of the sources in stories relating to Latinos were actually Latino further indicates that Latinos do not have as much visibility on the news pages as may be warranted.

This research is particularly valuable, especially since it provides a longitudinal perspective on the earlier content studies cited in the literature review. In this case, the findings indicate that, in most of the cities surveyed, the newspapers present a more integrated picture than would have been anticipated from earlier research. At the same time, the study provides an indication as to which sections of the paper are making more progress, and it provides a clear direction for areas needing improvement.

A Stylistic Analysis of Newspaper Coverage
of Mexican Americans

The research in chapter 7 on the style of writing in the reporting of Latino affairs is probably the most innovative set of findings in the CASA research. While the Flesch readability ratio is not a new research technique, the application of readability studies to the coverage of a particular minority group in different sections of the newspaper advances the use of the method. In identifying both the differences and similarities in readability between different sections of the newspaper and between Latino and non-Latino stories, the researchers have identified potential avenues for future research.

Some of the differences, such as the fact that editorials have more big words and are more difficult to read, are not surprising. Others, however, are more provocative. Future researchers can use these findings as a basis for comparing the readability of local and national news stories, as well as of stories found in different sections of the newspaper. The applicability of the research findings is primarily for newspaper editors and reporters who, given this information, can develop reporting and writing styles that are both informative and understandable. Again, the topic of Latino coverage was the rationale for executing such a study. Yet the findings will be applicable to other areas not directly linked to Latinos.

CONCLUSIONS

At this point, an assessment of the contribution of the CASA project to Latino studies and mass communication is at best premature. The most accurate and thoughtful evaluation should come in a few years, after other scholars and professionals have had the opportunity to use the content of these studies in their own work. The CASA project provides a rich and detailed set of resources from which to continue work in the field of Latinos and mass communication. As the contents of this book are referred to, critically analyzed, and thoughtfully applied, the importance of the CASA project will be more fully appreciated.

As work on this topic continues, it is our hope that consideration of Latinos will become more important to those involved with mass communication. At the same time, it is our hope that recognition of the importance of media will become more central to the thinking of those concerned primarily with Latinos. For research on Latinos and mass communication to become more fully integrated into both disciplines, it must be carried out by people who see it as integrated into a whole fabric of knowledge, not as a fragmented part. When seen in this light, the findings have a greater opportunity for use in developing theory and policy. When the work is isolated, or performed on an ad hoc basis, it is perceived and treated as a part of a fragmented or sideline field. Hopefully, the CASA project has demonstrated that Latinos no longer should be treated as a sideline issue for either media corporations or mass communication researchers.

10

IMPLICATIONS FOR MEXICAN AMERICANS, MEDIA PROFESSIONALS, AND COMMUNICATION RESEARCHERS

Enormous amounts of data are contained in earlier chapters. In keeping with the conventions of publishing scientific research, the findings of each study have been presented straightforwardly, with few interpretative comments. The summary in chapter 8 continued that format, synthesizing major results for easy reference. Here, we take time to draw subsets of implications from the studies that we believe to be particularly important for three of the target audiences of this volume: Mexican Americans, media professionals, and communication researchers. Each section then attempts to bring into focus some of the findings that pertain most directly to that reader group. By no means do we wish others to bypass these sections; rather they have been formulated in terms of particular implications that should be of interest to all but especially salient for those focal groups.

IMPLICATIONS FOR HISPANICS

Multiple implications for Hispanics, especially Mexican Americans, can be derived from these studies. Three broad categories of implications will be developed here:

1. Education
2. Self-knowledge
3. Potential for change in the commercial media

Education

Here, we will discuss implications for media education, research education, and media consumer education.

Media Education. It seems urgent that Hispanic communities take steps to encourage and provide incentives for the media education of Hispanics in schools and universities. Without qualified personnel available, the media are not in a good position to include Hispanics on their staffs. However, with such representation, the media are more likely to be responsive to Hispanic needs. With qualified Hispanic personnel, the media should better be able to provide content that meets the standards of quantity and quality that have been asked for by community leaders and other media critics. For example, more media models would be provided for Hispanic youth, promoting cultural pride and a strong concept of self.

Media education in this sense implies a special dual social responsibility on the parts of both the person trained and the employing media organization. There is the responsibility to serve the Hispanic community, not merely to hire (or be hired as) an employee with a Spanish surname, not merely to offer a poor-quality show in Spanish once a week and to consider the obligation to the Hispanic community met.

Media personnel sensitive to community needs and issues need to be recruited. For this purpose, communities may consider fund-raising programs for media education scholarships, among other means of providing education opportunities. Participation by the local media in the form of offering internships would help channel the talent back to the community.

From the youth and adult studies as well as the content analysis of news coverage, the complaints of lack of adequate treatment of Hispanics in media reports can be remedied by a more thorough understanding of the Hispanic communities where the media operate. This can best occur when sensitive Hispanics reach *decision-making positions* through training and demonstrated competence.

Research Education. Research education for Hispanics in communication and the social sciences seems crucial. This implication was derived during the conduct of this research project. Too few qualified Hispanics were found to collaborate with this project. If more qualified personnel had been available, the quality of the research might have benefited from the added cultural sensitivity of Hispanic researchers who know their own communities. Learning to ask questions and to arrive at reliable, statistically valid answers is not a simple process. When more qualified Hispanics can participate in and direct projects of this type, even more comprehensive and relevant results should be obtained.

Communication research education also would enable more community leaders, media personnel, and media critics to ask penetrating research questions, and to be cautious of allegations and claims before empirical evidence is accumulated. More Hispanics should be encouraged to explore this skill area for the subsequent benefit of their own communities.

Media Consumer Education. The set of studies shows some critical differences in media evaluations, images, and satisfactions. Hispanic community leaders are very critical of the media and perceive more instances of racism in the media. The typical Hispanic and Anglo citizen is generally less critical of media content and coverage.

Media consumer education includes teaching how to gain access to the media, how to produce shows for public access channels on cable, how to get public service announcements aired on radio, where to call to have social news included in the newspaper, and so on. It includes teaching how the agenda of a medium can be affected, e.g., to object to or applaud coverage through letters to the editor, calls, and letters to television and radio stations. It includes educating Hispanics to recognize stereotyped or negative media portrayals. Organized and informed groups can make changes in the media through the appropriate channeling of complaints or information about events and topics in which they are interested. Media consumer education can take place at all school levels, in church, in the context of citizen groups, and through the media.

This research project is a demonstration that media institutions, when made aware of public sentiment, are willing to change; the media do seek to serve the larger components of their publics. Initiatives by interested and assertive Hispanic citizens likely contributed to Gannett's interest in and funding of this project. Bringing issues to the attention of the media may prompt the media to act. Media consumer education consists in part of breaking the communication silence between Hispanics and the media. If media audiences say all is well, no change can be expected.

Self-Knowledge

Perhaps the most important implication of this set of studies is the self-knowledge derived by Hispanic communities. If Hispanic communities know themselves and their relationship with the media, they can act in an informed manner (1) to exert pressure on established media institutions; (2) to do nothing if things are as desired; (3) to create media institutions with Hispanic roots that are responsive to Hispanic interests and concerns; (4) to promote education, specifically media education; (5) to promote political activity; and (6) to dispel myths.

These findings identified a disparity between Hispanic leader projections and the Hispanic community's self-reported media behaviors and attitudes. Awareness of that disparity is educational for Hispanic leaders; it gives them a broader perspective of their own community.

Self-knowledge can be derived from research projects only if the results of such projects are widely disseminated. We do not yet know how widely this research will be shared among the communities studied and among others with similar characteristics. Conferences were held and newspaper reports have appeared. Hispanic scholars, media decision makers, and the public throughout the U.S. have access to this book. However, a primary responsibility to diffuse this research, to promote the self-knowledge advocated here, and to critique this research project must fall to concerned Hispanics. Using this and other projects as a base, Hispanics should go on to conduct research that updates their understanding of themselves and that addresses the shortcomings of this and other projects.

Commercial Media Change

This project exemplifies what a commercial enterprise can do through research to serve its audiences. After the project started, some community leaders reported changes in local news media that may well have resulted from awareness of the research. Several newspapers involved began to hold meetings with Hispanic representatives to better understand "what is going on." Those leaders believed there was more coverage of Hispanic communities, new consideration of Spanish sections in the local newspaper, and more prominence given to Hispanic achievements and culture. If indeed those perceptions were accurate, the media's responsiveness may signal the potential of better media services to the Hispanic communities that participated by contributing their time and information.

Future research may investigate changes in the content of the media that accompanied this set of studies.

IMPLICATIONS FOR THE MEDIA

This entire volume is replete with useful data for people charged with managing media institutions. The first recommendation that should be made to such individuals is to study the data carefully, for there are many implications apparent for gathering and presenting news that will serve both the Hispanic and non-Hispanic communities better. However, this chapter will serve to highlight some important policy issues for media managers as they attempt to understand and implement change based on this research effort. It is evident that these data have extensive implications for content decisions in newsrooms, staffing decisions including hiring and structuring of personnel activities, and promotional and community activities in the Hispanic community that could and should be attempted by media leaders. We close this section with some words of caution for managers as they attempt to use these data.

Changing the Product

Anyone in a management position in the newspaper industry knows that one of the pitfalls of dealing with researchers is that a simplistic answer to most problems uncovered by research is simply to add more newshole and give the people what they think they want. Anyone who makes such a suggestion today is naive at best and a fool at worst. We assume that most print media managers will have to apply these data to the newshole they now have. They cannot, in most cases, just add newshole at will; the problem then becomes one of better using the resources now available.

Careful attention to the adult report, the content analyses, and the computer-assisted stylistic analyses reveals that breadth of coverage in these daily newspapers is a consistent problem. On the local level, people from all parts of the community are not being covered on a consistent basis. Some communities do a better job than others in including Hispanic people but some of our analyses lead us to believe that Hispanics are never born, seldom marry, and almost never die. They do not make the paper. Although the content analyses indicate that Hispanics are covered in specific sections of the newspapers, there needs to be more attention to covering this group in the same ways that others in the community are covered.

One of the most positive findings in all this research suggests that the best way to serve Hispanics is simply to serve the entire community with more breadth of coverage in the daily newspaper. Hispanics constitute a younger group, and their tastes are very similar to those of young people studied all across this country. What we have is a recurrence of the young reader problem so often discussed in the newspaper industry. Content preferences identified in the adult chapter should be analyzed, and balance and rotation should be attempted to satisfy those preferences. Ways must be found for newspapers to present content on a regular basis that interests readers aged 18 to 40. Many of the interests of young people in general are of special interest to Hispanic readers. When newspapers provide such a rotation of breaking news and features, more people including Hispanics and non-Hispanics will be more favorably disposed to the paper, which should result in increased circulation.

It should be stressed that there is not great dissatisfaction with newspapers among the Hispanic community. Those who are presently reading the newspapers are relatively satisfied with the product they receive on a daily basis. However, many Hispanics just are not reading the paper at present. One critical issue for media management is how to increase circulation in this segment of their markets. There are no easy answers but certainly the onus is first on people in newsrooms to provide content of general interest to everyone in the communities. Without proper display and coverage of such items, there is low probability of increasing circulation among present nonreaders. More people coverage, sharper editing of the wire to include more national topics of interest, and a commitment to coverage of all segments of the local community should go a long way toward attracting new readers while at the same time holding those who are now relatively satisfied with the product.

It is not clear that we must make the same assumptions about a fixed newshole when it comes to the broadcast media. The sure-to-come access on cable systems, the move toward more all-news channels, and the rising pressure for more local news programs all suggest that the broadcast newshole may in fact be viewed as one with the potential for greatest expansion. Hispanics are a prime target for broadcast news programs and features. They are heavy television and radio consumers and are very satisfied with what local television and radio provide them. Whether the broadcasts are in Spanish or English, there is a huge potential for television and radio to satisfy the content needs of Hispanic Americans. While the myth of the television- and radio-dominated Hispanic household is not supported by these data in that both Anglos and Hispanics use these media in very similar ways, it is still clear that television and radio news departments have much to gain by paying attention to the content preferences of Hispanics. The market is there for increased local news coverage of their communities, and features and documentaries about a variety of issues would be watched and listened to by this group. While it is not necessarily true that the print and broadcast media are in direct competition for this group, the data do suggest that all people are very sophisticated about their likes and dislikes. As suggested in the discussion of the print media, content changes that attract more Hispanics are likely to attract more people in general to the media. Some very similar interests and needs are being expressed by both Anglos and Hispanics. The media satisfying those needs first and best will profit in many ways.

The youth survey provides additional evidence that print media should continue to cultivate young people. Hispanic parents already encourage their children to read the paper, and Hispanic children use newspapers for a variety of social learning purposes. Hispanic and Anglo youth presently read the local newspaper with equal frequency. They are also equal in their use of the newspaper to satisfy news-seeking motives. These young people represent a tremendous potential of new subscribers for daily newspapers. We find no evidence of an age group generally alienated from print media. Media managers should direct more attention to getting newspapers into the schools and the homes of Hispanics. The long-term payoff of such an attempt should be great.

Young people are generally interested in and heavy consumers of the broadcast media. The fact that non-Hispanic and Hispanic youth use television to the same degree as a source of news might surprise some. Well-produced news and educational programs are being watched and will be watched by all youth. Special attention to satisfying the news-gathering needs of young people has probably not received as much focus from media managers as it warrants. Since Hispanics presently have more access to cable systems and are attuned to the broadcast media, changes in content to better satisfy their news ought to be a high-priority item both for Spanish language broadcasters and those using English.

The content and stylistic analyses raise several questions for media managers. The content analyses showed no systematic exclusion of Hispanics in any newspaper we studied. However, the papers varied greatly in the amount of newshole dedicated to Hispanics and Hispanic issues. Specific sections, such as sports, contain a lot of play on Hispanic people. Announcements, local happenings, and other day-to-day activities in the Hispanic community are less well covered in most newspapers. The editorial pages are less likely to contain issues of most concern to Hispanic readers. All of this suggests special attention to enterprising local efforts to cover and display news of the local Hispanic community. This must be done consistently. These data also suggest that photojournalists in these communities are doing a relatively good job of covering the Hispanic community. Editors also use this art when they have it. This suggests that coverage of Hispanic people can be done and that when it is done, it will be noticed and appreciated.

The stylistic analyses probably raise more questions for media managers than they answer. First, it was a complete surprise to us that in two markets, stories mentioning Hispanics and written about Hispanic events were two full grade levels lower in reading level than comparable local stories without Hispanics. Moreover, in two other markets, the complexity of writing increased almost two grade levels when the content was about Hispanics compared to similar stories about non-Hispanics. It is perplexing that story type was such a big predictor of ease of comprehension. The fact that newspapers differed on their readability scores is not surprising, nor was it unexpected that the local report would be at a lower reading level than the wire report or the editorial page. Prior research had found similar trends. No one can say for sure exactly what level of readability a newspaper should aim for, but the wire report and the editorial page in many of these dailies clearly exceeds the average education level of the entire community.

That there were such dramatic differences in the reading levels of stories about Hispanics and non-Hispanics in four of the six newspapers was a curious finding. One implication for management is for increased editing of the wire report and editorial page in selected communities. The differences in Hispanic and non-Hispanic stories may be attributable to specific staff differences in the newspapers. If staff differences are responsible for such findings, training programs and increased editorial vigilance might be one appropriate management response to reduce the readability differences. Certainly the data raise enough questions to pique the curiosity of those in editorial positions.

Product changes can be made in both print and broadcast media to allow these institutions to serve the Hispanic community better. The suggested changes, moreover, will result in better service to the entire community. Given so many similarities of preference in these communities, changes in content and format can appeal to a broad-based segment of the community. In all cases, the policy implications are clear. It is not enough to run a once-a-week feature or documentary on some Hispanic issue; the entire community must be covered and the interests of Hispanics and non-Hispanics served on a consistent, predictable basis.

Changing the Staff

It has been stated that these data underscore the need to increase the number of Hispanic reporters, editors, and management executives. If the media are to represent the communities they serve, people most sensitive to those communities must be placed in positions of responsibility. This is one way to change the staff.

While most would agree that media managers should take steps to change staffs by adding more minorities, including Hispanics, there is also a responsibility to change the attitudes and behaviors of staff members, mostly non-Hispanics, who presently occupy positions in media organizations. Reporters, editors, and managers have had very little training to be culturally sensitive, for which schools of journalism across this nation must share some blame. Very few journalism programs have courses in intercultural communication, media management, or other topics specifically designed to develop sensitivity to the cultural diversity in communities across this country.

Nor has the industry itself done a particularly good job of developing training programs for the people who cover minority communities. Although the industry has made some progress in supporting programs for minority journalists, it has been less forward-looking in training staff to cover all parts of the community as it exists.

We are not suggesting that such training and educational programs are a substitute for the hiring of more minority journalists, but we *are* suggesting that it may be necessary to drag educators, media managers, and journalists into the 1980's, their heels perhaps dragging, to make everyone more capable of covering a more culturally diverse society. That is certainly another way to change the staff of any media organization.

Changing the Nature of the Job

Two of the principal investigators on this project are currently working on a large research project, funded by the American Society of Newspaper Editors, to determine the variables that affect "what is news" on a day-to-day basis. It is evident from this project that the nature of beat assignments is an important determinant of what ends up in the newspaper and therefore what is considered "news." A continuing question arose during Project CASA concerning whether the best way to increase coverage of the Hispanic community was to assign people to a "Hispanic beat." Proponents of such a structure in the newsroom argue that such a beat assignment would assure that people were out covering the Hispanic community on an exclusive basis and would therefore get to know that community. It was further argued that such an assignment structure would allow these reporters to develop sources and become identified to the Hispanic public, resulting in more and better stories. Some newspapers studied in Project CASA did use Hispanic beat assignments, with varying degrees of support from the newsroom staff involved.

Critics of such beat assignments suggest that when there is a Hispanic beat, other members of the staff simply ignore anything that happens in the Hispanic community. They claim that such a structure unnecessarily restricts the content of the news by giving too much to do to too few people. They suggest instead that all staff members, from the city side, features, sports, business, etc., must be encouraged, cajoled, even forced to cover all aspects of the community, including Hispanics. Only then will the entire community be covered as it should be on a day-to-day basis. The obvious rebuttal to them is that such a structure has resulted in less than adequate coverage of the Hispanic community for too many years.

There is no simple answer to this problem. One solution obviously lies in changing the staff both by additions and by training. However, that is neither a quick nor an easy solution to a problem that deserves immediate attention. Part of the problem must be placed squarely on the shoulders of the assignment editors, department or section editors, and the managing editors of newspapers. Clearly, the assigning of beats in the Hispanic community is a quick way to produce more copy about Hispanics. This is probably worth considering as a first step. But more needs to be done to ensure better coverage. Feature editors, sports editors, business editors and a number of people on the city side need to proactively plan for a variety of people to cover the Hispanic community. Reactive management responding only to police blotters and announcements of Mexican festivals produces a kind of coverage criticized by both Hispanic community leaders and the public at large. In communities with large Hispanic populations, someone needs to be responsible for a continuing audit to make sure that such coverage is being undertaken and that it gets the play it deserves. Perhaps an ombudsman—be it a member of management, an editor, or a reader's committee—is justified in communities with large Hispanic populations. Only when there is a systematic audit of just what is being covered, along with accountability residing with one or more people in the newsroom, can one expect significant changes across the entire staff.

Changing the Many Publics

Certainly these data have much to say to people outside media organizations, and it is important for management to communicate these results. Several audiences have an interest in these findings. Clearly, Hispanic leaders and organizations will be most interested in anything a media manager has to say about them and their constituencies. Many of the publishers involved in this project began meeting with leaders shortly after the results were available. The publishers both received feedback and provided information about the attitudes and behaviors of Hispanics in a broad geographic area. Many felt that it was the start of a long-overdue dialogue. In too many media organizations, the newspaper publisher or the station manager is seen as having the obligation to "meet the public," while others in the organization lead a more insular existence. Perhaps one of the implications of this research is that more people ought to be involved in communicating with community leaders and others about issues that affect the gathering and reporting of news. Perhaps newspapers and other media organizations ought to try more "town meetings," where such issues are discussed among management, staff, and residents of the community.

Another way of communicating with a broader audience is through improved promotional activities originating in media companies. Media organizations are notoriously bad at telling their own story. Slogans, rack cards, and cute spot announcements are no substitute for solidly informative promotional campaigns that tell exactly what the newspaper, television station, radio station, or magazine has to offer its consumers. In an age of jingles, the time has come for promotional departments to take seriously the obligations of community involvement and comprehension. An in-house ad or a promotional spot might increase short-term consumption or sell a few Sunday newspapers, but it is no long-run solution to the problem of providing better understanding of just what the media can offer Hispanics and, for that matter, the rest of the community.

The newspaper industry is also going to have to attack the problem of nonreaders in the Hispanic community. As we have said, some of that is going to have to be done by changes in content and staffing over time. Some newspapers presently make no attempt to circulate in predominantly Hispanic areas. They feel that the return on investment in such circulation attempts makes it unwise. They also feel that the demographics are not ones that will attract new advertisers and therefore feel justified in making minimal attempts to increase penetration in specific areas. The data in our studies should dispel the notion of the typical Hispanic as an uninvolved non-consumer of print media. The future of many newspaper franchises is inextricably interwoven with the growth and development of a solid base of Hispanic readers.

Another audience that must be reached is those responsible for media-buying decisions. Media buyers have had very little data to rely on about Hispanics and their buying habits. This research clearly indicates that Hispanics can be reached through both the print and broadcast media. They depend on these media for news, entertainment, and for information about where to buy the things they need. Given the initial interest shown in this research by media buyers and agency personnel, the Hispanic community is not likely to be ignored by Madison Avenue in the future. It is also evident that the media can reach the Hispanic in either English or Spanish. Buyers should not hesitate to make print buys targeted at Hispanic audiences; not only are target Hispanic audiences large, but Hispanics for the most part are very capable in two languages. Given the relative lack of attention to these people from either the news side or from advertising interests, Hispanics represent a large untapped market for advertisers and a huge potential source of new revenue for media organizations.

Some Caveats for Media Management

We must offer a few words of caution before moving on to implications for future research. First, the question of Spanish-language sections, columns, or stories remains perplexing given these data. Discussion of whether these newspapers should run items in Spanish has occurred for a long time, certainly predating this research project by many years. Non-Hispanics are simply not generally fluent in Spanish, and the commitment of newshole to the Spanish language certainly reduces the available new for large segments of the community. In an era of very precious newshole, such a decision could have serious repercussions for any newspaper. It is also evident from this data that many non-Hispanics would respond very negatively to the printing of *any* part of their newspaper in a language other than English. Some newspaper management has been criticized even for running advertisement copy in *both* English and Spanish. Some newspapers can experiment with Spanish-language copy and probably face little down-side risk. The attitudes in some communities and the size of the newshole make this a distinct possibility. In other communities, the prevailing racial attitudes and the size of the newspaper might preclude such an attempt at this time.

With the advent of short-wave broadcasting, opportunities for cable access, and satellite technology in the print industry, the possibility of more specialty publications in Spanish is good. Whether these take the form of regional newspapers publishing in Spanish, special inserts transmitted by satellite to subscribing newspapers, or more Spanish-language broadcasting, it is clear that media organizations will soon recognize the huge market potential of this growing minority.

Another caveat is that you cannot run a newspaper or broadcast organization by referendum. This project should point out the pitfalls of management's assumption that *anyone* speaks for a community. It has been our experience in newsrooms that a very few vocal citizens with phone or pen in hand can have a tremendous impact on news decisions. We have called this approach to change *management by telephone referendum*. Changes are made or not made on the assumption that all these callers must be representative of some larger body "out there." Publishers and other managers also use this same referendum approach to management. Often their referendum comes from the local country club or business community, but the point is still the same. A very small number of people are *presumed* to be representative of a larger public. We are not suggesting that media managers ignore the views of people they have identified as community leaders in attempting to better serve Hispanic Americans. We do suggest, however, that the attitudes of such leaders may differ significantly from the rest of the public. Therefore, we think it is necessary to use whatever techniques are available to continually update information about the wants, needs, and desires of the community as a whole.

One of those techniques is obviously systematic research on media use and satisfaction in the community. This project represents such an attempt at assessment. This also leads us to our last caveat: Research should always be a tool and never a rule. No amount of data on preferences can substitute for sound journalistic judgment. It is often the responsibility of journalists to produce what the public needs to know rather than exclusively what they want to know. Research can be used to make better management decisions, and we think the end result can be a better product for the consumer. With that in mind, we turn to a final section on Project CASA's implications for future research into the media attitudes and behaviors of Hispanic Americans.

IMPLICATIONS FOR RESEARCH

Throughout this book, we have offered some specific suggestions for future research issues. We have proposed possible extensions of the current lines of investigation and highlighted questions deserving further exploration. Now we wish to address some of the more significant methodological and substantive implications raised by this project.

Methodological Implications

Entering this project, we were convinced of the value of acquiring multiple perspectives. At its conclusion, we are even more convinced of the superiority of this comprehensive approach to data collection. The data collected from the adolescents served to cross-validate that acquired from the adults; where the same information was requested from both groups, we received highly consistent replies. Analyses of content and style further served to confirm or render invalid impressions advanced by our respondents; we learned, for instance, that the underrepresentation of Hispanics in the newspapers was severe in some content areas, as thought, and not so in other content areas. Similarly, community leaders voiced opinions and concerns that echoed issues and suspicions expressed by newspaper executives and editorial personnel. Had we not collected views from both groups, we might have attributed the disparity in views toward the media between Hispanic leaders and the larger Hispanic public as indicative of Hispanic leaders being out of touch with their constituencies. Instead, we were able to conclude that leaders, whether they be from the media or community organizations, by virtue of their positions share a perspective that is more critical and problem-oriented; they are much more likely to attract negative feedback and to be sensitive to individual instances of poor media performance. Had we not also collected data from the public at large, we would not have realized that leaders and their publics present different pictures of Hispanic media use and evaluation; had we only sought one perspective, we would have obtained a distorted and incomplete understanding of what is and what can be.

In a like vein, the results of this project reinforced the importance of gathering quantitative as well as qualitative data. Much of what has been written about Hispanics in the past has relied on highly general and subjective analyses of Hispanic culture, values, beliefs, and practices. Our open interviews with community leaders and newspaper personnel were current and somewhat more specific; they still yielded subjective rather than objective data. It now appears to us that many of these previous analyses and hypotheses—for example, that of the strong oral tradition and the dominating influence of the family in Hispanic culture—may have served to perpetuate myths and stereotypes. We believe the results of this project weaken many assumptions and misconceptions about the communication patterns of Hispanics. Without the benefit of hard data to substantiate our claims, we believe our conclusions would carry much less credibility, both with Hispanics and with non-Hispanics. Certainly Hispanic leaders would be less inclined to accept that newspapers are covering Hispanics to a reasonable degree in some areas (e.g., sports) without seeing the actual data for numbers of occurrences and inches of copy. Nor would journalists be as inclined to believe that Hispanics share many of the same news interests as non-Hispanics if the comparative ratings across a large number of people were not available. That so many unexpected findings emerged from these data argues for a more determined effort in the future to acquire objective, empirical information about Hispanics and the mass media.

Another value of this project was the use of a Spanish-language version of the adult questionnaire. The use of this instrument was not without its difficulties and costs. It was extremely time-consuming to develop, particularly because of disagreements over what was an acceptable translation. It necessitated the hiring of only bilingual interviewers and required twice as much training time. It also yielded a relatively small number of interviews actually conducted in Spanish, a return rate that might make its use prohibitive for commercial research firms. Nevertheless, it had important advantages. It did pick up 15 percent of the Hispanic population that would not otherwise have been capable of being surveyed. Consequently, it significantly improved the representativeness of our sample and the generalizability of our results relative to other studies. The opportunity to choose the language in which to be interviewed may also have improved the completion rate among Hispanics, who might have appreciated efforts to adapt to their needs. Finally, the use of bilingual interviewers may have produced a side benefit of allaying suspicions and any reluctance to participate among Hispanic respondents. We had been forewarned that we would have a high refusal and termination rate among Hispanics. That did not materialize, perhaps because of the specific methods we used.

One concern posed by members of our advisory panel at the time of planning the project was the use of telephone interviews to collect the adult data. Of special concern was the potential underrepresentation of such subgroups as migrant workers, highly mobile individuals, and indigent families without telephones. While our budget prevented us from even considering in-person interviews, we believed going into the project that we could still achieve a relatively representative sample, primarily overlooking those who would be least likely to be consumers of local media. We compensated for mobility to a large degree by the use of random-digit dialing, a procedure we recommend for anyone conducting telephone research. We also discovered, based on asking the adolescents about the presence of phones in their homes, that the penetration was very high, ranging from 88 to 96 percent in Hispanic homes. We therefore feel the problem of underrepresentation was less serious than anticipated; from a pragmatic standpoint, we believe we missed people who might have been equally or even more unreachable by other methods. Finally, the offsetting advantages of using long-distance telephone interviews were many. Interviewers could be closely supervised to insure uniformity in interviewing style and to resolve problems as they arose. Physical appearance cues of ethnicity were not available to inhibit cooperation among any of the ethnic groups surveyed or to contaminate results by eliciting socially desirable responses; only vocal indicants were evident for some interviewers. Finally, the anonymity of the telephone survey should have increased candor and honesty; the occasional expression of socially undesirable responses indicated to us that it did.

One other aspect of our methods that merits discussion is the use of analyses of content and style. In this area, we encountered some difficulties that were not resolved to our total satisfaction, primary ones being who should qualify as Hispanic and what topics should be treated as Hispanic-related. We relied predominantly on the 1980 Census List of Spanish surnames in making judgments, which by definition yields some errors of commission and omission. For example, we were told of prominent people in the community, likely to appear in the news, who were Mexican American but had Anglicized surnames or were not Hispanic but had Spanish surnames. We do not know how to solve this problem in future research other than to rely on multiple criteria and discard those instances that are most questionable. Another problem, this one with the stylistic analysis, was that Hispanic stories were required to focus primarily on a Hispanic issue and/or on an individual with a Spanish surname. More detailed stylistic analyses could benefit from distinguishing between Hispanic issue stories and Spanish-surname stories, Hispanic versus non-Hispanic bylined stories, Hispanic sports stories versus Hispanic local news stories, and parallel relevant distinctions. Finally, a problem that will forever plague content and stylistic analysis is the massive amount of coding needed to draw even a few simple conclusions. The incredible time investment required will no doubt deter similar undertakings, but we believe the significant findings uncovered in this project made the current investment worthwhile.

Substantive Implications

Three of the most provocative findings to come out of this study are the relatively favorable evaluations of the media held by Hispanics; their heavy dependence on the media for news, information, and entertainment; and the considerable similarity between Hispanics' and Anglos' media use and opinions. Given that there may be some resistance among Hispanics and Anglos alike to accept these findings, it is important that these kinds of unexpected findings be put to further test; replications on a large scale are needed.

At the same time, it is essential to determine how well these findings fit other Hispanic subpopulations and other geographic areas. We have stressed that this sample was primarily Mexican American. We do not know if these results also apply to Cubans, Puerto Ricans, and other groups of Hispanic origin. Neither do we know how well they apply outside the Southwest or in much larger communities. We believe we had a good mix of rural and urban environments, but we are also aware that major cities like Chicago and New York may have problems and experiences not captured by this project. This is yet another direction for expansion.

If future research continues to show high similarities in the media needs and preferences of Anglos and Hispanics, subsequent attention should focus more on the demographic differences, such as age, education, and income, that separate frequent and satisfied media users from nonusers and dissatisfied users. Hispanics have proclaimed their heterogeneity; such a direction for future research would affirm this by recognizing that ethnicity per se may not be the best way of categorizing people.

Just as more data are needed on Hispanic consumers of media, as compared to non-Hispanics, so are more needed on media products and their coverage of Hispanics compared to non-Hispanics. Specifically, content analysis of television and radio programming is needed to parallel what we have already learned from these selected newspapers about how much actual coverage there is of people and issues and how prominently it is featured. The CASA research team has begun that effort. A more comprehensive analysis of all media, including magazines, could also explore how issues of special interest to Hispanics but not tied to them alone—such as the changing role of women and job discrimination—are treated. Do they incorporate the views of Hispanics or acknowledge the issue's salience to Hispanics? And how thoroughly do they cover such topics?

As for other general topics that could profit from future examination, several are readily apparent. The youth survey more thoroughly explored entertainment uses of the media than did the adult survey; those same assessments should be made of adults. The role of other media beyond newspapers and television also deserves a more thorough analysis. For example, what functions does radio fulfill and how credible is the medium? Which kinds of magazines have the greatest appeal? All the Spanish-language media—what they offer, how much they are used, whether users are satisfied—also need to be investigated. As ancillary topics, more knowledge is needed about what sources Hispanics seek out for their various information needs, how their family and interpersonal communication patterns affect and are affected by media exposure, and how language preferences shape relationships with the media. Pursuit of these and other topics should add important shadings to the picture of Hispanics and the mass media.

BIBLIOGRAPHY

Abrams, O. Minority news: the experiment ends. *Columbia Journalism Review,* Jan/Feb, 1977, 54–55.

Aguirre, A., Jr. The sociolinguistic situation of bilingual Chicano adolescents in a California border town. Unpublished manuscript. Angelo State University, 1977. (ERIC Document Reproduction Service No. ED 152 063)

Anisman, P. H. Some aspects of code switching in New York Puerto Rican English. *The Bilingual Review,* 1975, *2* (1 & 2), 56–85.

Antunes, G. & Gaitz, C. M. Ethnicity and participation: A study of Mexican Americans, Blacks, and Whites. *American Journal of Sociology,* 1975, *80* (5), 1192–1211.

Baird, F. L. An Anglo view of Mexican Americans. *Public Service,* 1974, *1* (2), 1–6. (ERIC Document Reproduction Service No. ED 101 897)

Barba, C. Are you missing the 30th market? *Television/Radio Age,* Oct 23, 1978, 85.

Barker, G. C. Social functions of language in a Mexican-American community. *Anthropological papers of the University of Arizona, No. 22.* Tucson, Az.: The University of Arizona Press, 1972.

Barrera, A. Carrascolendas. *Public Telecommunications Review,* Jul/Aug, 1976, 20-24.

Bean, F. D., Curtis, R. L., & Marcum, J. P. Familism and marital satisfaction among Mexican Americans: The effects of family size, wife's labor force participation and conjugal power. *Journal of Marriage and the Family,* 1977, *39* (4), 759–767.

Bittner, J. R. & Shamo, W. G. Readability of the "mini page," *Journalism Quarterly,* 1976, *53* (4), 740.

Blatt, G. The Mexican American in children's literature. *Elementary English,* Apr, 1968, 446-451.

Bogatz, G. & Ball, S. A summary of the major findings in "The second year of Sesame Street: a continuing evaluation." Educational Testing Service, Princeton, Nov, 1971. (ERIC Document Reproduction Service No. ED 122 802)

Brennan, E. & Ryan, E. B. Reported language usage and verbal fluency of bilingual Mexican-American adolescents. *Anthropological Linguistics,* 1973, *15* (9), 398–405.

Bureau of Elementary and Secondary Education (HEW/OE). Descriptions of children's television series produced under the Emergency School Aid Act. Washington, D.C.: Division of Equal Education Opportunities, Oct, 1976. (ERIC Document Reproduction Service No. ED 129 302)

Burgoon, J. K., Burgoon, M., & Wilkinson, M. Writing style as a predictor of newspaper readership, satisfaction and image. *Journalism Quarterly,* 1981, *58* (2), 225–231.

Casavantes, E. Pride and prejudice: a Mexican American dilemma. *Civil Rights Digest,* 1970, *3* (1), 22–27.

Chavira, R. A case study: reporting of Mexican emigration and deportation. *Journalism History,* 1977, *4* (2), 59–61.

Cheng, C. Letting down the "ethnic turf" defenses. *Public Telecommunications Review,* Jul/Aug, 1976, pp. 38–41.

Children's Television Workshop. A report of three studies on the role and penetration of Sesame Street in ghetto communities. Daniel Yankelovich Inc., New York, Apr, 1970. (ERIC Document Reproduction Service No. ED 122 819)

Children's Television Workshop. A report of three studies on the role and penetration of Sesame Street in ghetto communities. Daniel Yankelovich Inc., New York, Jun, 1971. (ERIC Document Reproduction Service No. ED 122 819)

Children's Television Workshop. Report on the role and penetration of Sesame Street in ghetto communities. Daniel Yankelovich Inc., New York, Apr, 1973. (ERIC Document Reproduction Service No. ED 122 821)

Children's Television Workshop. Summary of the script and program review of Sesame Street by the Chicano Study Center, University of California in Los Angeles, New York, 1974. (ERIC Document Reproduction Service No. ED 122 825)

Christian, J. M. & Christian, C. C., Jr. Spanish language and culture in the southwest. In J. Fishman (Ed.), *Language Loyalty in the United States.* The Hague: Mouton and Co., 1966.

Clark, M. *Health in the Mexican-American culture.* Los Angeles: University of California Press, 1959.

Clemente, F. & Sauer, W. Voluntary associations and minority status: comment and extension. *American Sociological Review,* 1975, *40* (1), 115–117.

Cohen, A. D. Bilingual schooling and Spanish language maintenance: an experimental analysis. *Bilingual Review,* 1975, *2* (1 & 2), 3–12.

Cole, S. & Goebel, J. B. Mexican American and White reaction to same race stimulus persons as a function of belief similarity. Paper presented at the Annual Meeting of the Midwestern Psychological Association, Chicago, May, 1974. (ERIC Document Production Service No. ED 102 447)

Cooney, J. Quarterly reports for January-March 1977 and April-June 1977. Children's Television Workshop. New York, 1977. (ERIC Document Reproduction Service No. ED 142 238)

Corenblum, B., Fischer, D. G., & Anderson, K. Occupational differences and attribution of trait adjectives to ethnic groups. *Psychological Reports,* 1976, *39* (2), 535–542.

Davis, S. Viewpoints, *Television/Radio Age,* Jan 1, 1979, 47.

Delia, J. G. Dialects and the effects on impression formation. *Quarterly Journal of Speech,* 1972, *58* (3), 285–297.

del Solar, D. Toward "unfringed" and open programming: some workable solutions. *Public Telecommunications Review,* Jul/Aug, 1976, 30-33.

Driedger, L. Ethnic self-identity: a comparison of in-group evaluations. *Sociometry,* 1976, *39* (2), 131–141.

Dunn, E. Mexican-American media behavior: a factor analysis. *Journal of Broadcasting,* 1975, *19* (1), 3–10.

Duran, D. & Monroe, M. The Latino communications project: an investigation of communication patterns and organizational activity among Mexican, Cuban, and Puerto Rican residents of Chicago. University of Wisconsin, Madison, Library School, 1977. (ERIC Document Reproduction Service No. ED 157 535)

Dworkin, A. G. Stereotypes and self-images held by native-born and foreign-born Mexican Americans. In J. H. Burma (Ed.), *Mexican-Americans in the United States: A Reader.* Cambridge, Mass.: Schenikman, 1970.

Eiselein, E. B. & Marshall, W. "Fiesta"—an experiment in minority audience research and programming. *Educational Television,* Feb, 1971, 11-15.

Eiselein, E. B. & Marshall, W. Mexican-American television: applied anthropology and public television. *Human Organization,* 1976, *35* (2), 147–156.

Elías-Olivares, L. Language use in a Chicano community: A sociolinguistic approach. *Working papers in Sociolinguistics,* No. 30. Austin, Texas: Southwest Educational Development Laboratory, 1976. (ERIC Document Reproduction Service No. ED 125 810)

Filep, R., Millar, G., & Gillette, P. The Sesame Mother Project. Final report. Institute for Educational Development, El Segundo, California, Aug 27, 1971. (ERIC Document Reproduction Service No. ED 055 676)

Fishman, J. & Casiano, H. Puerto Ricans in press. *Modern Language Journal,* 1969, *53* (3), 157–162.

Flores, N. Z. & Hopper, R. Mexican Americans' evaluations of spoken Spanish and English. *Speech Monographs,* 1975, *42* (2), 91–98.

Funk, S. G., Horowitz, A. D., Lipshitz, R., & Young, F. W. The perceived structures of American ethnic groups: the use of multidimensional scaling in stereotype research. *Sociometry,* 1976, *39* (2), 116–130.

Galavision. Assorted collection of brochures, 1980 movie list, customer agreement, and May and June, 1980 program guides. New York: 250 Park Avenue.

Galavision: Pay TV with a difference. *TVC.* September 15, 1979.

Gast, D. Minority Americans in children's literature. *Elementary English,* 1967, *44* (1), 12–23.

Giles, H. Communicative effectiveness as a function of accented speech. *Speech Monographs,* 1973, *40* (4), 330–331.

Good, P. Is network news slighting minorities? *TV Guide,* Mar 5, 1977, 4–8.

Goodman, M. E. & Beman, A. Child's-eye views of life in an urban barrio. In *Spanish-speaking people in the United States: Proceedings of the 1968 Annual Spring Meeting of the American Ethnological Society.* Seattle: University of Washington Press, 1968.

Gray, W. S. & Leary, B. E. *What makes a book readable with special reference to adults of limited reading ability: an initial study.* Chicago: The University of Chicago Press, 1935.

Greenberg, B. S. & Baptista-Fernandez, P. Hispanic-Americans: the new minority on television. In B. S. Greenberg (Ed.), *Life on Television,* Norwood, N.J.: Ablex, 1980, 3–12.

Grieshop, J. I. & Harris, M. B. Effects of mode of modeling, model age, and ethnicity on rule-governed language behaviors. *Journal of Educational Psychology,* 1974, *66* (6), 974–980.

Gromatzky, I. Consumer education for Mexican Americans. Paper presented at the National Conference on Educational Opportunities for Mexican Americans, Austin, 1968. (ERIC Document Reproduction Service No. ED 016 563)

Guernica, A. Cable television . . . the medium for Hispanics? *Agenda,* May/Jun, 1977a, 25–27.

Guernica, A. The development of the National Latino Medical Coalition. *Agenda,* Jul/Aug, 1977b, 29–31.

Guernica, A. Chicano group to get its own TV station. *Agenda,* Nov/Dec, 1977c, 28–30.

Gutierrez, F. Mexico's television network in the United States: the case of Spanish International Network. *Proceedings of the Sixth Telecommunications Policy Research Conference.* Lexington: Lexington Books, 1978a, 135–159.

Gutierrez, F. Through Anglo eyes: Chicanos as portrayed in the news media. Paper presentation at the Association for Education in Journalism Conference, Aug 13–16, 1978b.

Gutierrez, F. Latinos and public broadcasting: an agenda for the 1980s. Paper presented at the Latinos in Public Broadcasting: Towards the 1980s conference, San Diego, Jan, 1980a.

Gutierrez, F. Latinos and the media in the United States: an overview. Paper presented at the International Communication Association Conference, Acapulco, May, 1980b.

Gutierrez, F. & Schement, J. Spanish-language radio in the southwestern United States. University of Texas at Austin, Center for Mexican American Studies, Monograph #5, 1979, 57–65.

Harvey, F. A., Quiroga, B., Crane, V., & Bottoms, C. L. Evaluation of eight ''Infinity Factory'' programs. Executive summary. Education Development Center, Inc., Newton, Mass., Jun, 1976a. (ERIC Document Reproduction Service No. ED 129 329)

Harvey, F. A., Quiroga, B., Crane, V., & Bottoms, C. L. Evaluation of eight "Infinity Factory" programs. Part I: analysis of the eight-show series. Education Development Center, Inc., Newton, Mass., Jun, 1976b. (ERIC Document Reproduction Service No. ED 129 330)

Holladay, H. P. A study of communication preferences of Mexican-American parents. Unpublished manuscript. California State College, Los Angeles, 1971. (ERIC Document Reproduction Service No. ED 152 469)

Hoppe, C. M., Kagan, S. M., & Zahn, G. L. Conflict resolution among field-independent and field-dependent Anglo American and Mexican-American children and their mothers. *Developmental Psychology*, 1977, *13* (6), 591–598.

Hopper, R. & Williams, F. Speech characteristics and employability. *Speech Monographs*, 1973, *40* (4), 296–302.

Hornburger, J. The minority image in children's books. Paper presented at the National Council of Teachers of English Conference, San Diego, Nov 26–29, 1975. (ERIC Document Reproduction Service No. ED 116 179)

Hsia, H. J. A preliminary report on motivation and communication patterns of Black, Chicano, White, and affluent White in a typical southwest U.S. city. Paper presented at the Association for Education in Journalism Conference., Fort Collins, Colorado, Aug 19–23, 1973. (ERIC Document Reproduction Service No. ED 081 009)

John, V. & Berney, T. D. Analysis of story telling as a measure of the effects of ethnic content in stories. Final report. Yeshiva University, Office of Economic Opportunity Research Report #577, New York, Mar, 1967. (ERIC Document Reproduction Service No ED 014 326)

Justin, N. Mexican-American reading habits and their cultural basis. *Journal of Reading*, 1973, *16* (6), 467–473.

Klare, G. R. *The measurement of readability*. Ames, Iowa: Iowa State University Press, 1963.

Knight, G. P. & Kagan, S. Acculturation of prosocial and competitive behaviors among second- and third-generation Mexican-American children. *Journal of Cross-Cultural Psychology*, 1977, *8* (3), 273–283.

Knudson, K. H. & Kagan, S. Visual perspective role-taking and field-independence among American and Mexican-American children of two ages. *The Journal of Genetic Psychology*, 1977, *131* (2), 243–253.

Koeller, S. A. The effect of listening to excerpts from children's stories about Mexican Americans on the self-concepts and attitudes of sixth-grade children (Doctoral dissertation, University of Colorado, 1975). *Dissertation Abstracts International*, 1976, *36*, 7186A. (University Microfilms No. 76-11, 589)

Korman, F., & Valenzuela, N. Patterns of mass media use and attitudes about mass media among selected Anglo and Chicano opinion leaders. *Aztlan*, 1973, *4* (2), 335–342.

Korzenny, F., Armstrong, G. B., & Neuendorf, K. Cultural identity and communication style among Mexican Americans. Paper presented at the Speech Communication Association Convention, San Antonio, Nov, 1979.

Kuvlesky, W. P. Use of Spanish and aspirations for social mobility among Chicanos: a synthesis and evaluation of Texas and Colorado findings. Paper presented at the annual meeting of the Rocky Mountain Social Science Association, Laramie, Wyoming, 1973. (ERIC Document Reproduction Service No. ED 075 128)

Lampe, P. E. Mexican American self-identity and ethnic prejudice. *Cornell Journal of Social Relations*, 1975, *10* (2), 223–237.

Laosa, L. M. Carrascolendas: a formative evaluation. University of California at Los Angeles, Mar, 1974. (ERIC Document Reproduction Service No. ED 090 968)

Laosa, L. M. What languages do bilingual children use with whom?: research evidence and implication for education. Paper presented at the Meeting of Teachers of English to Speakers of Other Languages, Los Angeles, 1975. (ERIC Document Reproduction Service No. ED 116 456)

Laosa, L. M. Viewing bilingual multicultural educational television: an empirical analysis of children's behaviors during television viewing. *Journal of Educational Psychology,* 1976, *68* (2), 133–142.

Larez, M. Statement before the FCC. League of United Latin American Citizens, San Francisco, Jan 10, 1973. (ERIC Document Reproduction Service No. ED 071 441)

Lewels, F. Racism in the mass media—perpetuating the stereotype. *Agenda,* Jan/Feb, 1978, 4-6.

LeCorgne, L. L. & Laosa, L. M. Father absence in low-income Mexican-American families: children's social adjustment and conceptual differentiation of sex role attributes. *Developmental Psychology,* 1976 *12* (5), 470–471.

Lewin, K. *Resolving Social Conflicts.* New York: Harper and Brothers, 1948.

Littlefield, R. P. Self-disclosure among some Negro, White and Mexican-American adolescents. *Journal of Counseling Psychology,* 1974, *21* (2), 133–136.

Lopez, R. & Enos, D. Spanish-language-only television in Los Angeles county. *Aztlan,* 1973, *4* (2), 283–313.

Lynch, M. D. Stylistic analysis. In P. Emmert & W. D. Brooks (Eds.), *Methods of Research in Communication.* Boston: Houghton Mifflin Company, 1970.

Madson, W., Rubel, A. J., & Heller, C. S. *Mexican-American youth: forgotten youth at the crossroads.* New York: Random House, 1966.

Marshall, W., Eiselein, E. B., Duncan, J., & Bogarin, R. *Fiesta: minority television programming.* Tucson, Az.: The University of Arizona Press, 1974.

Martinez, T. How advertisers promote racism. *Civil Rights Digest,* 1969 2 (4), 5–11.

McClure, E. & Wentz, J. Code-switching in children's narratives. Paper presented at the Mid-American Linguistics Conference, University of Kansas, 1975. (ERIC Document Reproduction Service No. ED 119 524)

Miller, M. V. Variations in Mexican-American family life: a review synthesis of empirical research. *Aztlan,* 1979, *9* (2 & 3), 209–231.

Mirandé, A. The Chicano family: a reanalysis of conflicting views. *Journal of Marriage and the Family,* 1977, *39* (4), 747–756.

Morgan, B. M. An investigation of children's books containing characters from selected minority groups based on specific criteria (Doctoral dissertation, Southern Illinois University, 1973). *Dissertation Abstracts International,* 1974 34, 6364A. (University Microfilms No. 74-6232)

Moznette, J. & Rarick, G. Which are more readable: editorials or news stories? *Journalism Quarterly,* 1968, *45* (2), 319–321.

Mulac, A., Hanley, T. D., & Prigge, D. Y. Effects of phonological speech foreignness upon three dimensions of attitude of selected American speakers. *Quarterly Journal of Speech,* 1974, *60* (4), 441–420.

NASB (National Association of Spanish Broadcasters). News/Noticias, 1979–1980, *1* (1–3), *2* (1–3).

Neuendorf, K., Korzenny, F., & Armstrong, B. Cultural identity and television behaviors of Hispanic-Americans. Paper presented at the International Communication Association Conference, Acapulco, May, 1980.

Parra, J. A. Bilingual programming for Latinos: the media's missing link. *Public Telecommunications Review,* Jul/Aug, 1976, 14-18.

Pasqua, T. Newspaper readers' news values: an exploratory comparison of Chicanos and Anglos. *Aztlan,* 1975, *6* (3), 347–361.

Passel, J. S. & Word, D. L. Constructing the list of Spanish surnames for the 1980 census: an application of Bayes' theorem. Paper presented at the Annual Meeting of the Population Association of America, Denver, Apr, 1980.

Patella, V. M. & Kuvlesky, W. P. Situational variation in language patterns of Mexican-American boys and girls. *Social Science Quarterly,* 1973, *53* (4), 855–864.

Patella, V. M. & Kuvlesky, W. P. Bilingual patterns of non-metropolitan Mexican-American youth: variations by social context, language use, and historical changes. Paper presented at the Annual Meeting of the Rural Sociological Society, San Francisco, Aug, 1975. (ERIC Document Reproduction Service No. ED 133 108)

Peñalosa, F. Toward an operational definition of the Mexican American. *Aztlan,* 1970, *1* (1), 1–52.

Price-Williams, D. R. & Ramirez, M. Divergent thinking, cultural differences, and bilingualism. *The Journal of Social Psychology,* 1977, *103* (1), 3–11.

Pyrczak, F. Readability of "Instructions for form 1040." *Journal of Reading,* 1976, *20* (2), 121–127.

Ramirez, A. Social influence and ethnicity of the communicator. *The Journal of Social Psychology,* 1977, *102* (2), 209–213.

Ramirez, A. & Lasater, T. M. Ethnicity of communicator, self-esteem, and reactions to fear-arousing communication. *Journal of Social Psychology,* 1977, *102* (1), 79–91.

Ramos, R. A case in point: an ethnomethodological study of a poor Mexican-American family. *Social Science Quarterly,* 1973, *53* (4), 905–999.

Rapp, M. A. "Junta de Amigos"—a "first" in central Michigan. *Educational Television,* Jun, 1971, 21–28.

Razik, T. A. A study of American newspaper readability. *Journal of Communication,* 1969, *19* (4), 317–324.

Rich, A. L. & Ogawa, D. M. Black stereotypes of non-Black communicators: a descriptive study. Paper presented at the International Communication Association Convention, Atlanta, 1972. (ERIC Document Reproduction Service No. ED 066 907)

Rodrigues, R. J. Awareness of multicultural language and learning styles research: an urging. Paper presented at the Annual Meeting of the Conference on College Composition and Communication, Kansas, Mo., Mar/Apr, 1977. (ERIC Document Reproduction Service No. ED 147 862)

Romero, F. E. A study of Anglo-American culture value concepts and their significance in secondary education. *A Research Contribution for Education in Colorado,* 1966, *3* (2), 1–8. (ERIC Document Reproduction Service No. ED 023 506)

Rosenthal, M. Indicators of growth abound in Spanish media community. *Television/Radio Age,* Oct 23, 1978, A17–A27.

Ryan, E. F. & Carranza, M. A. Evaluative reactions of adolescents toward speakers of standard English and Mexican American accented English. *Journal of Personality and Social Psychology,* 1975, *31* (5), 853–863.

Sanchez, L. Treatment of Mexican Americans by selected U.S. newspapers, January-June 1970. Unpublished M.A. thesis, Pennsylvania State University, Jun, 1973.

Schement, J. R. Literature on the Chicano audience in review. *Aztlan,* 1977, *7* (1), 119–124.

Seggar, J. Television's portrayal of minorities and women, 1971–75. *Journal of Broadcasting,* 1977 *21* (4), 435–446.

Sena, J. R. The survival of the Mexican extended family in the United States: evidence from a southern California town (Doctoral dissertation, University of California, Los Angeles, 1973). *Dissertation Abstracts International,* 1974, *34,* 887A. (University Microfilms No. 73–18, 651)

Singleton, J. Cross-cultural approaches to research on minority group education. Paper presented at the 69th annual meeting of the American Anthropological Association, New Orleans, Nov, 1969. (ERIC Document Reproduction Service No. ED 040 245)

Spanish-language market study. *Television/Radio Age,* Nov 7, 1977, S1–S24, A18–A20.

Stanford, M. On predicting the effects of a bilingual children's educational television program (Doctoral dissertation, University of Texas, Austin, 1973). *Dissertation Abstracts International,* 1974, *34,* 6015A. (University Microfilms No. 74–5333)

Stephan, W. G. Stereotyping: the role of ingroup-outgroup differences in causal attribution for behavior. *Journal of Social Psychology,* 1977, *101* (2), 255–266.

Steward, M. S. & Steward, D. S. Effect of social distance on teaching strategies of Anglo-American and Mexican-American mothers. *Developmental Psychology,* 1974, *10* (6), 797–807.

Subervi-Velez, F. Mass media exposure and perceived discrimination among Latinos of Chicago. Paper presented at the Association for Education in Journalism Conference, Houston, Aug, 1979.

Subervi-Velez, F. The effects of communication and socioeconomic status on the political participation of Puerto Ricans, Mexican Americans, and Cubans in Chicago. Paper presented at the International Communication Association Convention, Acapulco, 1980.

Tan, A. Evaluation of newspapers and television by Blacks and Mexican-Americans. *Journalism Quarterly,* 1978, *55* (4), 673–681.

Tankard, J. W. & Tankard, E. F. Comparison of readability of basic reporting texts. *Journalism Quarterly,* 1977, *54* (4), 794–797.

Task Force on Minorities in Public Broadcasting. A formula for change. Corporation for Public Broadcasting, Nov, 1978.

Tejada-Flores, R. Latino Consortium Newsletter, KCET–TV, Los Angeles, 1979.

Tijerina, A. A. Assessment of needs and coping mechanisms of elderly Mexican Americans. Unpublished manuscript, University of Houston, 1977. (ERIC Document Reproduction Service No. ED 170 104)

Tyler, J. S. Kinder en Ingles: English for the Spanish-speaking preschooler. *Educational Television,* Dec, 1970, 17-19.

Uribe, O., Jr. & Martinez, J. S. Analyzing children's books from a Chicano perspective. Far West Laboratory for Educational Research and Development, San Francisco, 1975. (ERIC Document Reproduction Service No. ED 129 458)

U.S. Bureau of the Census, Current Population Reports, Series P–20, No. 339, *Persons of Spanish Origin in the United States: March 1978,* Washington, D.C.: U.S. Government Printing Office, 1979.

Valenzuela, N. Media habits and attitudes of Mexican Americans. Surveys in Austin and San Antonio. University of Texas at Austin, Center for Communication Research, Jun, 1973.

Valenzuela, N. Public television and the Mexican-American audience. Corporation for Public Broadcasting, Office of Communication Research Report, 214, Jan, 1974.

Van Wart, G. Carrascolendas: Evaluation of Spanish/English educational television series within Region XIII. Final report. Evaluation component. Education Service Center, Region 13, Austin, Jun, 1974. (ERIC Document Reproduction Service No. ED 092 089)

Velasquez, R. & Warner, P. L.A. Hispanic community to receive 4 new channels. *Hollywood Reporter,* Jan 7, 1980, 14.

Ward. V. Ethnicity and mobility orientations: a study of the Mexican Americans of southern Colorado. Unpublished M.A. thesis, Colorado State University, 1972.

Weigel, R. H. & Quinn, T. E. Ethnic differences in cooperative behaviors: a non-confirmation. *Psychological Reports,* 1977, *40* (2), 666.

Weisgerber, R. & Coles, G. Evaluating the potential of films for improving self-image in minority group children. Final report. National Center for Educational Research and Development, (DHEW/OE), Washington, D.C., Dec, 1971. (ERIC Document Reproduction Service No. ED 061 726)

Whitehead, J. L., Williams, F., Civikly, J. M., & Albino, J. W. Latitude of attitude in ratings of dialect variations. *Speech Monographs,* 1974, *41* (4), 397–407.

Whitney, J. Image making in the land of fantasy. *Agenda,* 1978, *8* (1), 7–11.

Williams, B. Why migrant women make their husbands tamales. Unpublished manuscript, American University, 1975. (ERIC Document Reproduction Service No. ED 145 333)

Williams, F. The psychological correlates of speech characteristics: on sounding "disadvantaged." *Journal of Speech and Hearing Research,* 1970, *13* (3), 472–488.

Williams, F. & Naremore, R. C. Language attitude: an analysis of teacher differences. *Speech Monographs,* 1974, *41* (4), 391–396.

Williams. F. & Natalicio, D. Evaluating Carrascolendas: a television series for Mexican-Americans. *Journal of Broadcasting,* 1972, *16* (3), 299–309.

Williams, F., Valenzuela, N., & Knight, P. Prediction of Mexican-American communication habits and attitudes. University of Texas at Austin, Center for Communication Research, Jun, 1973.

Williams, F., Van Wart, G., & Stanford, M. Carrascolendas: national evaluation of a Spanish/English educational television series. Final report. University of Texas at Austin, Center for Communication Research, Jun, 1973. (ERIC Document Reproduction Service No. ED 078 679)

Williams, F., Whitehead, J. L., & Miller, L. M. Ethnic stereotyping and judgments of children's speech. *Speech Monographs, 1971, 38* (3), 166–169.

Williams, F., Whitehead, J. L., & Traupmann, J. Teachers' evaluations of children's speech. *Speech Teacher,* 1971, *20* (4), 247–254.

Williams, J. A., Babchuk, N., & Johnson, D. Voluntary associations and minority status: a comparative analysis of Anglo, Black, and Mexican Americans. *American Sociological Review,* 1973, *38* (5), 637–646.

Wolin, M. How Spanish-language media is shortchanged by Nielson. *Los Angeles Herald Examiner,* Apr 4, 1980, A1, A14.

Zaffirini, J. A social-categories perspective on mass media habits and attitudes of Mexican-American college students (Doctoral dissertation, University of Texas, Austin, 1978). *Dissertation Abstracts International,* 1978, *39,* 1910A. (University Microfilms No. 78–177, 38)

AUTHOR INDEX

Page numbers in italics indicate where a complete reference can be found.

SUBJECT INDEX